7102

Holger Müller

The MiG-21

The Legendary Fighter/ Interceptor in Soviet and Worldwide Use

1956 TO THE PRESENT

Schiffer Publishing Ltd

4880 Lower Valley Road • Atglen, PA 19310

Dedication: To Suzanne and Arno

Copyright © 2018 by Schiffer Publishing Ltd.

Originally published as *MiG-21* by Motorbuch Verlag, Stuttgart
© 2012 Motorbuch Verlag
www.motorbuch-verlag.de
Translated from the German by David Johnston

Library of Congress Control Number: 2018937193

Designed by Matthew Goodman
Type set in Aurora & Helvetica Neue

Photographs were taken by the author unless otherwise noted.

ISBN: 978-0-7643-5636-0
Printed in China

Published by Schiffer Publishing, Ltd.
4880 Lower Valley Road
Atglen, PA 19310
Phone: (610) 593-1777; Fax: (610) 593-2002
E-mail: Info@schifferbooks.com
Web: www.schifferbooks.com

For our complete selection of fine books on this and related subjects, please visit our website at www.schifferbooks.com. You may also write for a free catalog.

Schiffer Publishing's titles are available at special discounts for bulk purchases for sales promotions or premiums. Special editions, including personalized covers, corporate imprints, and excerpts, can be created in large quantities for special needs. For more information, contact the publisher.

We are always looking for people to write books on new and related subjects. If you have an idea for a book, please contact us at proposals@schifferbooks.com.

Contents

Foreword

After I was called up to serve in the East German National People's Army (*Nationale Volksarmee*; NVA) in September 1988, I was disappointed to learn that the aircraft I would be working on was the MiG-21. Having been an aircraft enthusiast since childhood, I had hoped that I would be allowed to work on one of the newer types flown by the NVA: the MiG-23, the Su-22, or even the brand-new MiG-29. The MiG-21, on the other hand, simply exuded boredom. Illustrated over and over again in every relevant magazine, everything was known about it. There didn't seem to be any secrets or innovations. This soon proved to be false. Whereas the standard lectures revealed that there were a multitude of MiG-21 variants, it was the stories told by the instructing officers, who had been trained in the Soviet Union, that first peaked my curiosity. Suddenly, they were talking about variants of the MiG-21 that had never been seen in this country. And after more than twenty years of close association with the aircraft, my opinion of it has changed. No other aircraft so markedly influenced military aviation during the Cold War as did the MiG-21. In addition to the numbers in which it was built, it was the type's widespread service in more than fifty nations that made and still makes the aircraft exceptional. The aircraft was, for fifty-seven years, produced in four nations, and has been in production longer than any other combat aircraft.

The MiG-21 owes its exceptional position to two qualities: first, it combines a simple design with the most-sophisticated aerodynamics in a way that few other types do; second, when the Soviet air force entered the Mach 2 age with the MiG-21 more than fifty years ago, the socialist superpower was probably enjoying the most successful period in its history. The damage caused by the Second World War had been repaired and the worst excesses of Stalin's rule were over. Soviet engineers had overtaken their American counterparts on the way to the cosmos. The Soviet sphere of influence was growing all around the world. The socialist states of Europe, which had fallen under Soviet control during the Second World War, were being joined by many young national states in Africa, Asia, and Latin America, which aligned themselves with the Soviet Union and thus increased its influence in world politics. All these nations received Soviet arms, and almost all of them received the MiG-21.

The MiG-21 proved to have an extremely long operational life. In some air forces, because of its simple, robust technology and comparatively lower operating costs, it even outlived its successors, the MiG-23 and MiG-29. Of the roughly 11,000 MiG-21s built in the Soviet Union, Czechoslovakia, and India, and the roughly 2,000 Chinese J-7/F-7 copies, several hundred examples remain in service today. The type's robustness and efficiency make the MiG-21 a suitable candidate for modernization measures, which also compensate for its greatest weaknesses.

There is no true successor to the MiG-21. Mikoyan-Gurevich failed to develop a cost-effective, single-engine type to follow the MiG-21. The MiG-29, created at a time when economic criteria seemed less important than sheer performance, is too expensive and too complex for many users. The cost of procuring and operating most Western types, even single-engine aircraft such as the Mirage 2000 and F-16, is well beyond those of the MiG-21. The only types in keeping with the concept of a small, light, and robust aircraft that can also operate from unpaved strips are the Swedish JAS-39 Gripen and the Chinese-Pakistani JF-17, which because of political and economic conditions can never see widespread use like the MiG-21. It is therefore not presumptuous to predict that no other combat aircraft will ever achieve the worldwide importance that the MiG-21 had and still has. This is especially true since there is a good chance that the MiG-21 will experience its sixtieth and perhaps seventieth anniversary of entering service.

As a topic, because of the length of time it was in production, the numbers in which it was produced, the multitude of versions, and its widespread service, the MiG-21 is virtually inexhaustible. So as not to exceed the scope of this work, therefore, I have restricted myself to what became reality in significant quantity and is sufficiently documented.

Holger Müller
August 2018

Acknowledgments

The author would like to express his sincere thanks to Dietrich Banach for his valuable support, especially on the China chapter, and his numerous suggestions; Jürgen Vogt for his extensive and detailed corrections and additions; Guido E. Bühlmann for his unique photos; Stefan Büttner and Alexander Golz for their terrific photos, but also for their years of companionship; Radek Vavřina for his detailed drawings; Karlheinz Foh for added information from a radioman's point of view; and Michael Wegerich for his organizational support.

Furthermore, the author would like to thank all those who contributed in any way to the completion of this book, whether through work, photos, texts, or the opening of doors:

Wing Commander Asad, Capt. Agnė Balčiauskytė, Zivojin Bankovic, Air Marshal Muhammad Enamul Bari, Uwe Beyreuther, Piotr Butowski, Lt. Col. Laurenţiu Chiriţă (†), Lt. Jan Chramosta, Harel Cohen, Maj. Marian-Ion Dobre, Col. S. Dobrew, Brig. Gen. Nebojša Đukanovic, Maj. Timothy Dunne, Col. (GS) Gerfried Elias, Lt. Col. (GS) Heinz-Jochen Ewert, Olga Franczak, Siegmar Frenzel, Dessislava Gentcheva, Dr. Rainer Göpfert, Maj. Hadushi, Marco Hanisch, Air Vice Marshal M Naim Hassan, Paul van den Heuvel, Group Captain MD Sharahul Huda, Alexandru Huiber, Wing Commander Mahmud Mehedi Hussain, Lt. Franjo Ivić, Col. Želko Jelenić, Col. Jaromir Jurečka, Maj. Karaj, Ralf Keil, Group Captain M. Saeedul Hasan Khan, Col. Petar Kovačević, Lt. Shkelzen Krypi, Lt. Col. Géza Koronczai, Lt. Col. Kuleci, Lt. Ieva Kuzminaite, Lt. Col. Mladen Labaš, Lt. Col. (GS) Holger Leukert, Col. Lleshaj, Lt. Col. Lleshi, Chris Lofting, Thomas Ludwig, Sergey Vladimirovich Luppa, Jitka Macháčková, Col. Abidemi Timothy Marquis, Doina Matanie, Lt. Metaksov, Col. Gelu Miron, Adela Maria Mureşan, Col. Tsvetomir Neshevskiy, Dirk Peisker, Lt. Stoyan Petkov, Lt. Col. Adrian Pirvu, Gerolf Plüch, 1st. Lt. Michal Prejzek, Lt. Col. Puhac, Major Gen. Rumen Radev, Air Commordore M. Mafidur Rahman, Lutz Richter, Walerij D. Romanenko, Maj. Nikolai Rusew, Brig. Gen. Sarfraz, Juliane Schneider, Ulrich Schneider, Lt. Col. (GS) Carlo G. Schnell, Maj. Lian Someşan, Simone Stadermann, *Oberleutnant* Klára Stejskalová, Ilana Sternfeld, Maj. Stoyanov, Dr. Michal J. Stolár, Dmytro M. Sudorgin, Capt. Šunić, Col. Antal Taligas, Lt. Col. Liliana Tanase, Leena Tiainen, Dr. István Toperczer, Lt. Nadejda Topurova, Col. Dancho Tsonev, Karoly Vandor, Maj. Dejan Vasić, Col. Dusan Viro, Lt. Col. Milan Virt, Dănuţ Vlad, Viktor Vorat, Alice Walther, Simon Watson, Wolfgang Wehner, Lt. Wetov, Dr. Jürgen Willisch, Col. David J. Wilmot, and Buck Wyndham.

CHAPTER 1
Development History
The Path to the Standard Soviet Fighter Aircraft

Following the end of the Second World War, the arms race between the two superpowers, the United States and the USSR, and their allies, resulted in the creation of new combat aircraft in rapid succession. As new types entered production and service, design work was already under way on the next generation—as a rule, at least until the mid-1960s—which had to surpass their predecessors, especially in terms of speed. And so, at a time when the North American F-100 and Mikoyan-Gurevich MiG-19, both capable of Mach 1, were just entering service, development began in several countries on combat aircraft that were to be capable of speeds of Mach 2 and greater. Decisive factors in achieving this goal were the availability of sufficiently powerful engines and the aerodynamic layout of the aircraft, especially with respect to the shape and sweep of the wing and the configuration of the engine air intakes.

Until Mach 1 was achieved, almost all designs had a swept wing, but research into flow behavior at high speeds revealed that other wing shapes could also offer advantages. Designers were unable, however, to agree on which wing type was best suited for a Mach 2 combat aircraft. As a result, in the 1950s, types designed for this speed range appeared with very different wing configurations. The F-4 Phantom II had broad chord swept wings with dihedral on the outer wings, the Lockheed F-104 Starfighter had short-span trapezoid-shaped wings, the English Electric Lightning had swept wings with ailerons at right angles to the direction of flight, and the Saab J-35 Draken had a double delta wing. The Convair F-106 Delta Dart and Dassault Mirage III had tailless delta wings.

In the Soviet Union in the early 1950s, the Central Aero- and Hydrodynamic Institute (TsAGI) began extensive calculations and wind tunnel experiments to determine the optimum wing configuration and air intake design for speeds in excess of Mach 1. Furthest advanced was research into the swept wing, since this had been used by several transonic and supersonic production aircraft. It had been learned that the use of wings with greater than 55 degrees of sweep resulted in a large thickness-chord ratio and thus, in view of the high aerodynamic loads, especially in aerial combat, provided a layout with sufficient stiffness. The delta wing, which provided high lift with low drag, a low wing loading, and less drag in the supersonic speed range, was also considered. The extended fuselage attachment along the wing root increased the strength of the entire airframe, and the thick wing offered space for fuel tanks. Theoretical calculations suggested that a wing with 60 degrees of leading-edge sweep and a thickness-chord ratio of 5 percent could meet requirements with respect to flight characteristics in all speed ranges and also suffice in terms of mechanical load capacity.

Such delta wings proved to lave diminished longitudinal stability, however. Because computer-assisted flight control systems were not yet available, the only possible solution was the optimal arrangement of the horizontal tail surfaces to the wing. At the same time, the massive decrease in elevator effectiveness at supersonic speeds resulted in the classic combination of fixed horizontal stabilizer and movable elevator being replaced by an all-flying tail, a single movable surface that combined the functions of stabilizer and elevator.

Finally, stable operation of the engine required that air entering the engine be reduced to subsonic speeds, which required an appropriate air intake design. Here, too, foreign designers came up with a variety of solutions: on the F-4

Phantom II and F-106 Delta Dart, intake ramps controlled the flow; the F-104 Starfighter and Mirage III used fixed or axially movable shock cones, while the English Electric Lightning had a complete fixed cone; and on the J-35 Draken, an intake without movable parts slowed the airflow through internal shock waves.

A subsequent assessment of the aerodynamic concepts was, however, possible only on the basis of actual flight tests; consequently, it was decided to built prototypes with swept and delta wings for comparative purposes. Design Bureau No. 155 Mikoyan-Gurevich (OKB MiG), which was responsible for creating a tactical combat aircraft for the air force (*Voyenno-Vozdushnye Sily*, or VVS), was not the only one to choose this method. OKB Sukhoi, which was responsible for designing a heavy interceptor fighter for the air defense (*Protivo Vozdushnoy Oborony Strany*, or PVO) on the basis of the same research, also selected this path. Unlike Sukhoi, which developed operational types from both designs—the Su-9/11 interceptor with delta wings and the Su-7 fighter-bombers with swept wings—at the end of testing, Mikoyan-Gurevich would make a decision as to which concept had proved to be the ideal solution to meet the requirements profile. Several hurdles had to be cleared before that stage was reached, however.

In addition to selection of the wing configuration, TsAGI provided recommendations for all fundamental decisions that had to be made, and gave guidelines concerning dimensions and design layout. The institute favored a conventional design with a separate horizontal tail. For the air intake, it suggested a longitudinally movable, central-intake shock cone, whose position could be changed to match airspeed and dynamic pressure.

Finally, there was one item missing for development of the planned type—a sufficiently light and powerful power plant. This was created in parallel with design work by Mikoyan-Gurevich under the designation AM-11 (later called RD-11 and finally R11) by OKB-300 (formerly Mikulin) under Sergey K. Tumansky and permitted a return to a light, single-engine design after the previous MiG-19 had to be designed with two engines because a sufficiently powerful power plant was unavailable.

Design work on the new type began as Project E under the leadership of chief designer Anatoliy Grigoryevich Brunov. Because of the need to compare swept and delta wings in practice, the two prototypes were almost identical apart from

their wings. An initial swept-wing design called the E-1 was dropped because no suitable engine was available, and the E-2, with the same wing layout, was the first type that was actually built. Since the R11 engine on which the project was based was not available when the prototype was built, the AM-9B (or RD-9B), which powered the production MiG-19, was installed in its place. While the MiG-19 had two of these power plants, the E-2 was powered by just a single engine producing 5,732 pounds of thrust and 7,171 pounds with afterburner. These figures were far below what the R11 was expected to produce; consequently, the prototype's performance was nowhere near what was projected. This interim solution nevertheless made it possible to carry out principal testing of the airframe, systems, and aerodynamic concept without losing time through ongoing engine development.

The first design of the new fighter aircraft displayed a whole range of features that were to appear on the production aircraft as well. The shape of the fuselage with its thirty-seven formers and the design of the vertical and horizontal tails and the undercarriage were largely the same as those of the first generation of the MiG-21. The aircraft was designed so that the pilot in his cockpit, the aircraft systems, the armament, and the engine could be accommodated in the smallest-possible airframe with minimal frontal area. Significant parts of the forward fuselage were the air intake with the movable shock cone (which had been recommended by TsAGI). Because of the minimized dimensions of the fuselage and wings, the main undercarriage could not be completely retracted into one or the other component. The designers therefore turned to a solution in which the undercarriage legs retracted inward into wells in the wing, while simultaneously a pivoting mechanism placed the mainwheels in a vertical position and they were retracted into the fuselage. Because the available cross section was insufficient to completely accommodate the wheels, the fuselage had bulges above and below the wing root, enabling the wheels to be fully retracted.

The swept wing had an area of 226 square feet, with the leading edge swept at 55 degrees. It was a two-spar design with stressed skin and a 6 percent thickness-to-chord ratio. The outer area of the leading edge consisted of two-part automatic slats. On the trailing edge were hydraulically operated split flaps and two-part ailerons, which together with spoilers provided roll control. The control surfaces were

The development of the best-known delta-wing aircraft began with swept wings; however, the original E-2 design and the E-50 high-altitude fighter prototype with additional rocket engine (seen here) developed from it were abandoned in favor of the superior delta concept. *Piotr Butowski Collection*

controlled by rigid control rods. A hydraulic booster assisted pitch control by the all-moving tailplane. Retractable speed brakes were located on both sides of the fuselage, beneath the leading edge of the wing.

Created just after the MiG-19, the E-2 shared a number of features with its predecessor that disappeared in the following development stages. In addition to the AM-9B afterburning engine with hydraulically controlled nozzles, these included large maintenance hatches on the upper sides of the fuselage and three 30 mm NR-30 cannon. There was one on each side of the fuselage beneath the cockpit, while the third was located under the fuselage slightly to the right of the centerline. The E-2 thus did not have a fuselage pylon for carriage of an external fuel tank like the later types, since the space required for it was taken up by the central cannon.

Equipment was comparatively spartan and consisted of a radio and IFF equipment, radio compass, beacon receiver, and radio rangefinder.

Work on the E-2 prototype was completed on December 25, 1954, and after completion of ground trials, on February 14, 1955, Georgi Mossolov took the aircraft up on its maiden flight. After just a few flights the trials were halted to allow installation of the R11 engine, which was now ready.

The E-4 was built with delta wings for comparison with the E-2 swept-wing prototype. While the fuselage, vertical and horizontal tail surfaces, equipment, and armament of both types were identical, the E-4 had triangular wings with 57 degrees of leading-edge sweep and a thickness-to-chord ratio of 4.5 percent. The trapezoidal ailerons were aerodynamically balanced and moved 16 degrees up and down. To provide additional lift at low speeds, the aircraft had rectangular split flaps in the area of the trailing edge. A large boundary layer fence was located on the undersurface of the wing, just outboard of the main undercarriage. Hydraulic boosters assisted operation both of the all-moving horizontal tail and the ailerons.

The E-4 made its first flight on June 16, 1955, with test pilot Georgi Sedov at the controls. The aircraft was powered by the AM-5 engine without afterburner that had also been envisaged for the swept-wing E-1, which had not yet been canceled. At the end of the year, this engine was replaced by the afterburning RD-9, which had been developed from the AM-5, giving it a performance similar to that of the E-2. Further modifications included shortening the ailerons while increasing range of movement to 20 degrees, increasing the dihedral of the all-moving horizontal tail, replacing the single boundary layer fence under the wing with three fences on top of the wing, and clipping the wingtips, giving the wings a trapezoidal shape in place of the previous triangular one.

The type was first shown to the public on July 26, 1956, during the Tushino air parade. It flew a total of 109 times until flight testing ended on September 20 of the same year. The trials included investigation of the spin behavior of a delta wing and its aerodynamics at speeds up to Mach 1.45.

In July 1956, American U-2 spy planes began overflying the Soviet Union, and there was an urgent need to put a stop to them. At that time, however, the Soviet Union lacked the necessary means. Existing aircraft could not reach the U-2's operating altitude of 60,000 feet and higher. Previously, surface-to-air missiles capable of engaging targets at that altitude had been limited to a ring of sites around Moscow and were not available in the rest of the country. The development of high-speed, high-altitude bombers in the West had been foreseen, however, and in 1954 the MiG design bureau had been tasked with building a fighter aircraft with mixed rocket-turbojet propulsion, capable of speeds up to 1,200 miles per hour (mph) and with a service ceiling of up to 70,000 feet. At the same time, OKB-1 under Leonid Duzhkin was directed to develop a suitable rocket engine for the aircraft. The E-2 provided the basis for the new aircraft. Development began in February 1954, in the course of which the aft fuselage and fuel system of the original design had to be revised. The S-155 rocket engine, with a thrust of 8,385 pounds, was installed in a bulge at the base of the vertical tail directly above the turbojet engine and was powered by a combination of special kerosene and nitric acid. As a result of

these modifications, the vertical tail of the aircraft, designated the E-50, was smaller than that of the E-2, and its fuselage was somewhat longer. The mixed-power prototype made its first flight on January 9, 1956, with Valentin Muchin at the controls. The first aircraft was lost on July 14 of the same year after engine failure, after which a second was built. It made its first flight on January 3, 1957. Because of the rocket engine, it reached a maximum speed of more than 1,490 mph (Mach 2.3 at 59,000 feet) and a dynamic service ceiling of 83,661 feet. The burn duration of the rocket engine was limited, however, to three minutes at full power and sixteen minutes at minimum thrust. A third prototype also had a lengthened nose, modified air intake, and increased rocket fuel capacity. It was also the first to be armed, with three 30 mm NR-30 cannon. This aircraft crashed on August 7, 1957, before it could be transferred to the Air Force Research Institute at Aktyubinsk (GK NII VVS) and used against the U-2.

Not until the R11 engine became available was it possible to open up the new aircraft's entire performance envelope and thus determine which wing configuration was best suited to its planned role. As soon as the new engine became available, therefore, the construction of new prototypes was begun, in which different paths were taken. While the first E-2A was created by converting the E-2 to the new engine, for testing of the delta wing a new prototype was built with the designation E-5.

The modifications that resulted in the E-2A went beyond the exchange of power plants. The wheelbase and track of the undercarriage were changed and the hydraulic system was divided into two subsystems. The automatic leading-edge slats were deleted because in several cases they had caused critical flight situations. Instead, a large boundary layer fence in the center of each wing prevented spanwise flow from reaching the wingtips and thus improved aileron effectiveness.

The first flight by the converted E-2A was made by chief test pilot Georgi Sedov on February 17, 1956. Like the E-4, the E-2A was revealed to the public over Tushino on July 26 of the same year. During flight testing, which was often interrupted by frequent engine changes, the E-2A achieved a speed of 1,180 mph and a service ceiling of 59,000 feet. Production of Product 63 began in State Aircraft Factory No. 21 (GAZ 21) Sergo Ordzhonikidze in Gorki (now again called Nizhni Novgorod). The initial production run of six aircraft was

Flight testing of the delta wing, a characteristic feature of the MiG-21, began with the E-4 prototype. *Piotr Butowski Collection*

designated MiG-23, and the first was delivered on July 1, 1957. Since it was becoming apparent that the delta wing variant was superior, the type was not put into production. The aircraft that were built were used by the LII testing center and OKB MiG for flight tests associated with development of the E-5, and later were used by various training facilities. Development of a mixed-power version with the designation E-50A was canceled. It was envisaged that production aircraft would have two wing pylons for the carriage of armament. This was to include AES-57 unguided rockets (in UB-16 pods) and TRS-190 or AES-212 bombs up to 1,100 pounds.

The E-5 also differed from the E-4 in more than its new engines. In addition to dividing the hydraulic system, the differences included air inlets at the roots of the stabilizers for improved engine cooling and a third air brake on the centerline of the aft fuselage. After the conclusion of ground testing, the first prototype, designated E-5/1, made its maiden flight with

test pilot Vladimir Nefyodov at the controls on January 9, 1956. This flight can be seen as the first flight ever by a MiG-21, since the E-5 was the first variant that had the most-significant features of the future production aircraft—the delta wing and the R11 engines. By October of the same year, the aircraft completed thirty test flights, which were hampered significantly by the engine in its early form. In one case, disintegration of the engine resulted in serious damage to the aircraft.

Numerous modifications were made to the aircraft between October 1956 and February 1957. These included lengthening the fuselage by 15.75 inches, replacing the hydraulic boosters for the stabilizer and ailerons with improved models, and installing an automatic incidence control to match horizontal tail deflection with speed and altitude. After a second round of test flights that lasted until July, which confirmed the correctness of the modifications,

The forefather of all MiG-21s: with its delta wing and R11 engine, the E-5 had all the essential features of the later production model. *Piotr Butowski Collection*

further changes were made. This resulted in another series of flight tests that continued until the end of May 1958.

A second prototype of the E-5 was used for takeoff and landing tests on unpaved runways, for which the aircraft was fitted with a nonretractable ski undercarriage. Ski-shaped skids as well as circular ones were used, rotating about a vertical axle. The latter could be pivoted 15 degrees, so that only a small area touched the ground, and behaved similarly to wheels. The tests showed that the system was usable in principle, but also revealed many technical and piloting problems.

In the course of development work the E-5's wingtips were clipped, resulting in the definitive outline of the future production model. Even while testing of the prototypes was still in full swing, State Aircraft Factory No. 31 (GAZ 31) Georgi Dimitrov in the Georgian capital of Tbilisi began preparations for production of a small series of aircraft now for the first time designated the MiG-21. Prior to this, the E-5

made its public debut over Tushino on July 26, 1956. Preliminary work for the MiG-21 without a version letter, which had been given the product code 65, began in the summer of 1956. According to the production factory's files, seven of these aircraft were completed by the beginning of 1958, both for use in the continuing development process and for service trials. What is still not known is whether these aircraft were officially taken on strength by the VVS or were used solely for test purposes.

On the basis of its experience with the swept- and delta-wing prototypes, in 1957 the MiG OKB developed an aerodynamically optimized concept that received the OKB designation E-6 and was supposed to represent the starting point for quantity production. The key element of the new version compared to its predecessor was the more powerful and durable R11F-300 engine. Further changes included a redesign of the intake and shock cone and of the aft fuselage, including the tail surfaces, an upgrade of the aircraft's equipment, and a reduction in the number of cannon to two, while simultaneously placing a wing pylon on each wing. These could carry rocket pods or single or mixed gravity weapons with a maximum total weight of 2,200 pounds. Deletion of the third, centerline cannon made space for the addition of a ventral pylon for carriage of an external fuel tank. The most noticeable external change was the replacement of the two stabilizing fins beneath the aft fuselage with a central fin, the so-called false keel. Also new was a braking parachute to reduce landing roll, which was housed in a compartment on the left side beneath the rear fuselage. Flown by Vladimir Nefyodov, the aircraft made its maiden flight on May 20, 1958. Just eight days later it was forced to make an emergency landing after vibrations developed and then the engine failed. The hydraulic system failed when the aircraft was just above the ground. The electrical backup for the horizontal tail reacted too slowly and the aircraft overturned. Test pilot Nefyodov died in the hospital, where doctors had initially failed to appreciate the severity of his injuries.

To quickly make up for the loss of the prototype, an E-5 was converted from one of the small series of aircraft manufactured at Tbilisi. Designated the E-6/2, the aircraft was completed in August, and on September 15, 1958, Konstantin Kokkinaki took it into the air on its first flight. A third prototype was also built, the E-6/3, which unlike its predecessors had antisurge shutters on both sides of the nose and auxiliary input doors just in front of the wing roots. The aerodynamic configuration of the MiG-21 was thus complete, and the new type was ready for state acceptance trials, which were to take place at Aktyubinsk in the summer of 1959. Immediately afterward, GAZ 21 in Gorki and GAZ 31 in Tbilisi began series production of the MiG-21F; however, this ended in Tbilisi after ten aircraft had been built, possibly to make room for production of the MiG-21 two-seat version, which began in 1962. In Gorki, however, this was the start of mass production that was to continue for a total of twenty-five years.

The first production MiG-21F was test flown at Gorki on February 8, 1960. On March 5, 1960, factory pilots ferried the first MiG-21Fs to the 32nd Guards Fighter Regiment (GvIAP) at Kubinka near Moscow, where two squadrons were to be equipped with the type. All of the unit's pilots made their first flights on the type within two months. This had been preceded by conversion training of pilots and ground personnel at the factory in Gorki and at the GK NII VVS.

GAZ 21 delivered eighty-three MiG-21Fs by the end of 1960, all of which were destined for the Soviet air force. In October of the same year, five MiG-21Fs of the 32nd GvIAP were sent to Aktyubinsk to test this version's arsenal of weapons, which consisted of cannon, unguided rockets, and bombs.

While the MiG-21 was an aircraft whose performance attracted international attention, its weaponry and equipment were essentially of early 1950s standard. The type's armament was improved with the addition of the K-13 (R-3S) infrared-guided air-to-air missile, which entered production in early 1960. To test the integration of the missile into the MiG-21's weapons system, three MiG-21F fighters were converted into E-6T prototypes and fitted with new wings and APU-13 launch rails. The resulting version was given the designation MiG-21F-13. GAZ 21 delivered the first aircraft in July 1960; the last, in late 1962. After this, Factory No. 30 Znamya Truda (Banner of Labor) in Moscow continued production for another two years. Gorki built MiG-21F-13s both for domestic requirements and export, while those made in Moscow were for foreign users only.

The aircraft was thus produced at all three intended locations, with their responsibilities divided as follows: single-seat fighters for the Soviet air forces were built in Gorki, while export versions were produced in Moscow. Tbilisi produced the two-seat version both for domestic and foreign use. But there is no rule without an exception: the previously mentioned preproduction series single-seaters and the first generation were built in Tbilisi. Several versions for domestic use and export were made in Gorki, and the first two-seaters for export were made in Moscow. The following was true, however: not until a new version was in production for the Soviet air forces was the previous version released for export.

With the arrival of the MiG-21F-13, which was delivered to the VVS from 1960 to 1962, the new type, which because of its characteristic shape was called the *balalaika* (referring to the musical instrument), began equipping fighter units nationwide. The F-13 version of the MiG-21 was first displayed publicly at the air parade at Tushino in July 1961, and the West gave it the code name "Fishbed."

In parallel with preparations for quantity production of the MiG-21 in the Soviet Union, license production in allied countries was also initiated. China and the USSR reached a production agreement in late 1957. The political rift between the two nations, which reached its high point in mid-1960, then brought the preliminary work for production of the MiG-21 in China to a halt. Only after the Soviet side relented at the beginning of 1961 was work resumed, though very slowly. An aircraft assembled from Soviet parts flew for the first time in 1964, followed by the first Chinese-built prototype in 1966. Because of the Cultural Revolution and its ruinous effects on parts of the Chinese economy, it was not until the early 1970s that series production achieved a noteworthy output. From then on, Chinese industry developed a line of types based on the MiG-21 that were designated J-7 or F-7, and these differed considerably from the original. These will be dealt with later in a separate chapter (see p. 123).

The first talks concerning license production of the MiG-21 in Czechoslovakia began in late 1958. A contract between the governments of the nations was signed in the first half of

1960, and in July of the same year the first plans and design drawings arrived at Aero Vodochody. Then, one year later, the Soviet Union delivered a pattern aircraft and components for four others. The first MiG-21F-13 assembled in the ČSSR made its initial flight on April 20, 1962.

The original plans for license production in Czechoslovakia envisaged that a total of 430 aircraft would be completed by 1965. For economic reasons this number was first reduced to 246 examples and finally to 180—while simultaneously stretching the production period. In fact, 196 aircraft were completed, including preproduction aircraft. The Czechoslovakian air force received 168 of the MiG-21F-13s built by Aero, while in 1969 another twenty-six were purchased by the United Arab Republic (the brief federation of Egypt and Syria). One of the preproduction aircraft served as a static test airframe. Series production ended with the completion of the last aircraft on June 17, 1972. All other

With the E-6, development of the MiG-21 had matured to the point that it was ready to enter production. The mounting of air-to-air missiles on the wingtips was a feature that was not adopted for series production. *Piotr Butowski Collection*

Despite what the dummies on this monument suggest, the MiG-21F did not carry guided air-to-air missiles. *Guido E. Bühlmann*

versions of the MiG-21 to serve with the Czechoslovak air force came from the Soviet Union.

While production of the MiG-21F-13 was still going on, the E-6/2 and E-6/3 were used to test air-to-air missile mountings, including wingtip-mounted launch rails. This configuration was not a success, however, and the underwing rails previously used were retained. The E-6T/1 prototype was fitted with the new, more powerful R11F2-300 turbojet, and it set two official Fédération Aéronautique Internationale (FAI, or World Air Sports Federation) world records. On October 31, 1959, Georgi Mosolov reached an average speed of 1,483 mph over a straight course of 9.3 to 15.5 miles (15–25 kilometers). On September 16, 1960, Konstantin Kokkinaki achieved a speed of 1,335 mph over a 62-mile (100 kilometer) closed circuit. In both cases the reported designation of the aircraft was E-66.

In the next stage of development, the E-6T/1 was fitted with a rocket engine in a pod under the fuselage. Additional modifications included two ventral fins under the fuselage instead of the false keel, and an increase in fuel capacity by

adding a tank just behind the cockpit. On April 28, 1961, Georgi Mosolov, flying this machine (which was officially designated E-66A), reached a world record altitude of 113,891 feet.

In 1960–61, a converted MiG-21F, designated the E-6/9, was used to test the MiG-21 as a nuclear weapons carrier. In addition to a special fuselage pylon, the machine was also equipped with a bombsight for this purpose. These nuclear capabilities were not included on production aircraft until some time later.

The E-6V/1 and E-6V/2 prototypes had modifications to shorten takeoff and landing distances and to improve low-speed handling characteristics. These soon became standard on all MiG-21s. The R11F2S-300 engine allowed for the extraction of bleed air, which was used for boundary layer control on the landing flaps. Special fittings on the aft fuselage enabled two rocket-assisted takeoff (RATO) units to be attached. The braking parachute was located at the base of the vertical tail in a cylindrical container.

Chapter 1: Development History

Early MiG-21F-13s, like their predecessors, still had the bulges on the aft canopy framework, which indicated the installation of the KK-3 ejection seat. *Popsuyevitch collection*

To overcome one of the weak areas of the first generation of MiG-21s, its lack of all-weather capability, in 1958, work began on a prototype called the E-7, which was equipped with the ZD-30 radar. To accommodate the bulky radar and its TsD antenna, the intake cone and the diameter of the entire intake area had to be made larger. The cannon was deleted to make up for the increased weight resulting from these modifications. The E-7's armament consisted entirely of missiles. The first prototype of the new version, designated E-7/1, which also had a ground control interception system and larger mainwheels, made its maiden flight in August 1959. After the loss of this aircraft, three months later its place was taken by the E-7/2, with a larger vertical fin, more-streamlined wing pylons, and an autopilot. By the time this machine was also lost in a crash in May 1960, the E-7/3 and E-7/4 prototypes were already available. With the R11F2-300 engine, a new fuel tank in the fuselage spine behind the cockpit, two more integral tanks in the wings, and a broader-chord tailplane, these machines had the configuration of the MiG-21PF, which defined the shape of the second MiG-21

generation and entered production at Gorki in June 1960. The first deliveries to the Soviet military took place in 1961; the last, in 1965. Moscow delivered the export model of this version in 1964 and 1965.

After production of the MiG-21PF had ended, the E-7/4 was specially prepared for world record flights. On September 16, 1966, Marina Solovyova set a female speed record over a 310-mile (500 kilometer) closed course at 1,281 mph. On October 16, Yevgeniya Martova achieved 559 mph on a 1,242-mile circuit, and on February 18 of the following year, 1,322 mph on the closed 62-mile (100 kilometer) closed course.

Since development of the MiG-21 initially concentrated exclusively on the single-seat version for the combat role, there were no two-seat training versions with which to train the pilots of the first- and second-generation MiG-21s. Development of a two-seat version of the MiG-21 therefore began in late 1959. The aircraft was based on the E-6T and had a larger cabin with tandem seats for the student and instructor. Accommodating the rear seat required considerable

MiG-21F-13 in the ultimate configuration, as produced both at the Gorki and Moscow factories. *Guido E. Bühlmann*

modification of the structure of the forward fuselage and redesign of the aft fuselage. The size of the canopy necessitated a departure from the previous forward-opening, one-piece canopy and the adoption of a three-part arrangement consisting of a fixed windscreen and two canopies that opened to the right for the two crew members. To offset the increased weight, the cannon armament was deleted. The aircraft was capable of carrying a single machine gun in a fuselage pod.

On October 17, 1960, Pyotr Ostapenko made the first flight in the E-6U/1 prototype. Three more were built until the new MiG-21U could be put into production at Tbilisi for the Soviet air forces. Production lasted from 1962 to 1966 and reached 180 aircraft. The MiG-21U was also built in Moscow for export from 1964 to 1968.

Various changes were introduced during production. The most noticeable of these was replacement of the narrow-chord tailplane with a broader-chord one, with transfer of the braking-parachute container to the root of the tailplane. The model change was made both in Tbilisi and Moscow in 1966.

As the two-seater entered production, development of the single-seat versions continued. Research aircraft for the development of a successor to the MiG-21PF were no longer pure prototypes; instead, they were converted production aircraft. One was used to test a new vertical tail with a further increase in chord, which was to remain standard until production ended. A second retained the narrow-chord tailplane but had the blown flaps tested on the E-6V/1 and a braking-parachute container at the base of the tailplane. Attachment points were also fitted to the rear fuselage for takeoff-assist rockets.

The first production version with at least one of these innovations was the much-simplified MiG-21FL export variant, which had the revised braking-parachute container and the broad tailplane, but not the SPS flap-blowing system. These aircraft were produced at Gorki from 1961 to 1965, but assembled at Moscow between 1965 and 1967.

After a lengthy planning phase, in August 1962 India finalized a contract with the USSR to produce the MiG-21 under license. In addition to production of the MiG-21FL, it

From this perspective, the most-noticeable new features of the MiG-21PF—its larger intake shock cone housing the radar, high-mounted pitot tube, and fuel tank in the dorsal spine—all are visible.

covered the manufacture of the R11 engine and the K-13 air-to-air missile. Components for the aircraft, which were assembled in India, came from Gorki. The first MiG-21FL assembled in India left the Ozar factory (Nasik) at the end of 1966. The first engine made in Koraput was delivered two years later. Then, on October 19, 1970, the first MiG-21 made entirely from parts produced in India was completed. The last MiG-21FL was handed over to the Indian air force in 1973. In total, 196 aircraft of this version were delivered.

The MiG-21PFS, deliveries of which to the Soviet air force began in 1963, was the first production version to have the SPS flap-blowing system. The early PFS still had the narrow-chord tailplane, but this was later supplanted by the broad-chord version. In the last development phase, this version also received a new ejection seat and the associated two-part cockpit canopy with a fixed windscreen and sideways-opening hood. Externally these aircraft were almost identical to the MiG-21PFM, the only difference being the equipment installed in the aircraft.

Logically, a standard production MiG-21PFS with new avionics served as the prototype for the MiG-21PFM. Externally there was no difference between the two versions; however, the first PFMs still had the forward-opening canopy and ejection seat of their predecessor. Testing of the new type began in October 1962, and production began at Gorki in 1965 and Moscow in 1966. New features were added during production, such as the ability to carry a cannon pod and use guided air-to-surface missiles. These modifications for use against ground targets made the MiG-21PFM into a multirole combat aircraft, albeit one with limited capabilities by today's standards. Consequently, the number produced at Gorki and Moscow reached almost 1,700 examples, a total that would be exceeded only by the later MiG-21bis.

At the beginning of the 1970s, a number of PF- and PFM-version aircraft were converted into M-21 and M-21M target drones at repair facilities; for example, at Lvov (present-day Lviv, formerly Lemberg). Thus modified, the drones are used to train fighter pilots and surface-to-air missile units.

The requirement to develop a tactical reconnaissance aircraft from the MiG-21 led to modifications that subsequently became part of all later development. While the first prototype MiG-21R, converted from a MiG-21PF, differed from its predecessors only in having a reconnaissance pod carried on the fuselage stores pylon, the following aircraft, which were converted from MiG-21PFS fighters, had four wing pylons

and a continuous fuselage spine with a larger fuel tank. This determined the external shape of the third MiG-21 generation. The factory in Gorki began production of the MiG-21R in 1965, both for the Soviet air force and for export, and it continued until 1971—not least because no follow-on version for this specialized role was developed. A number of aircraft were produced specially for Egypt, with cameras installed in the fuselage, as the MiG-21RF.

After the single-seat versions, the two-seat trainer was also equipped with the SPS flap-blowing system. The new version with this modification and new ejection seats was designated the MiG-21US. The main external difference compared to the final version of the MiG-21U was the periscope on the rear cockpit canopy, which despite the broader ejection seats provided the instructor in the rear seat with a view forward. A total of 347 examples of the MiG-21US were built at Tbilisi between 1965 and 1971.

In view of the advantages with respect to range and the carriage of external loads that resulted from the MiG-21R configuration, it was only logical that the next fighter version was based on the reconnaissance version. It was the first to make use of the improved RP-22 radar. A MiG-21PF served as a prototype to test the device, followed by two others based on the MiG-21PFM. Flight testing of the new version, which was designated MiG-21S and was operated only by the Soviet military, began in September 1963, while quantity production began at Gorki in 1966 and ended in 1968.

Equipping the MiG-21S with the new R13 engine and installing a cannon resulted in the MiG-21SM. A converted MiG-21S served as the prototype for this version. As a result of its more balanced armament, the MiG-21SM was produced in significantly greater quantities than its predecessor. Production in Gorki—once again exclusively for the Soviet air forces—ran from 1968 to 1971.

An export version of the MiG-21SM was developed with reduced capabilities. The early MiG-21M variant had two significant steps back compared to the SM; namely, the RP-21 radar and the R11 engine. Most of the following MiG-21MF version at least had the R13 engine. The MiG-21M was built in Moscow from 1968 to 1971. HAL Nasik began deliveries of the Indian license-production version in 1973, with the last of 158 examples leaving the factory on November 12, 1981. Production of the MiG-21MF in Moscow—with a few exceptions exclusively for export—lasted from 1970 until the end of the MiG-21 production program at GAZ 30 in

This MiG-21U with the narrow-chord tailplane typical of the first production batches was used in the ČSSR to test ejection seats. *Guido E. Bühlmann*

A MiG-21FL, produced under license in India, with the GP-9 cannon pod beneath the fuselage. Note the split flaps without the SPS flap-blowing system. *Simon Watson*

1974. The factory in Gorki continued production of the MiG-21MF for two years in a slightly modified form.

Integration of significant features of the single-seaters developed to date—a three-axis autopilot and R13 engine—into the two-seat airframe resulted in the MiG-21UM, the final training version. Production of this version began at Tbilisi in 1971, and 1,133 examples were completed, a significantly higher number than its predecessors.

Operational experience with the versions from the PF had shown that the MiG-21 could definitely be used as a fighter-bomber—more usable in fact than the Su-7, which had been developed for the role but never lived up to expectations. The fixed-cannon installation and provision with four underwing stores stations had further improved the MiG-21's suitability for air-to-ground operations. The aircraft's rather limited range remained a weak point, however. Since more-economical engines were not available, the only option was to increase fuel capacity. Because fuel tanks were already in every available space, increasing volume could be achieved only by enlarging the airframe at the place where only minor interference with the structure was necessary—in the fuselage spine. The more powerful R13F-300 engine was fitted to compensate for the increased weight. The result was the MiG-21SMT, which was built in Gorki from 1971 to 1973. The SMT was one of the MiG-21 versions capable of delivering nuclear weapons (see "Nuclear Weapons").

OKB MiG developed the MiG-21MT as a reduced-capability version of the MiG-21SMT. It differed from the base model mainly in having the RP-21 radar. Common to both versions was the large saddle tank, which in some situations caused center-of-gravity (cg) problems resulting in problematic flight behavior. Though produced in the Moscow factory responsible for exports, the small series of fifteen MiG-21MTs that was built was used exclusively by the Soviet air force.

Despite its limited range and armament, the MiG-21PFM's well-balanced handling characteristics made it popular with pilots. *Guido E. Bühlmann*

After the unsatisfactory experience with the oversize dorsal spine of the MiG-21SMT/MT, a design compromise had to be found for subsequent developments that would enable a satisfactory range and acceptable handling characteristics. This consisted of reducing the size of the fuel tank in the fuselage spine to something between the dimensions of the MiG-21SM and SMT. The introduction of the feature took place—as it so often did—as production went on. The modified version was still called MiG-21SMT, but received the new product code 50bis.

With the new fuel tank, which was shorter and less bulky, the MiG-21 single-seater had found its ultimate outer shape, which it would retain until series production ended. All further development steps concentrated on the aircraft's inner workings—the engine, equipment, and armament. An evaluation of air combat experience in the late 1960s and early 1970s had revealed that most aerial combat took place at medium and low altitudes. The MiG-21, which had been conceived as a high-altitude interceptor, was therefore completely redesigned in order to improve its air-to-air combat capabilities, especially at lower altitudes. The key step was the adoption of the R25 engine, which, at virtually the same weight, delivered more thrust, especially at low altitudes, and provided better response. The airframe was redesigned to endure the higher structural loads at low level. The number of changes justified the new version designation "bis," which—borrowed from the French—means "again" and proves the MiG-21bis to be a quasi-new design. Produced in two principal equipment variants, either with a fighter ground control interception or instrument landing system, this final version of the MiG-21 was produced longer and in greater numbers than all other versions. Production of the MiG-21bis began at Gorki in 1972 for domestic requirements, and in 1975 for export. HAL in India began license production of the MiG-21bis—parallel to production of the MiG-21M—in 1977, and this continued until 1984. HAL delivered a total of 220 aircraft.

The MiG-21R reconnaissance version had improved range, thanks to its saddle tank and external tanks beneath the wings. Mission-specific equipment was carried in the pod beneath the fuselage.

The MiG-21RF was developed especially for the Egyptian air force. Its cameras were housed in the fuselage.

Finally, in 1985, by which time the MiG-29 was already in production, the last new-build MiG-21 left the factory halls in Gorki. One year earlier the factory in Tbilisi had delivered the last MiG-21UM.

Production by GAZ 21 in Gorki reached 5,765 aircraft, of which 1,812 were exported. GAZ 30 in Moscow built 3,203 MiG-21s, the majority of which were exported. GAZ 31 in Tbilisi built a total of 1,677 aircraft of this type—roughly in equal numbers for domestic use and export. Total Soviet production was thus 10,645 MiG-21s, which were built over a period of twenty-six years. License production brought the total number of MiG-21s built to 11,414 aircraft—surpassed by just one jet aircraft, the MiG-15!

The evolution of the MiG-21 would thus have come to an end, had the OKB MiG not recognized—surely also influenced by the economic shift launched by Communist Party general secretary Mikhail Gorbachev—that because of the difficult economic situation in most countries using the MiG-21, a complete replacement with a new type was unlikely. Instead, it had to be assumed that the MiG-21 would remain in service longer than planned, and therefore it would have to be updated to match current technology.

The first attempt to integrate modern weaponry took place at the end of the 1980s. Beginning in 1990, OKB MiG together with the Nizhni-Novgorod Aircraft-Building Plant SOKOL—as it is called today—launched the MiG-21-93 modernization program, and in 1991, it named India as the first potential customer. At the beginning of 1993, Indian Hindustan Aeronautics Limited (HAL) and MiG signed the first agreement to develop a modernized version of the MiG-21. After negotiations with various parties, the Indian government finally decided in favor of the MiG-21-93, and on March 1, 1996, the final contract was signed for the modernization of a total of 125 MiG-21bis. The work would be carried out by HAL, while the newly formed production consortium MiG MAPO would produce the complete concept and deliver

Because it was equipped with the older RP-21 radar and R11 engine, the MiG-21M export version was less capable than the MiG-21SM, which was built at the same time for the Soviet air force. *Guido E. Bühlmann*

many components. A prototype of the MiG-21-93 was first shown at Aero India 1993, and the aircraft made its first flight on May 22, 1995.

Sokol modified three MiG-21bis to become prototypes of the MiG-21-93. In preparation for modification work by HAL, beginning in 1996, two Indian-made aircraft were converted into prototypes at Gorki. The new version, alternatively called the MiG-21bis UPG, MiG-21 UPG, or MiG-21 Bison, made its first flight at Nizhny-Novgorod on October 3, 1998. The two prototypes were delivered in December 2000 and August 2001; the first machine modernized in India left the factory in Nasik, where it made its first flight on the 31st of the same month.

The MiG-21's modernization potential was also recognized outside the Soviet Union and Russia. Romania, unlike most eastern European nations, made a realistic assessment of its economic prospects and in the early 1990s decided to modernize its MiG-21 fleet. While Israeli Aircraft Industries (IAI, now Israel Aerospace Industries) was initially favored as

a partner, that same year Elbit, another Israeli company, was selected to provide systems for the program, which was designated MiG-21 LanceR.

The prototype of the LanceR A, the fighter-bomber variant, took to the air for the first time on August 22, 1995, followed by the two-seat LanceR B in May 1996, and the LanceR C interceptor in November 1996. The decision to modernize the MiG-21 proved to be correct: with the LanceR, the Romanian air force had a completely NATO-compatible combat aircraft with comparatively low operating costs. As well, the project gave impetus to the modernization of the domestic aviation industry and especially for AEROSTAR Bacău, where all the work on the aircraft was carried out.

It was not by chance that Romania chose exclusively Israeli companies as partners for the modernization of the MiG-21. Since the 1960s, the Israeli aircraft industry had gathered experience with Eastern Bloc aircraft through the testing of equipment captured in the Arab-Israeli wars. With the fall of the Soviet empire, a new market for the

The MiG-21MF was the first export version to be powered by the R13 engine.

Despite efforts to achieve commonality of equipment with the single-seat versions, even the third-generation MiG-21UM two-seat trainer had no radar.

The development of the MiG-21 series reached its zenith in
the early 1970s, with the MiG-21bis. This version remained
in production unchanged until 1985.

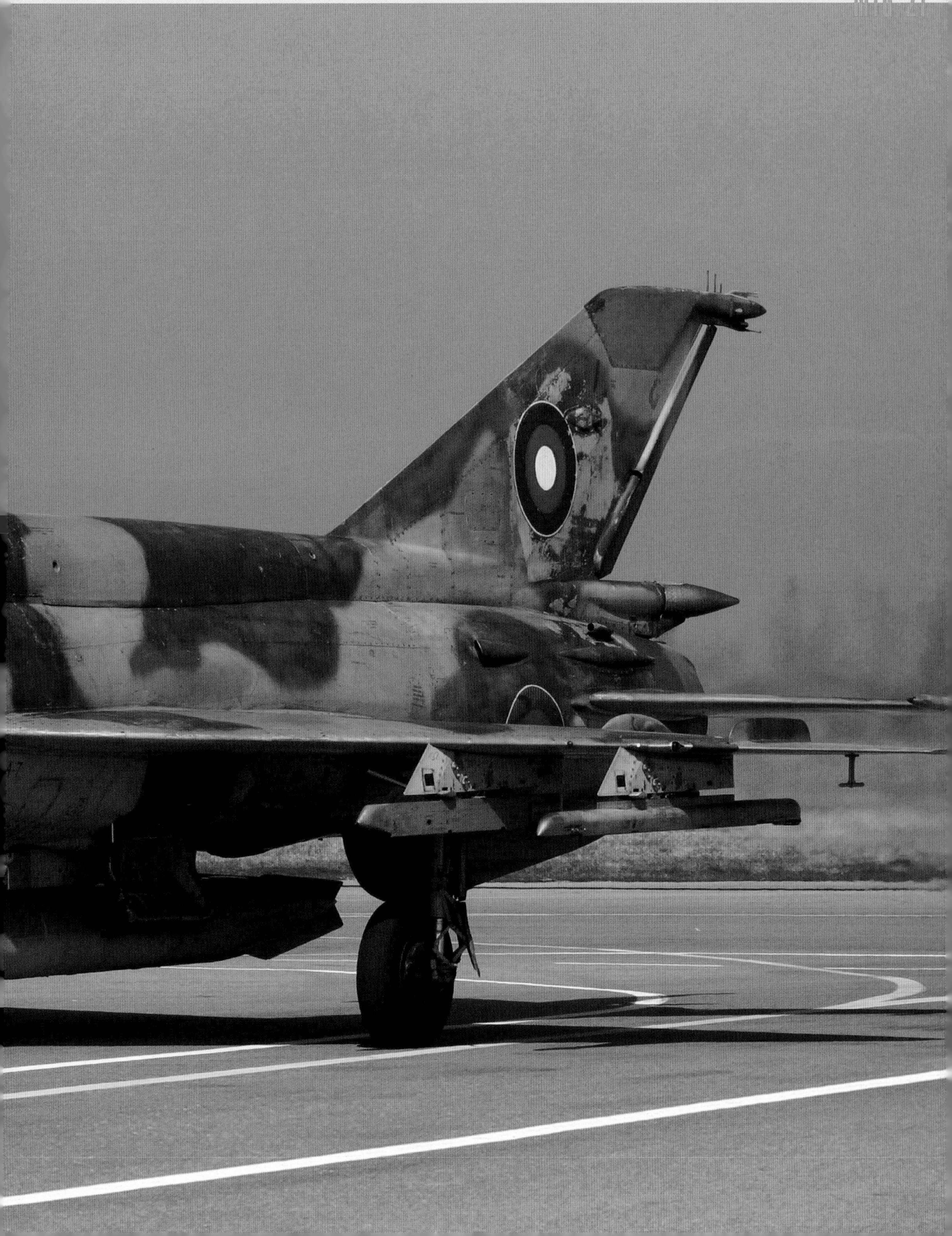

MiG-21bis built under license in India differed from the
Soviet originals in having a different array of antennas.
Stefan Büttner

Finland received the last production MiG-21s in 1985–86.

This testbed, based on a MiG-21SM, represented a first attempt to integrate modern weapons systems in the MiG-21.

The MiG-21-93, which was shown worldwide in the early 1990s, was capable of carrying almost the same range of armaments as the MiG-29, two generations newer.

modernization of systems with their origins in the Soviet Union opened up in which this experience could be put to good use. At the 1993 Paris Air Salon, IAI and AEROSTAR displayed a prototype that at least externally had significant features of the MiG-21 2000, as the program was called. When, a short time later, Romania broke off contact with IAI for reasons that were not officially given and instead launched the LanceR program with its competitor Elbit, IAI developed its MiG-21 modifications alone. The prototype made its first flight—albeit in a configuration that was far from production standard—on May 24, 1995. The first true MiG-21 2000 flew in April 1998. IAI subsequently won Cambodia, Zambia, and Uganda as customers, but numbers lagged behind those of its competitor.

Even the end of this modernization program has not meant the end of further development of the MiG-21. Despite the availability of more-modern designs, after the millennium China undertook new modifications to the J-7 family, which remains in production to this day. The MiG-21 can thus claim to have had not only the longest production life of any combat aircraft ever built, more than fifty-seven years, but also the longest development history of any military aircraft type.

The MiG-21 LanceR by system providers Elbit and AEROSTAR was marketed in and outside Europe; however, the only further users were Croatia and Mozambique. *Stefan Büttner*

The demonstrator for the MiG-21 2000 was a product of Israeli-Romanian cooperation. After Romania selected Elbit as its partner, Israeli Aircraft Industries continued the project on its own until it was ready for the market. *Stefan Büttner*

Technical Description of the MiG-21MF

General

The MiG-21MF is a single-seat supersonic fighter aircraft with limited all-weather capabilities, powered by a single turbojet engine. The airframe is of all-metal construction with delta wings in a midwing configuration, all-flying horizontal tail surfaces, and swept vertical tail.

Armed with missiles, cannon, and bombs, the aircraft is powered by a turbojet engine with afterburner and has a tricycle undercarriage. The pilot is accommodated in a sealable pressurized cockpit with ejection seat.

Specifications

Length including pitot tube	51.7 ft.
Length without pitot tube	47.6 ft.
Height	13.5 ft.
Normal takeoff weight	18,104 lb.
Maximum takeoff weight	21,299 lb.
Maximum speed at 42,650 ft.	Mach 2.1 (1,385 mph)
Maximum climb rate with full afterburner and two air-to-air missiles	29,500 ft./sec.
Static service ceiling	56,758 ft.
Dynamic service ceiling	75,459 ft.
Ferry range	1,066 mi.
Maximum endurance at 32,800 ft.	1 hr. 41 min.

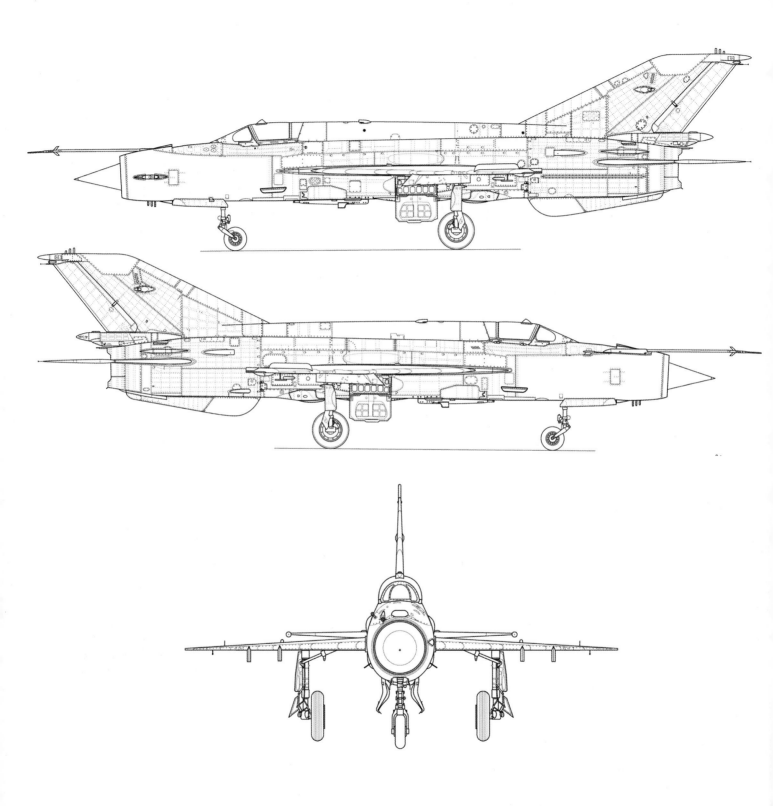

The layout of the MiG-21MF in detail.

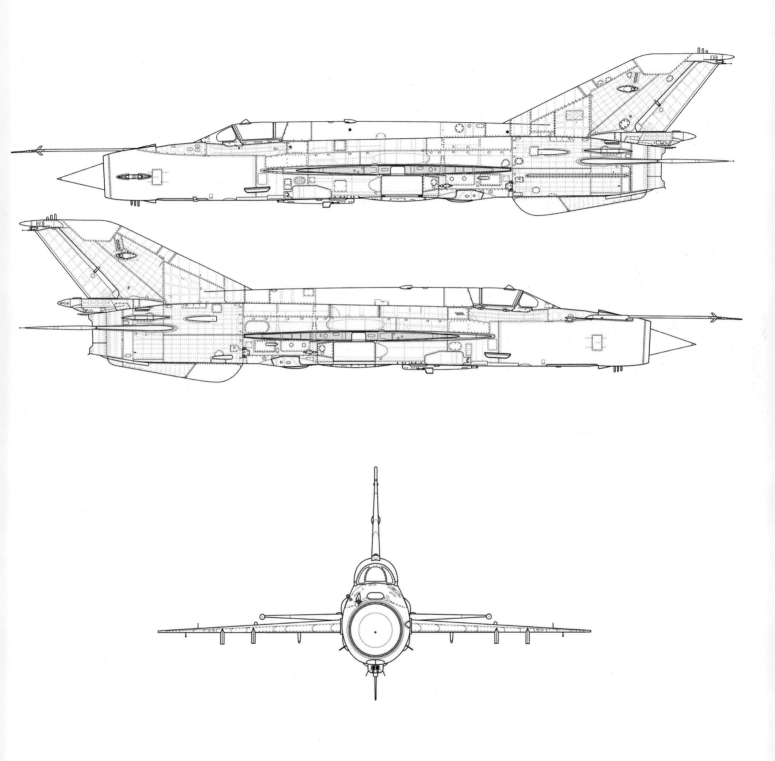

General

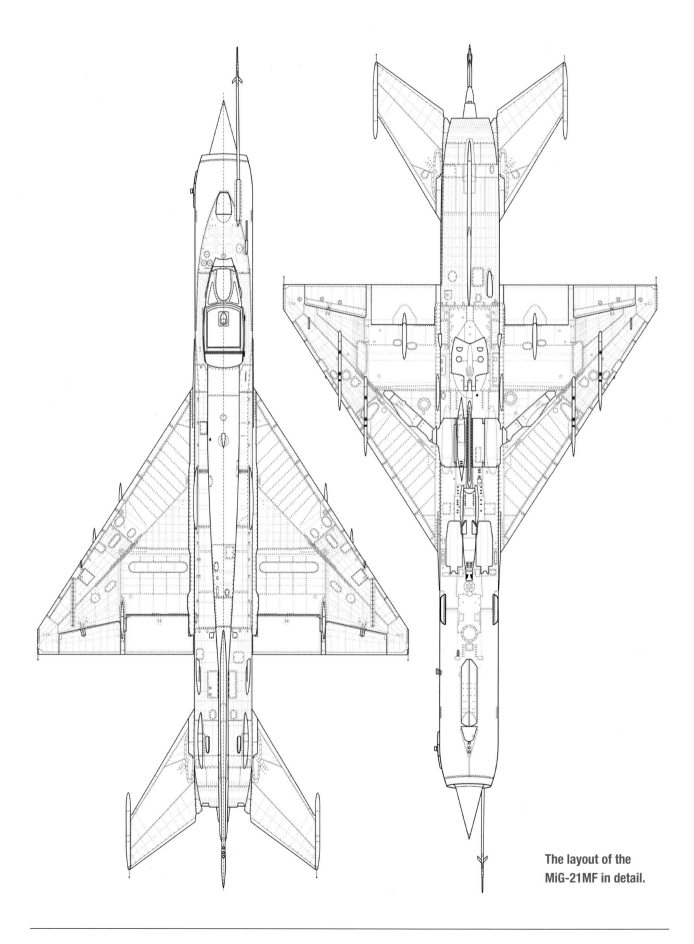

The layout of the
MiG-21MF in detail.

Chapter 2: Technical Description of the MiG-21MF

Schematic drawing of the air intake section with movable shock cone. The longitudinal axis of the shock cone is tilted 3 degrees from that of the aircraft. *Holger Müller Archive*

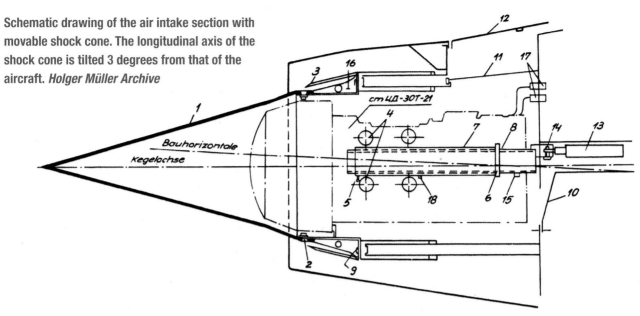

Illustration 60: Pictorial Schematic of the Cone Mechanism

1. Shock cone; 2. Cone attachment screw; 3. Removable ring; 5. Support bolt; 6. Removable thrust bearing; 7. Outer rail; 8. Inner rail; 9. Cone tip attachment screw; 10. Hatch in nosewheel bay; 11. Hatch in skin of shock cone; 12. Hatch in nose of aircraft; 14. Cylinder rod attachment bolt; 16. Cast ring; 17. Radar connection points; 19. Thrust bearing on inner rail; 20. Shock cone cylinder; 21. Guide rollers; 22. Construction horizontal line; 23. Shock cone axis

The forward fuselage of an Egyptian MiG-21MF. The wing-fuselage attachment points are clearly visible.

Despite the small fuselage cross section, the air intake in the nose of the aircraft can be seen well on this cutaway model of the MiG-21F-13.

Fuselage

The MiG-21's fuselage is of all-metal, semimonocoque construction, and it can be divided into two parts for removal of the engine and maintenance. The air intake passes through the fuselage nose and gives the aircraft its characteristic appearance. The pressurized cockpit sits over the air intake. The fuel tank is in the center part of the fuselage, and the power plant extends from the center section to the tail.

The fuselage consists of a longitudinal system (spars, auxiliary spars, and L-shaped stringers), a cross-system (formers), and skin. Most of the spars, the auxiliary spars, and the stringers are made of Dural, while several spars are also made of steel. Maximum fuselage diameter is 48.9 inches. The Dural skin varies between 0.04 and 0.14 inches in thickness.

The forward section of the fuselage is assembled from four main assemblies. The first extends from formers 1 to 3; the second, from formers 3 to 6; the third, from formers 6 to 11; the fourth and largest, from formers 11 to 28. The first section houses the fixed and movable parts of the air intake. The fixed part is formed by the intake ring, with the movable part formed from the shock cone, which ensures an optimal subsonic flow of air for the engine over a broad speed range. The shock cone assembly is located between formers 1 and 3 and is canted 3 degrees downward from the longitudinal axis. The radar is housed in the movable part of the shock cone assembly.

The shock cone system also provides boundary layer control to increase effectiveness of the air intake system. The air that is taken in is used to cool the radar components and is subsequently released through the nosewheel bay into the atmosphere. Since the temperature of the incoming air rises at higher airspeeds, the system contains a pressure valve that interrupts the flow of air at speeds greater than Mach 1.35. Also part of the assembly is the hydraulic cylinder, for moving the shock cone and the reservoir of deicing fluid for

Opening and closing of the canopy is entirely manual. A folding strut fixes the canopy in the open position.

In the intake section, boundary layer bleed air is drawn through the slot between the shock cone and the metal ring behind it.

the windscreen. The second fuselage section is divided by a horizontal bulkhead. Radio and special electrical equipment is located in the upper section beneath a cover attached by quick-release screws, in the so-called nose hatch. The lower half contains the nosewheel undercarriage bay. The nosewheel undercarriage is attached to a forged-steel element between formers 6 and 7a, and when retracted it is covered by two nosewheel doors.

The third fuselage assembly essentially houses the pressurized cockpit, which consists of formers, stringers, spars, and the canopy frame. The reinforced windscreen consists of three layers of silicate glass and has a thickness of 0.57 inches. The left and right windscreen quarter panels and the canopy are made of acrylic glass 0.4 inches thick. All joints are sealed with rubber bands and putty. The canopy is hinged on the right side and when open is held in place by a folding brace. The canopy frames are fastened to formers 9 and 10.

The TS-27 AMSch rearview periscope is on top of the canopy and consists of two separate mirrors, which are adjustable horizontally and vertically. The canopy can be locked and unlocked both from inside and outside the cockpit

The GSh-23 cannon mount allows the gun to be lowered for maintenance.

The fuselage center section with starboard forward speed brake, fuselage pylon with 211-gallon external fuel tank, wheel well door, and aft speed brake. When the external tank is fitted, the aft speed brake is automatically retracted and locked.

by means of a lever on the left side of the fuselage, and in the closed position it is held in place by four latches.

The aircraft batteries and the loop antenna of the ARK radio compass are located beneath the cockpit and are separated from it by the cockpit floor. The control rods running along the cockpit floor are beneath a removable false floor. Insulation in the sidewalls of the cockpit protects it against heat and sound. The lower part of the third section is covered by quick-release panels and hatches.

The forward part of the fourth main assembly is divided into upper and lower compartments. The underside of this section, between formers 13 and 16, is reinforced to take the GSch-23 cannon. Two load-bearing U-beams are installed between formers 13 and 16, and these are attached by two horizontal bars. These elements serve as a carriage for the cannon, which is covered by metal panels, some of which can be removed. The aft part of the cannon cover and the fuselage between formers 9 and 11 are covered with heat-resistant steel panels with a thickness of 0.03 inches.

The rubberized fuel tanks are located in the upper part of the fourth main assembly between formers 13 and 28. Fuel tank number 2 is located between formers 13 and 16; number 3, between formers 16 and 20; number 4, between formers 20 and 22; number 5, between formers 22 and 25; and number 6, between formers 25 and 28. Tank number 7, which is made of Dural, is in the fuselage spine behind the cockpit.

There are also three hydraulically operated speed brakes in the lower part of this section. The forward side-mounted speed brakes between formers 11 and 13 are made up of Dural shells, spars, stringers, and inner and outer skins. The speed brake mounts are on former 11, and the associated hydraulic cylinders are attached to former 13 by universal joint connections. The rear speed brake is located between formers 22 and 25 and is similar in design to the two forward brakes. It is attached to former 22, and its hydraulic cylinder is attached to former 25.

This tail section has been removed from the aircraft. The exhaust cone has also been removed, revealing the ring used to adjust the nozzle cross section.

Chapter 2: Technical Description of the MiG-21MF

The undercarriage bays are in the lower part of the section between formers 16 and 20, and when the landing gear is retracted they are covered by two hydraulically operated doors.

The engine bearer is in the upper part of the section between formers 22 and 28. On former 25 are the so-called engine thrust transfer bolts, over which all of the engine's thrust is transferred to the airframe. Side mounts fix the engine vertically and horizontally.

Atop the fuselage, the so-called grotto extends from former 22 to the tail fin main bearer. Beneath it are the control rods for the elevator and rudder control and some of the electrical and radio equipment.

The intake shaft, which extends from the intake ring to former 22, splits into two parts forward of the cockpit and reunites aft of the cockpit. The cockpit supply system's air-to-air cooler forms the wall of the rear part of the intake shaft.

The wing attachment points are located on formers 13, 16, 22, 25, and 28. Formers 28 and 28A join the fuselage nose and tail sections. The flange joint consists of three guide pins and eighteen connecting bolts, which are riveted to former 28.

The rear fuselage section is also a semimonocoque structure made up of formers, stringers, and skinning. Four of the thirteen formers are made of steel. The stringers have a U profile and are made of Dural. The skin is also Dural, with a thickness of 0.047 to 0.2 inches. The antenna of the MRP-56 marker receiver is located between formers 30 and 31. Between formers 31 and 34 there are hydraulic accumulators and electrically controlled hydraulic valves. This area is protected against heat by layers of fabric. Centrally mounted on the underside of the fuselage between former 28A and the end of the fuselage is the so-called false keel. The forward part of the false keel is formed by the removable Textolit antenna cover, while the aft part is made of metal. To avoid bulges caused by thermal loads, the inner skin of the aft fuselage consists of ribbed steel panels.

Each of the stabilizers is attached to a tubular steel bearer with four vertical bolts and one horizontal bolt. The stabilizer bearers are mounted on formers 35a and 36, using ball bearings so that they are movable. The vertical stabilizer is attached to the fuselage by two mounts on formers 34 and 36.

The rear fuselage section is ended by the removable engine exhaust ring and the braking-parachute container above it.

Wing

The wing has a triangular (delta) shape with a leading-edge sweep of 57 degrees. The trailing edge is perpendicular to the aircraft's symmetrical axis. On the trailing edge of the wing are the axially balanced flaps and ailerons. On the upper surface of each wing between ribs 9 and 10, there is a boundary layer fence, which improves the aircraft's stability at high angles of attack.

The wing is a design with ribs and spars. Lengthwise spars are attached by cross-ribs and the skinning, which is also part of the load-bearing system.

The longitudinal system consists of five spars plus stringers. The forward auxiliary spar is in the area of the leading edge of the wing and extends over the entire wingspan. The forward spar also extends over the entire wingspan and, with respect to the arrangement of ribs,

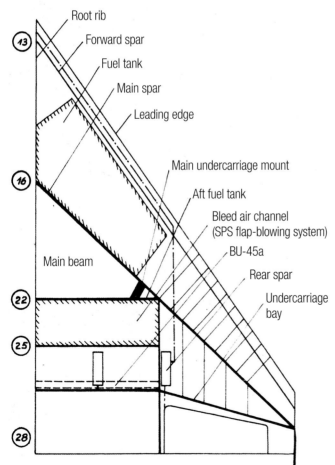

MiG-21 wing structure. *Holger Muller Archive*

Root rib
Forward spar
Fuel tank
Main spar
Leading edge
Main undercarriage mount
Aft fuel tank
Bleed air channel (SPS flap-blowing system)
BU-45a
Rear spar
Undercarriage bay
Main beam

Geometric Data

Wing area	247.5 ft.^{2}
Wingspan	23.5 ft.
Wing sweep angle	57°
Wing installation angle	0°
Wing dihedral angle	−2°

divides the wing into two parts: the ribs in front of the spar are arranged at right angles to the leading edge, while those aft of the spar are arranged parallel to the aircraft's longitudinal axis. The aileron control rods pass through holes in the forward spar face.

The main spar, which is at right angles to the aircraft's longitudinal axis, is between ribs 1 and 6 in the aft part of the wing. The main undercarriage leg mounts are at the junction of this spar and the fifth rib. The outer end of this spar is attached to the forward spar at the level of the sixth rib.

The root of the rear spar is on the first rib, while it ends at the sixth rib. The rear auxiliary spar extends over the entire wingspan. The longitudinal supports are at tight angles to the ribs and reinforce the skin as well as the wing's own stiffness.

The lateral support system consists of ribs that—as already mentioned—are arranged at right angles to the leading edge in the forward part of the wing and parallel to the aircraft's longitudinal axis in the aft part. There are twenty-five ribs in the forward part and eleven in the aft part. The wing skinning consists of Dural sheets whose thickness varies between 0.06 and 0.07 inches and over the integral fuel tanks is up to 0.14 inches. The wing is attached to the fuselage by five attachment points between formers 13 and 28.

Two integral fuel tanks are housed in each wing. All parts of the wing that come into contact with the fuel are protected by an anticorrosion finish. Each integral tank has its own fuel vent on the wing underside.

This top view reveals the captivatingly simple wing design with flaps and ailerons as the only moving parts. Also visible are the stabilators and the vertical fin and rudder.

Chapter 2: Technical Description of the MiG-21MF

The main undercarriage bay is located between the forward and main spars. In addition to the hydraulic cylinder for lowering and raising of the undercarriage, it also contains compressed air and oxygen bottles.

The ailerons on the rear part of the wing between ribs 6 and 11 and the aft auxiliary spar are of riveted construction with forward and aft spars, ribs, and skinning, which is 0.03 to 0.06 inches thick. A flutter-damping weight is installed in the leading edge of the aileron. The ailerons are attached to the wing by ball bearing hinges on ribs 6, 9, and 11.

The flaps are located between ribs 1 and 6 and the aft auxiliary spar. They consist of a spar, leading-edge fairing, ribs, a honeycomb-like filling, the trailing edge, the skinning, and hinges at both ends. The hydraulic operating cylinder is mounted on the underside.

Forward of the flap is a gas channel for carriage and equal distribution of the engine bleed air for the boundary layer control system.

The stores pylons for the installation of external stores are attached forward to the junction of the forward spar and rib 13 (inner pylon) and rib 18 (outer pylon) and aft to rib 5 (inner) and rib 8a (outer).

The BU-45A hydraulic aileron booster is located on rear rib 6a. The landing light is housed in the forward part of the wing between ribs 1 and 2.

Empennage

The tail unit is swept and cantilever. It consists of the vertical and horizontal tail surfaces and is symmetrical in profile. Elevator control is provided by two all-moving stabilizers without separate elevators. Each stabilizer consists of a forward, central, and aft spar plus ribs and skinning. Antiflutter weights are installed on the outermost rib of the stabilizer. The stabilizers are controlled by the BU-210B hydraulic booster in the vertical tail. Also located there is the hydraulic system's backup pump.

The vertical tail consists of the vertical stabilizer and rudder. The vertical stabilizer provides the aircraft's longitudinal stability. It consists of forward and aft longitudinal profiles, the stabilizer spar, and the skinning. The vertical stabilizer is attached at mounting points on formers 34 and 36. Components of the navigation, radio, and hydraulic equipment are housed in the vertical stabilizer.

The rudder consists of a spar, two profiles, ribs, and skinning with a thickness of 0.05 inch at the leading edge and 0.03 inch in the aft part. The rudder is mounted on the aft stabilizer profile with three ball bearings. On the trailing edge there is a trim tab to adjust the aircraft's longitudinal stability.

Geometric Data

Stabilator area	41.3 ft.²
Stabilator sweep angle	55°
Vertical fin area	
Vertical fin sweep angle	61° 27'
Rudder area	
Stabilator installation angle	0°
Stabilator dihedral	0°
Maximum stabilator deflection angle	
Nose up	+13°
Nose down	−28°
Rudder deflection angle	±25°

Specifications

Wheelbase	15.45 ft.
Track width	9.15 ft.
Mainwheels	KT-92B 800 x 200 W
Nosewheel	KT-102 500 x 180
Main undercarriage tire pressure	114 + 14 psi
Nosewheel tire pressure	100 + 14 psi
Shock absorber stroke main undercarriage	9 in.
Shock absorber stroke nose gear	3.4 in.
Nitrogen pressure main undercarriage	426 psi
Nitrogen pressure nose gear	526 psi
Wheel weight main undercarriage	140 lb.
Wheel weight nose gear	62 lb.
Brake pressure	270 psi

Because of its high-volume wheels, large track width, and robust undercarriage legs, the MiG-21 is also capable of operating from unprepared surfaces.

Undercarriage

The MiG-21's undercarriage is a robust tricycle design that enables it to take off from unpaved and unprepared surfaces (e.g., grass, roads). It consists of two main undercarriage legs and a nosewheel leg with steerable nosewheel.

The nosewheel leg with KT-102 nosewheel retracts into the nosewheel bay between formers 3 and 6. The main undercarriage legs are attached to the wings and retract into bays in the wing roots. During retraction of the undercarriage, the KT-92B mainwheels rotate 87 degrees relative to the undercarriage leg to align with the fuselage and are retracted into the undercarriage bays in the fuselage. All undercarriage legs are equipped with hydropneumatic shock absorbers with nitrogen gas filling. The nosewheel leg also has a flutter damper to minimize lateral vibration.

The undercarriage is operated by hydraulic cylinders and can be extended by compressed air in an emergency. The nosewheel leg can also be unlocked mechanically, after which gravity and dynamic pressure move it into the extended position, where it locks independently. In the retracted position, all undercarriage legs are held in place by mechanical locks. In the extended position, spreading rings in the hydraulic cylinders lock the main undercarriage legs in the down position. Hydraulic blocking also takes place. The nosewheel leg is mechanically locked at former 6. The nosewheel can pivot 47 + 1 degrees to both sides. All three wheels are equipped with disc brakes operated by compressed-air cylinders—eight for the nosewheel and twelve for the mainwheels. All brakes have an electromechanical antilock braking system. The PPS-2 indicator in the cockpit displays the position of the undercarriage.

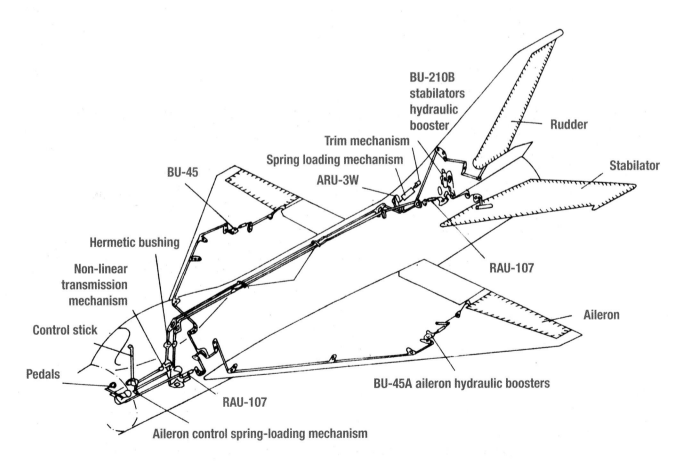

Schematic diagram of the aircraft control system. *Holger Müller Archive*

Chapter 2: Technical Description of the MiG-21MF

Specifications

Flap area	2 x 9.80 ft.²
Flap deflection angle	25° (takeoff position)
45° (landing position)	
Aileron area	2 x 6.35 ft.²
Aileron deflection angle	± 20°
Forward speed brake area	4.7 ft.²
Forward speed brake deflection angle	35°

Aircraft Controls

The aircraft's control system consists of all-flying horizontal stabilizers (stabilators), ailerons, rudder plus flaps, and speed brakes.

Elevator control is accomplished with the control stick, which is connected to the stabilators by rigid rods. The elevator control system includes the BU-210B hydraulic booster, which causes both stabilators to move simultaneously; a spring loading mechanism to simulate control force; the ARU-3W pitch control unit, which automatically adjusts stabilator deflection to speed and altitude; the trim mechanism, which takes the forces from the control stick and maintains longitudinal stability; the setting mechanism of the AP-155 autopilot in the form of the RAU-107A actuator and DSU-2 angle of attack sensor for independent control of the intake shock cone; and antisurge doors independent of the stabilators.

The aileron control system consists of two BU-45A hydraulic boosters, a spring-loading mechanism to simulate control forces at the control stick, a mechanism to reduce aileron effectiveness in the first third, and the AP-155 autopilot's RAU-107A actuator.

The rudder is controlled by pedals that are directly connected to the rudder by control rods without a booster.

The speed brakes and flaps are controlled hydraulically. The speed brakes are operated by a slide on the throttle

The air intake section's auxiliary input doors (beneath the cockpit) open automatically, while the antisurge doors (forward of the nosewheel leg) open only in flight to restore normal airflow to the engine.

lever; the flaps, by a three-position switch. The extended flaps are blown by the SPS boundary layer control system to improve low-speed handling characteristics and reduce landing speed. The system is activated automatically whenever the flaps are lowered to more than 30 degrees, and the control lever is between the SPS and maximum settings, provided the appropriate switch in the cockpit is in the ON position. The bleed air for the boundary layer control system is taken from the engine behind the compressor and flows through airlines in the fuselage and gas channels in front of the flaps. To reduce the engine's thermal load, the engine nozzle opens by 0.78 inch. The afterburner cannot be used when the SPS system is in operation.

Power Plant

The MiG-21 is powered by an R13-300 axial-flow turbojet engine with controlled afterburner. Air enters the intake section with automatically controlled shock cone and is fed to the engine. The air intake tunnel is divided into two halves forward of the cockpit. It later rejoins and is hermetically sealed against the engine. On the sides of the fuselage nose are automatically controlled antisurge shutters. These prevent pressure shocks in the air intake that could lead to a loss of engine performance or even to flow separation on the turbine blades. On the ground or at low flow speeds, the engine can also take in additional air through two uncontrolled auxiliary input doors on the sides of the fuselage.

The engine compartment is cooled by air that is drawn from the air intake tunnel. Additional systems receive their cooling air from separate intakes. On the ground the engine compartment is cooled by twelve circular valves with a diameter of 2.75 inches. The valves are opened by the pressure differential between the engine compartment and the environment caused by the flow of gases from the engine.

To ensure reliable engine starts in flight, the main combustion chamber's ignition system is automatically supplied with oxygen from a tank in the wing.

A fire-extinguishing system is installed to fight fires in the engine compartment and consists of IS-5 ionization sensors, the foam container, two circular spray manifolds, and the associated electrical system. The system is activated by pyrocartridges, and the foam is sprayed into the area between the engine and fuselage at a pressure of 1,450 pounds per

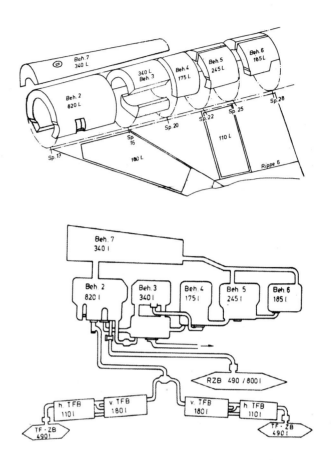

Schematic representation of the fuel tanks and their contents. *Holger Müller Archive*

square inch.

Fuel System

The fuel system provides the engine with a secure supply of fuel at all attitudes through the aircraft's entire speed and altitude range and ensures that the engine can be started reliably on the ground and in flight. It also cools the fuel pumps and the engine lubricant.

The fuel system consists of six fuel tanks in the fuselage, four integral tanks in the wings, up to three external fuel tanks, electric fuel pumps, the fuel usage control system, the low-pressure system to force fuel from the wing and external fuel tanks, the ventilation system, and the control system. With the exception of fuselage saddle tank 7, all the fuel tanks are produced from two elastic layers. The inner layer consists of fuel-resistant rubber with a thickness of 0.02 inches, while the outer is a rubberized fabric with a thickness

Filling of the fuselage and wing fuel tanks is accomplished by using the central filler point on the fuselage spine on all second-generation and later MiG-21s. The simultaneous filling of oxygen—as seen here—was actually forbidden because of the danger of an explosion.

External fuel tanks must be filled separately. Each tank has its own filling point in the aft part of the tank.

of approximately 0.04 inches. The rubber tank is an integral part of the fuselage structure.

Tank 2 holds 217 gallons; tank 3 (two part), 90 gallons; tank 4, 49 gallons; tank 5 (two part), 65 gallons; and tank 6 (two part), 49 gallons. Tank 7 in the fuselage holds 90 gallons. The integral wing tanks each have a capacity of 48 gallons (forward) and 29 gallons (aft).

The auxiliary fuel tanks hold 129 gallons (for installation under the fuselage and wings) and 211 gallons (fuselage only). The available volumes of fuel provided by the fuel system are therefore:
- no external tanks: 687 gallons
- with one fuselage-mounted external tank: 819 gallons
- with two underwing tanks (2 x 129 gallons): 938 gallons
- with one fuselage-mounted and two underwing tanks (3 x 129 gallons): 1,057 gallons
- with one fuselage-mounted tank (211 gallons): 885 gallons

The external fuel tanks are mounted on the ventral stores pylon and the outer wing pylons and can be jettisoned in flight. There is a pyrocartridge in each stores pylon, which is ignited when the appropriate switch is activated. The fuel tanks are of monocoque construction with a central former and tail fins. The fuel from the external tanks is transferred by compressed air to tank 2. The fuel from the fuselage and wing tanks is transferred to tank 3, the collector tank. The inverted flight valve in this tank ensures that the engine is supplied with fuel during inverted flight for up to fifteen seconds and up to five seconds in afterburner.

All internal tanks are filled through a central fueling valve atop tank 7, and special drainage lines link them to a central drain valve in the upper rear part of tank 7. Fuel is vented there; for example, when it is heated by the sun and expands. External tanks are filled individually by using fueling openings in the rear part of the tank. Fuel can be removed from the fuselage tanks by means of a drain valve on former 28. The wing and external fuel tanks are drained by using special drain plugs or by means of a special hose that transfers the fuel to a fuel truck. Deposits in the fuel can be drained by using tubular drain valves.

Centrifugal fuel pumps are powered by fuel-cooled electric motors. Type 495B pumps are present in tanks 3 and 4, and one type 422 pump is in tank 2. The system of fuel lines consists of supply lines (linking tank 3 and the engine), connecting lines (connecting all tanks with tank 3), fuel control lines (ensuring that tanks are emptied in sequence), pressure ventilation lines (to empty tanks without pumps, to ensure that pumps operate cavitation-free in all flight attitudes and provide fuel to the engine should the pumps fail), and drainage lines to vent the tanks. Other system components include filters, sampling valves, throttle valves and orifices, drain valves, and safety and float valves. All fuel is pumped in a specified sequence to tank 3 without affecting the aircraft's trim.

Indication of the actual fuel level is provided by an instrument preset to the amount of fuel onboard while on the ground. In the cockpit the pilot is alerted when the external fuel tanks and the first (fuselage tanks 2 and 7, wing tanks) and third (fuselage tanks 4, 5, and 6) tank groups are empty, and when minimum fuel level (119 gallons) is reached.

Specifications

Total capacity of both systems	9.5 gallons
Maximum operating pressure	3,058 psi

Hydraulic System

The hydraulic system consists of two independent subsystems. The main hydraulic system powers the intake shock cone, antisurge doors, flaps, speed brakes, undercarriage, and engine-nozzle-setting mechanism; supplies the second chamber of the BU-210B stabilator booster; causes the automatic braking of the wheels when the undercarriage is retracted; and doubles the supply to the BU-45A aileron booster. The hydraulic booster system feeds the control system's hydraulic boosters—the BU-45A aileron booster and the first chamber of the BU-210B stabilator booster.

Two NP-34M1-T plunger pumps provide pressure to each system. The hydraulic fluid is AMG-10. The hydraulic fluid reservoir is divided into two halves, each supplying one system. Each system also has one spherical and one cylindrical hydraulic accumulator for pressure storage and damping of pressure shocks. The hydraulic pumps are powered by the engine. An electrically powered NP-27T backup pump engages when hydraulic pressure falls below

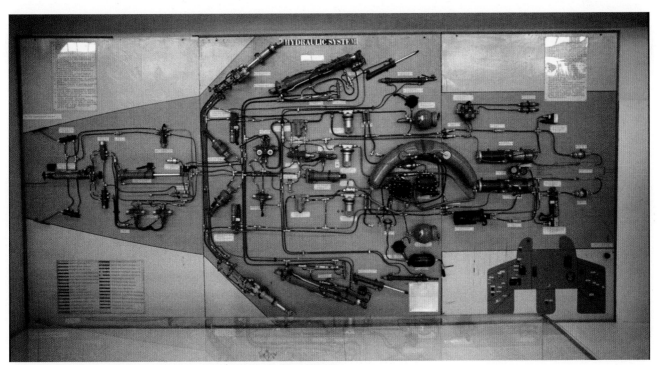

Hydraulic system components and their locations in the airframe.

56 pounds per square inch. The hydraulic lines are made of steel, while the return lines are aluminum.

Pneumatic System

The pneumatic system consists of two independent subsystems. The main system powers the wheel brakes, cockpit pressurization, braking-parachute release and jettison, windscreen deicing, cooling of the nose hatch, and jettisoning of the SPRD takeoff-assist rockets. The backup system provides emergency braking for the mainwheels and emergency lowering of the undercarriage.

Compressed-air bottles supply both systems. Two spherical tanks, each with a capacity of 122 cubic inches, one cylindrical tank with 269 cubic inches—all in the starboard main undercarriage bay—and finally two tanks in the main undercarriage legs charge the main system. Two spherical tanks, each with a capacity of 183 cubic inches in the port main undercarriage bay, are assigned to the backup

system. The braking-chute control system also has its own auxiliary tank. All tanks are filled from external sources on the ground.

The compressed-air connection is on former 20 in the main undercarriage bay. The two compressed-air valves—one for each subsystem—are also there. All compressed-air tanks are made of steel; the compressed-air lines, of aluminum.

Specifications

Capacity of the main system compressed-air tank	785 in.³
Capacity of the backup system compressed-air tank	159 in.³
Pressure of the main and backup systems	1,565–1,849 psi
Nosewheel braking pressure	213 psi
Main undercarriage wheels braking pressure	270 psi
Pressure in the cockpit pressurization system	25–36 psi

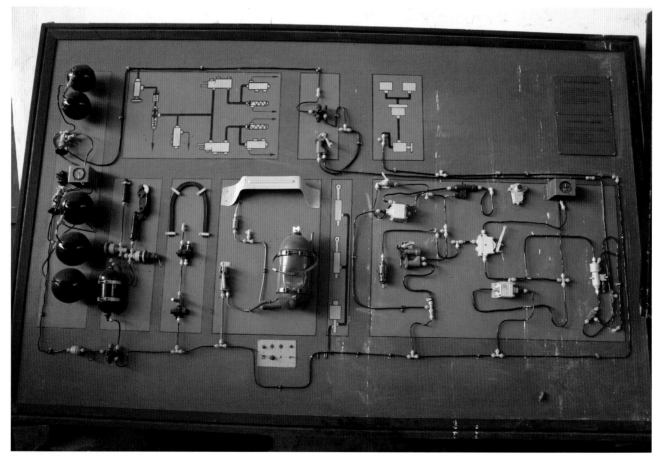

Pneumatic system

Both round and cross-shaped (seen here) braking parachutes were used by the MiG-21.

Braking-Parachute System

The purpose of the PT-21UK braking parachute is to shorten the landing roll distance. It is usually deployed immediately after touchdown at speeds of about 175 mph, but it can also be deployed at 6 to 10 feet above the runway and opened as speeds up to 200 mph. The braking chute has an area of 172 square feet and is completely opened 1 to 1.5 seconds after deployment.

The braking parachute is packed in a cylindrical bag and placed in the cylindrical braking-parachute housing. After the aircraft has slowed, the braking parachute is jettisoned, repacked, and placed back in the parachute housing.

Cockpit Environmental Control and Pressurization Systems

The cockpit supply system optimizes air pressure and temperature in all flight situations. The air to supply the cockpit is drawn from the engine compressor and delivered via an air-to-air cooler or a turbocooler. Defined cockpit pressure conditions and selected temperature are set by using pressure and temperature controls.

The pressurized cockpit is sealed by inflatable rubber tubes around the canopy frame and at all control rod and piping grommets.

Oxygen System

The oxygen system provides the conditions needed by the pilot for high-altitude flight and leaving the aircraft in the ejection seat. It ensures oxygen overpressure in the breathing system, which is regulated independent of altitude.

All piping systems are identified by color. Hydraulic lines and components are gray or metallic colors, compressed-air lines are black, oxygen lines and tanks are blue, fuel lines are yellow, and elements of the fire-extinguishing system are red.

The armament spectrum of the MiG-21MF consists of guided missiles, unguided rockets, bombs, and the integral 23 mm cannon. *Stefan Büttner*

The aircraft batteries are located in a container in the fuselage beneath the cockpit.

Cockpit equipment consists of many classic round instruments and switches.

Chapter 2: Technical Description of the MiG-21MF

Guido E. Bühlmann

Electrical System

The electrical system supplies instruments and equipment with different DC and AC voltages. Two 15 SZS-45 silver-zinc batteries, each with a capacity of 45 Ah, are the primary source of voltage. Two generators supply the system when the engine is running. These generators are powered via gearing from the engine's high-pressure turbine. The DC generator, which also serves as starter, delivers 28.5 volts; the AC generator, 115 volts at 400 Hz. If the DC generator fails, the batteries provide backup power. Power to subsystems with 115-volt/400 Hz one-phase alternating current is supplied by PO-750 and PO-1500 transformers; those with 36-volt / 400 Hz three-phase alternating current, by PT-125 and PT-500 transformers.

Equipment

The aircraft's avionics suite includes an RSIU-5 (R-802) radio, ARK-10 radio compass, MRP-56 marker receiver, KSI-2 heading system, AP-155 autopilot, RW-UM radio altimeter with warning-height preselector, SOD-57M transponder, SRZO-2 IFF system, RP-21MA radar, SARPP-12 flight data recorder, ARL-S LAZUR ground control intercept system, SPO-10 radar-warning receiver, and SORZ-1 central warning system.

Armament

The aircraft's onboard weapons system consists of one twin-barreled 23 mm GSh-23 cannon with 200 rounds of ammunition, the ASP-PF-21 gunsight, and a gun camera. Various guided and unguided weapons with a total weight of 2,200 pounds can be carried on four underwing stores stations.

Production Versions

More than twenty primary and many secondary versions of the MiG-21 appeared in rapid succession during the roughly two decades of MiG-21 development. While these differed in many details, they also shared enough features to enable them to be classified in four generations of production aircraft. For each of the first three generations of the MiG-21, there was also a two-seat training version for conversion and advanced training of pilots. All the two-seaters had just two underwing stores pylons, no cannon, and no radar gunsight.

Each MiG-21 version had both a type suffix and a product number. Both were used by the manufacturer and the air force, and consequently they also appeared in the aircraft documentation. As a rule the product number is given in the aircraft logbooks of aircraft built in Moscow, while the type suffix is usually recorded in logbooks of Gorki-built machines. The product number is therefore always needed to differentiate precisely between versions, ideally combined with the series number, because many modifications were undertaken during development and production of the MiG-21 without being reflected in the version designation.

Within the individual MiG-21 versions, there are also variants whose designations reflect equipment differences for various users. For example, there were two different variants of the MiG-21MF that had the product number 96A: the A and B. The former was for aircraft destined for Warsaw Pact countries; the latter, for all other nations.

First Generation

The first-generation MiG-21s were pure day fighters with no radar gunsight. They were armed with cannon and had two underwing stores pylons for bombs and unguided rockets.

MiG-21F (E-6, Product 72)

The first production version of the MiG-21 was equipped exactly like the E-6/3, the final prototype. Fuselage diameter was 4 feet, while the diameter of the air intake was 2.26 feet. The intake shock cone assumed three different positions depending on the aircraft's speed—below Mach 1.5, above Mach 1.9, and between these speeds. The pitot tube is mounted under the fuselage and can be tilted upward on the ground. The vertical tail is extremely narrow in chord — compared to later versions—and has an area of just 40.1 square feet. The cockpit canopy, which is hinged at the front and opens forward, has noticeable bulges at the rear, which are part of the KK-2 ejection seat system. The braking parachute is located in a container under the left side of the fuselage. Two small speed brakes are integrated into the cannon fairings on both sides of the fuselage. The MiG-21F is powered by an R11F-300 turbojet engine. Fuel capacity is 570 gallons in eight tanks. The wings have split flaps, each with an area of 10.1 square feet, and two wing stores pylons. Unlike those of all subsequent versions, the nose of these stores pylons is rounded. The nosewheel leg has a KT-38 wheel with dimensions of 19.7 x 7 inches. The MiG-21F has

MRK-10 nosewheel steering and a taxiing light on the nosewheel leg. The mainwheels have the designation KT-82 and measure 26 x 7.9 inches.

The MiG-21F is armed with two 30 mm NR-30 cannon in two fairings left and right beneath the cockpit. Remaining armament consists exclusively of unguided weapons. Up to 2,200 pounds of bombs can be carried on the underwing stores pylons, as well as S-5 unguided rockets in UB-16 pods and single S-21 rockets on PU-21 carriers. An external fuel tank can be mounted on the ventral stores pylon as required. The MiG-21F is equipped with an SRD-5 radar rangefinder, ASP-5NW gunsight, R-800 radio, MRP-56P marker receiver, ARK-54 radio compass, RW-U radio altimeter, SOD-57M transponder, and SRO-2 IFF set. An SIW-52 infrared sight can also be installed.

MiG-21F-13 (E-6T, Product 74)

The most obvious difference between the MiG-21F-13 and its predecessor is the deletion of the port NR-30 cannon. Instead, the aircraft can carry R-3S infrared-guided missiles on both wing pylons, which have a straight leading edge, in addition to bombs and unguided rockets. It retains the R11F-300 power plant. Beginning with the aircraft with Gorki construction number 0815, the number of integral wing tanks was increased from two to four, increasing total fuel capacity from 602 to 655 gallons in a total of ten tanks.

The side fairings on the rear canopy frame disappeared with the installation of the SK ejection seat from aircraft 0401 onward. From construction number 0815 onward, the nosewheel steering was deleted and the aircraft was steered by differential mainwheel braking controlled by the rudder pedals. Beginning with this aircraft, the MiG-21F-13 also had a larger vertical tail, with an area of 51.7 square feet.

The first operational version of the MiG-21, the MiG-21F, was used only by the Soviet air force.

Externally, the MiG-21F-13 differed from the preceding version primarily in the absence of the port cannon and the new wing hardpoints, which enabled it to carry air-to-air missiles.

Aircraft equipment now included an R-802 radio set and ASP-5ND sight. Like the earlier version, the F-13 does not have an autopilot. Either an SRO-1 (for export customers outside the Warsaw Pact—recognizable by the single antenna on the fuselage spine) or SRO-2 IFF set is used. An SPO-2 Sirena 2 radar-warning receiver is also fitted.

MiG-21F-13 (S-106, Z-159F, License Built in the ČSSR)

The sole difference between the MiG-21F-13 built under license in Czechoslovakia and Soviet-built aircraft was the replacement of the aft section of the cockpit glazing with a metal panel. There was also a reconnaissance version of this variant called the MiG-21FR, equipped with four AFA-39 cameras in a pod that was also made in the ČSSR. A total of seventy aircraft were modified for the reconnaissance role.

MiG-21U (E-6U, Product 66)

The MiG-21U was the first two-seat version of the MiG-21 for training of pilots and maintenance of currency. The MiG-21U's fuselage was based on that of the MiG-21F-13 and had the same intake section. The pitot tube was located atop the fuselage on the right side—which did not become standard on single-seat versions until the third generation. The ejection seats for the student and instructor are in a tandem arrangement. Instead of the forward hinged canopy of the single-seater, two separate canopies open to the right. The canopy is shaped to accommodate the SK seats, and a firing sequence ensures the safe ejection of both pilots.

Instead of the two side-mounted speed brakes, the two-seat version has a central speed brake in the same position.

While early-production aircraft had the narrow-chord tailplane of the MiG-21F-13, later aircraft had the broader-chord tail of the MiG-21PFS single-seater. The initial version is often designated Product 66-400, with the later one designated 66-600; however, there is no confirmation of this

On the MiG-21F-13 built under license in Czechoslovakia, metal panels replaced the glazing aft of the canopy. *Guido E. Bühlmann*

in official documents. Nevertheless, to easily differentiate between the two versions, these designations are used hereafter. The Romanian MiG-21U-600 with the serial number 5117 carries a placard with a construction number that begins with the product code 67 instead of 66. It is therefore conceivable that the allocation of product number 67 to this version was planned.

The strengthened undercarriage of all two-seat MiG-21U aircraft is similar overall to that of the second-generation MiG-21.

The aircraft is powered by the R11F-300 engine; total fuel capacity is 621 gallons. The MiG-21U and all subsequent two-seaters can be armed with unguided rockets and R-3S infrared-guided air-to-air missiles plus a 12.7 mm machine gun in a pod under the fuselage.

Second Generation

In the second generation of MiG-21s, the aircraft became an all-weather fighter with a radar gunsight but no cannon. It was capable of carrying bombs, unguided rockets, and guided missiles on two underwing stores pylons.

MiG-21PF (E-7, Product 76)

The MiG-21PF exhibits considerable external differences compared to the first-generation versions. The diameters both of the intake shock cone and the air intake were increased (the latter to 34.25 inches) to accommodate the RP-21 radar. As well, the UVD-2M system was fitted to continuously vary the position of the intake shock cone. The pitot tube was moved to a position atop the fuselage nose, and the glazing behind the cockpit disappeared. Instead, just behind the cockpit is located a new fuselage fuel tank (tank 7) with a capacity of 45 gallons, which tapers to the rear and

The fuselage and intake section of the MiG-21U was based on equivalent components of first-generation MiG-21s and were thus correspondingly slim in appearance.

The wide-chord tailplane was introduced on the twenty-fourth production batch of the MiG-21U, and was retained until production ended. *Stefan Büttner*

---

terminates in the so-called grotto. Total fuel capacity is now 726 gallons. The MiG-21PF is powered by an R11F-300 engine.

The undercarriage was strengthened with larger KT-92 mainwheels (31.5 x 7.9 in.). Because of the larger mainwheels, the fuselage undercarriage bays and the corresponding bulges in the external skin and undercarriage doors became larger. The forward speed brakes were redesigned and are larger in area.

Thanks to its radar, the aircraft's armament envelope was expanded to include the RS-2US radar-guided air-to-air missile (AAM). Deletion of the cannon weakened the aircraft's combat capability significantly. Also added to the MiG-21's arsenal from PF onwards was the S-24 heavy unguided rocket. The Vozdukh-1/Lasur ground control interception (GCI) system, the SRZO-2 IFF system, and the KAP-2 autopilot formed part of the aircraft's equipment. Absent was the RV-UM radio altimeter, which was restored in subsequent versions.

MiG-21FL (Product 77)

Created in parallel with the MiG-21PF was a simplified version with the designation FL, exclusively for export to countries outside the Warsaw Pact. A version of the less capable RP-21 radar, designated R1L, with even less range, was fitted. All MiG-21FLs, including those made under license in India, had the broader-chord fin high-mounted braking-chute container, but also wings with split flaps and no SPS blown flaps. The reduction in equipment made it possible to accommodate additional fuel aft of the cockpit, raising total capacity to 740 gallons.

The MiG-21FL's power plant was also a step back compared to the MiG-21PF—it was powered by the R11F-300 used in the MiG-21F-13.

MiG-21PFS (E-7SPS, Product 94)

The significant modifications incorporated in the MiG-21PFS

The larger shock cone and the dorsal fuel tank aft of the cockpit introduced by the MiG-21PF changed the aircraft's silhouette considerably. *Guido E. Bühlmann*

remained until the end of MiG-21 production. Beginning with the 226th aircraft, the vertical tail was increased in area to 58 square feet, and the new braking parachute (model designation PT-21UK) was moved from the underside of the fuselage to a tubular container at the base of the vertical tail. This made it possible to deploy the braking chute in the air, significantly reducing landing distance. Introduction of the SPS boundary layer control (flap-blowing) system had even greater effects on landing characteristics and low-speed flight, however. Landing speed was reduced from 186 to 168 mph to a minimum of 155 mph. For the first time it was possible to mount SPRD-99 takeoff-assist rockets on the side of the fuselage between formers 22 to 28.

Because of the larger wheels introduced by the MiG-21PF, the SPS system, the relocated braking chute, and the ability to use takeoff-assist rockets, the MiG-21 was capable of taking off and landing on unpaved and short strips.

MiG-21PFM (Product 94/94A)

While the first MiG-21PFM aircraft were delivered with the cockpit configuration of the earlier versions, in later aircraft the new KM-1 ejection seat designed by MiG itself replaced the earlier SK model, which was prone to failure. This eliminated the need to position the cockpit canopy in front of the seat as a shield during ejection. The previous one-piece canopy, which opened forward pneumatically, was replaced by a two-part design consisting of a fixed windscreen and quarter panels and a folding canopy that opened manually to the right.

Since deletion of the cannon had proved to be a serious disadvantage in aerial combat, in the course of production (from construction number 6413 onward at the Moscow factory), provision was made for the carriage of a GP-9 cannon pod with 23 mm GSh-23 cannon on the ventral pylon. The resulting loss of the ventral fuel tank and the

The MiG-21FL export version was the first single-seat variant to have the braking-parachute container at the base of the tailplane. *Simon Watson*

Late series MiG-21PFS with side-hinged canopy, KM-1 ejection seat, and broad chord tailplane were outwardly indistinguishable from MiG-21PFM.

The serial number 5311 on this MiG-21PFM is also its construction number. From this it can be concluded that aircraft from the fifty-third production batch did not have a cannon pod, which was introduced only in batch 64. *Guido E. Bühlmann*

additional drag produced by the GP-9 reduced the MiG-21PFM's range considerably, however. The PKI sight was used with the cannon.

The PFM was the first version of the MiG-21 capable of using a guided air-to-surface weapon, the Kh-66. The R11F2S-300, R11F2SK-300, and R13-300 engines were used in production versions of the MiG-21PFM. The KT-102 nosewheel unit with disc brake replaced the previously used KT-38 with hose brake.

MiG-21PFM (Product 94N)

Toward the end of MiG-21PFM series production in Moscow, one production batch was completed with the necessary wiring for the carriage of tactical nuclear weapons. The only external difference compared to the standard MiG-21PFM—the recess on the underside of the fuselage for mounting of the bomb pylon—was visible only if the fuselage stores pylon

was removed. In service the version designation was often shortened to PFMN. Henceforth, this will also be used here.

MiG-21E (M-21/M-21M)

MiG-21s of the PF and PFM versions were converted into remotely controlled target drones for realistic training of fighter pilots and surface-to-air missile units, with the designations M-21 (M for *Mishen* or target) and M-21M. Significant elements of the pilot's environmental system and the radar were removed to make space for a remote-control system, a new autopilot, additional antennas, control drives, and chaff/flare dispensers.

MiG-21US (E-6US, Product 68)

The MiG-21US training version was a development of the MiG-21U-600 with the SPS flap-blowing system and

Capable of carrying nuclear weapons, the MiG-21PFMN, which first appeared in the seventy-eighth production batch, did not differ from its predecessors externally but had special wiring and a recess in the fuselage for mounting of the pylon for the nuclear weapon.

Chapter 3: Production Versions

The MiG-21PFMs that were converted into target drones had numerous additional antennas and associated fairings—beneath the fuselage, on the fuselage spine, beside and on the vertical tail, and on the wingtips. *Guido E. Bühlmann*

The MiG-21US was equipped with KM-1 ejection seats, which led to the introduction of a periscope on the aft canopy, giving the instructor a view forward.

R11F2S-300 engine. Like the contemporaneous MiG-21PFM single-seater, the US version was equipped with the new KM-1 ejection seat. Associated with this was the installation of a periscope atop the canopy to provide a view forward for the instructor in the rear seat.

Late series MiG-21US aircraft had the KAP-155 autopilot and the associated angle of attack vane on the nose. Fuel volume was increased to 647 gallons.

Third Generation

The third generation of MiG-21s included all-weather fighters and reconnaissance aircraft with bomb, missile, and cannon armament. The aircraft have four underwing stores pylons and increased fuel capacity because of the saddle tank. Almost all aircraft of this generation were equipped with cannon armament.

MiG-21R
(E-7R, Product 03, Product 94R)

The designers of the MiG-21R faced two tasks: to incorporate the necessary equipment and increase the aircraft's range. Because of the little space available in the airframe, the equipment had to be placed in an external pod, which took the place of the ventral stores pylon. This eliminated the possibility of an external fuel tank there, so consequently a second underwing pylon was added beneath each wing, which could accommodate an external fuel tank or armament.

Four different reconnaissance pods could be carried by the MiG-21R. The type D was a daylight photo reconnaissance pod for low and medium altitudes and had vertical and oblique cameras. The type N was a night photo reconnaissance pod and contained a NAFA-47 camera. The object to be photographed was illuminated by cartridges released by the pod. The type R was for radar reconnaissance, and the type T was equipped with a television camera.

The antennas of the SPO-3R radar-warning receiver were housed in streamlined wingtip fairings. The RP-21M radar sight was similar to the previous version. The aircraft was powered by an R11FS-300 engine. During the MiG-21R's production run, the AP-155 autopilot was added to the production version. MiG-21s equipped with this system can be recognized by the DUA-3 angle of attack probe on the left side of the nose. Also absent from early-production MiG-21Rs was the SARPP-12 flight data recorder, which became standard equipment on later-production aircraft.

MiG-21RF (Product 94R)

Specially tailored to meet the requirements of the Egyptian air force, which was seeking a photo reconnaissance aircraft that could overfly the target area at high speed unhampered by a bulky reconnaissance pod, a small batch of the MiG-21RF version was produced by converting MiG-21R machines. Three cameras made by the British manufacturer Vinten were installed, partially recessed in the fuselage and partially housed in a fairing under the cockpit.

MiG-21S (E-7S, Product 95), MiG-21SN (E-7N, Product 95N)

The technical innovations introduced by the MiG-21R (saddle tank, two external stores pylons on each wing) were also incorporated into the MiG-21S fighter variant that entered production in 1966. The new RP-22 radar and the R-3R radar-guided air-to-air missile (a replacement for the RS-2US) were fitted for the first time. The MiG-21S did not have the integral cannon of the third-generation MiG-21, but like the MiG-21PFM it could carry the GP-9 cannon pod. The new pitot tube for the first time had vanes for measuring the angle of attack and yaw angle. The R11-F2S-300 was retained as power plant. The MiG-21SN was a version of the MiG-21S equipped to carry nuclear weapons.

The MiG-21R, the first representative of the third generation of MiG-21s, had a continuous dorsal spine and four wing hardpoints. The containers on the wingtips were found only on this reconnaissance version. *Alexander Golz*

Two variants of the reconnaissance pod carried by the MiG-21R: pod R for radar reconnaissance (left) and pod D for day photo reconnaissance (right).

The MiG-21RF developed for Egypt differed from the MiG-21R in that it had its cameras mounted in a bulged fairing beneath the cockpit (below).

MiG-21SM (E-7SM, Product 15)

The MiG-21SM differed from its predecessor, the MiG-21S, mainly in having a GSh-23 cannon semirecessed under the fuselage with 200 rounds of ammunition in a pallet in the fuselage. Also new was the R13-300 engine. For the first time, a mirror was mounted atop the canopy, and FOD deflectors were placed under the flaps. The MiG-21SM was capable of delivering nuclear weapons.

MiG-21M (Product 96A, Product 88)

The MiG-21M was a simplified export version of the MiG-21SM. The downgraded components were primarily the power plant and radar. The M was powered by the R11F2S-300 used in the MiG-21PFM and the slightly improved RP-21MA radar. The less powerful engine and the clearly greater gross weight affected the aircraft's handling qualities. New to this version was the SPO-10 radar-warning receiver, the antennas of which were mounted in bulges on the wingtips on the prototype and early-production aircraft—including some delivered to East Germany. Later aircraft had these antennas installed on the vertical tail.

MiG-21MF (Product 96A)

The MiG-21MF was also an export version of the MiG-21SM that employed more-powerful engines than the MiG-21M. Most examples of the MiG-21MF were delivered with the R13-300, but in some cases—including those delivered to Poland—the R11F2SK-300 was installed. The MF was equipped with the RP-21MA radar. The MiG-21MF had the mirror and FOD deflectors under the flaps introduced by the SM. Since these components were retrofitted to the MiG-21M by maintenance providers, they cannot be considered reliable criteria for differentiating between versions. Identical product and sequential construction numbers show that the M and MF were derivatives of one version.

MiG-21SMT (E-7SMT, Product 50, Product 50bis)

Because the Sukhoi Su-7 had failed to live up to expectations as a fighter-bomber, and no suitable replacement was available, a special fighter-bomber version of the MiG-21, the MiG-21SMT, appeared at the beginning of the 1970s. Since the MiG-21's range was insufficient for an attack aircraft, fuel capacity was increased by widening the saddle tank (tank 7) and lengthening it to the vertical tail. As a result, the capacity of this tank was raised to 238 gallons (divided into a forward tank holding 172 gallons and a rear tank with 66 gallons). Total fuel capacity without external tanks was 859 gallons. Although the SMT was powered by the more powerful R13F-300, which for the first time delivered a massive, short-term increase in thrust at low altitude thanks to a so-called special regime, the increased fuel load was detrimental to flight characteristics. As a result, beginning with construction number 50MM07, the MiG-21SMT was delivered with the

Even though this prototype at the museum in Monino has just two underwing stores pylons, the MiG-21S had four such pylons. A cannon pod could be mounted on the fuselage stores pylon.

The MiG-21SM was powered by the R13 engine and was the first version to have this power plant, which compensated for the type's higher gross weight. It and all subsequent versions had the GSh-23 cannon permanently mounted under the fuselage.

The MiG-21M was the export version of the MiG-21SM, which was used solely by the Soviets. Externally, the two types were largely similar, but there were considerable differences in equipment.

Chapter 3: Production Versions

smaller saddle tank of the later MiG-21bis. The resulting version was still designated the MiG-21SMT, but received product code 50bis.

The other equipment of the MiG-21SMT versions was largely similar to that of the MiG-21SM, including the RP-22 radar.

MiG-21MT (Product 96B)

Since the MiG-21MF was derived from the MiG-21SM, the MT was an export version of the MiG-21SMT that resulted from replacing the RP-22 with the the RP-21 radar. Most other systems were identical to those of the SMT.

MiG-21MF (Product 96D)

With the end of MiG-21 production in Moscow in 1974, the factory in Gorki also began building aircraft for export. At that time the MiG-21bis was in production for the Soviet air force;

the MiG-21MF, for foreign users. Several features of the MiG-21bis were adopted for the latter, obviously to rationalize production, such as cockpit instrumentation and wiring for the use of the R-60 AAM. The affected aircraft were often called the MiG-21MF-75, even though this was not to be found in the aircraft documentation. For simplicity's sake, however, this designation will be used henceforth.

The 96D variants of the MiG-21MF were delivered either with the R13-300 or R11F2SK-300 engine. Contrary to what has been claimed elsewhere, these MiG-21MFs were also equipped with the RP-21 radar.

Aircraft exported to Warsaw Pact countries had the R-832M radio.

MiG-21UM (E-6UM, Product 69)

The MiG-21UM was the final two-seat version of the MiG-21. Changes compared to the earlier US version included a new AP-155 autopilot with the DUA-3 angle of attack sensor on

The MiG-21MF was the first export version powered by the R13 engine. The type's equipment and armament—like the R-60 air-to-air missiles seen here—did not come up to current standards until they were upgraded.

The attempt to improve range by increasing internal fuel capacity (saddle tank) caused the MiG-21SMT to have problematic handling characteristics.

As production of the MiG-21SMT went on, a smaller dorsal fuel tank was fitted. Otherwise the two aircraft were identical.

the nose, the R-832 radio in aircraft from later production batches, and the R13-300 engine, although the R11F2S-300 was still used in some aircraft. Because of the MiG-21UM's relatively low weight, the R13-300's second afterburner stage was not fitted.

The two-seater was also equipped with the IP-K, PIO-2, and PUO-155 fault simulators, which enabled the instructor to simulate a variety of equipment failures and assess the student's response to them.

Fourth Generation

The fourth generation of the MiG-21 was created as an all-weather multirole combat aircraft with improved aerial combat capabilities at low altitudes. The engine and airframe were largely redesigned.

MiG-21bis (E-7bis, Product 75)

Unlike previous generations, the fourth generation of the MiG-21 has but one version, the MiG-21bis.

The obvious external feature of the MiG-21bis is its new saddle fuel tank, which is broader and longer than that of the MiG-21M/SM/MF. However, it is shorter and narrower than that of the SMT and thus represents the best possible combination of capacity and flight characteristics.

The MiG-21bis is equipped with the RP-22 radar, and it is the first version to be exported with this radar, the export version of which is designated A-23 Almas. The MiG-21bis is powered by the R25-300 engine. The new engine's greater airflow requirements resulted in changes to the air intake, which is 1.2 inches larger in diameter but 1.6 inches shorter. Fuel volume is 760 gallons.

Ammunition capacity for the GSh-23 cannon is now 250 rounds. Unlike its predecessor, the MiG-21bis can carry UB-32 rocket pods for thirty-two unguided S-5 rockets—though only on the inner stores pylons. When equipped with two UB-

The export version that was never exported: built in small numbers, the MiG-21MT was used exclusively by the Soviet air force. *Dirk Peisker*

The MiG-21MFs produced at Gorki were finished in an elegant gray color, which was significantly better suited to the interceptor role than the green-brown camouflage worn by aircraft built in Moscow.

With the exception of the radar, all technical innovations were incorporated into the final two-seat version, the MiG-21UM. The aircraft shown here is even fitted with the modern Parol IFF set.

Chapter 3: Production Versions

Since, obviously, not all of the equipment of the early 1970s could be installed in a single airframe, there were two versions of the MiG-21bis—one with the LAZUR ground control interception system and the one shown here, with the RSBN navigation system.

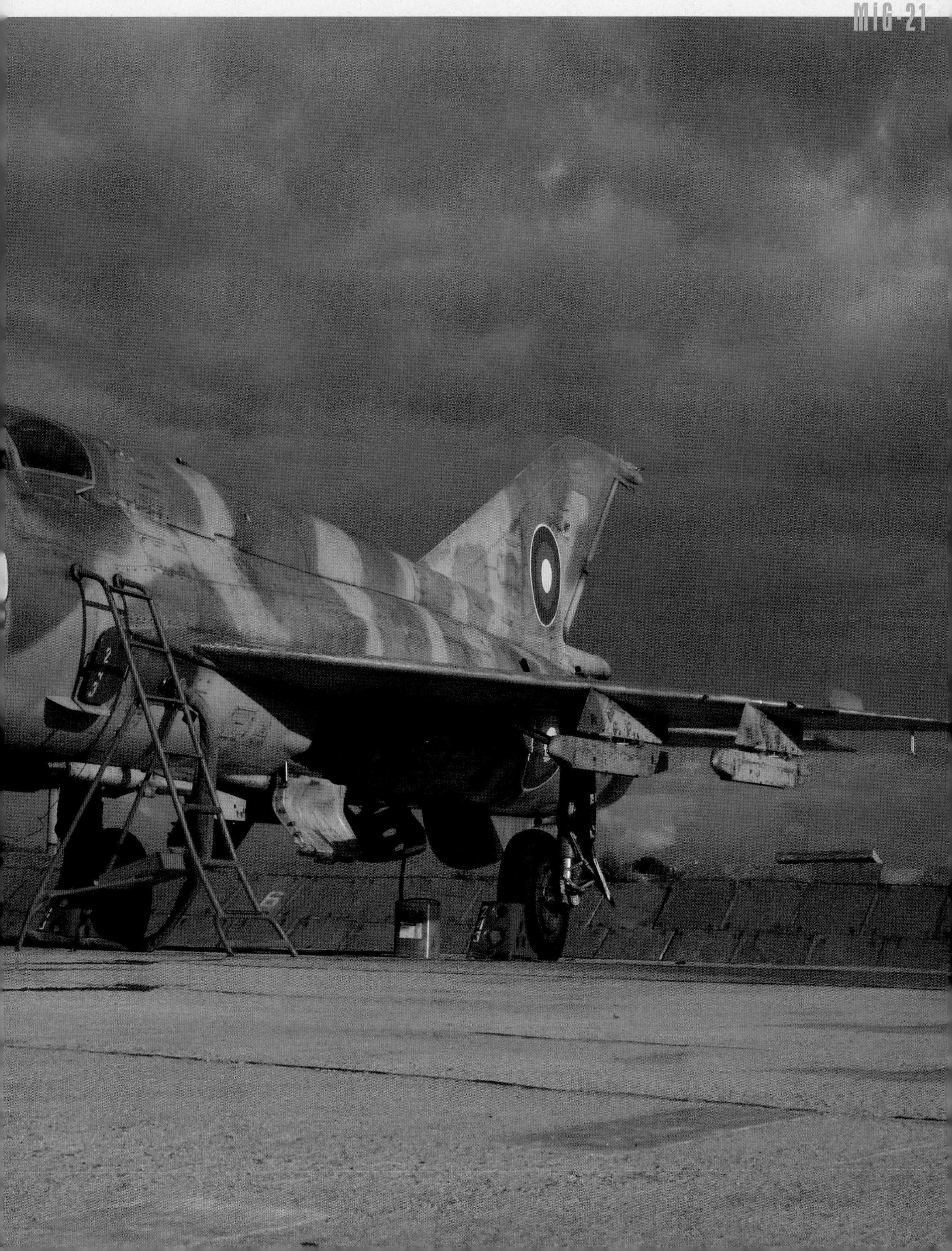

Although the MiG-21bis externally differed little from its predecessors, the longest built version was essentially a new design.

16 and two UB-32 rocket pods, total armament load is ninety-six rockets.

The MiG-21bis can be equipped either with the LAZUR fighter guidance system or the RSBN navigation system. Carriage of both systems is obviously not possible for space and/or weight reasons. There is no difference in the factory designation to differentiate between the two versions, while in the East German air force, for example, the LAZUR variant was designated 75A; the RSBN version, 75B. The manufacturer's identical production codes designate aircraft for export to Warsaw Pact nations (A) and other nations (B).

Power Plants

In May 1953, the staff of Experimental Design Bureau (OKB) No. 21 at Moscow-Luzhniki, under the direction of Alexander Alexandrovich Mikulin, began projecting a new turbojet engine for an OKB MiG fighter project designated E-1. Development of the engine proceeded under the designation AM-11 until Mikulin was replaced in January 1955. After Sergey Konstantinovich Tumanski took over OKB-300, the engine was renamed the RD-11.

In May 1956, the R11-300 engine, the 300 being the OKB suffix, successfully completed state acceptance trials with a 100-hour ground run. Previously, on January 9, the E-5, first prototype of the MiG-21, made its first flight powered by this engine, albeit without the afterburner that was fitted later.

The following derivative of the engine, with the designation R11F-300, then entered quantity production at Factory 500 at Moscow-Tushino. The engine flew for the first time in the E-6 prototype and powered the early MiG-21F and F-13 production versions.

In 1962, factory number 26 in Ufa began building the R11 engine. The F2 derivative, with greater afterburning thrust, was created there, as were the F2S, with bleed air for boundary layer control (SPS), and the F2SK, with a nozzle correction device in the area of the afterburner (SKDS). The new R13 and R25 engines were subsequently developed at Ufa under new chief designer Sergey Alexeyevich Gavrilov.

The R11 also powered the Yak-28 in addition to the MiG-21. The R11 and R13 were used in various versions of the Sukhoi Su-15. The R95Sch engine without afterburner was developed from the R13 to power the Sukhoi Su-25.

R11 (Product 37)

The R11-300, the first development stage of the MiG-21 engine, produced 8,385 pounds of static thrust at maximum power and 11,240 pounds of thrust with afterburner. Like the E-5 preproduction version of the MiG-21 powered by this engine, the R11-300 was built for only a short time and in small numbers. The following detailed descriptions therefore refer exclusively to production engines built in large numbers.

The R11F-300 (Product 37F) was a twin-shaft turbojet engine consisting of an axial compressor, annular combustion liners, twin-shaft turbine, and afterburner with variable nozzle.

The low-pressure compressor and turbine form the low-pressure spool, while the high-pressure compressor and turbine form the high-pressure spool. Both spools are coupled purely gas-dynamically, ensuring stable functioning of the compressor even in areas outside design limits. The axial speeds of the air in the compressor stages change as engine-operating conditions (speed, altitude, external temperature, throttle lever position) change. This leads to redistribution of the gas-dynamic loads between the two compressor sections, whereby the revolution ratio of the spools automatically changes. The twin-shaft design makes it possible to dispense with variable geometries, apart from the intake section and shock cone, resulting in a comparatively simple control system.

The engine functions in conjunction with a supersonic intake section, which—like the outer shape of the engine nozzle—is part of the airframe design. To guarantee reliable operation, subsystems for lubrication, cooling, ventilation, power and fuel supply, control, drainage, starting, monitoring, and fire extinguishing are present. The systems that supply power to the airframe, engine, and other equipment are mounted on an accessory board on the engine.

As thrust increases, the engine can operate at the following power settings: idle, minimum, maximum, minimum afterburner, and maximum afterburner. Between the idle and maximum regimes, changes in thrust are accomplished continuously by changing engine revolutions. In the afterburner regimes, thrust changes are also continuous; however, at maximum revolutions, the intensity of afterburning is influenced by varying the afterburner nozzle. Power levels are set with the throttle lever in the cockpit, which is connected to the engine by control rods.

The engine can be operated within the following flight parameters:

- Maximum allowable speed: 808 mph (at 42,650 ft.)
- Maximum allowable Mach number: 2.1 (at 42,650 ft.)
- Minimum allowable speed: 218 mph (at 49,213 ft.)
- Minimum allowable speed: 310 mph (at 49,213 ft.)
- Maximum altitude: 75,460 feet

The air intake section makes a significant contribution to the stable and effective operation of the engine. The intake cross-section with the large-volume cone in its center is located in the fuselage nose. The system of external shock waves produced by it ensures that the supersonic flow is slowed with little pressure loss. To smooth the flow, the boundary layer (about 1.5 percent of the air throughput) is bled off by a 0.25-inch annular slot at the end of the cone. The flow channel, shaped as a Laval nozzle, causes the air to accelerate again, until another shock wave, independent of the external system, in the inner part of the intake achieves the ultimate slowing of the incoming air to subsonic speed. The air intake section is controlled by three principal variants of geometry variation. Controlled by the UVD-2M system, the shock cone is moved axially independent of compressor pressure ratio and stabilator deflection. The auxiliary input doors open when the engine is throttled back at high Mach numbers, and the blow-in doors open if there is negative pressure in the intake section.

R11 engine, complete with afterburner and nozzle.

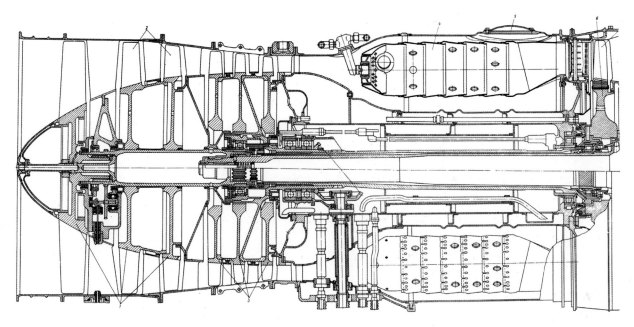

Longitudinal section of the 37F-2S(K) engine
1. low-pressure compressor rotor; 2. compressor blades; 3. high-pressure compressor rotor; 4. combustion chamber; 5. SPS tapping flange; 6. high-pressure turbine rotor; 7. low-pressure turbine rotor; 8. turbine blades; 9. afterburner diffusor; 10. afterburner ignition chamber; 11. afterburner chamber and nozzle

The compressor's job is to take in, deliver, and compress as much air as possible to a specified pressure level. In the 37F engine it is divided into two cascades per every three stages, with each cascade powered by its own turbine. The first three stages of the compressor form the low-pressure compressor, which is powered by the second turbine stage (the low-pressure turbine), while the first turbine stage (the high-pressure turbine) powers the last three stages of the high-pressure compressor. Each compressor stage consists of rotor and stator blades. The relative speed of the air in the spool of the first four stages is supersonic, which increases the air throughput and the degree of compression but reduces the degree of effectiveness.

The energy required for the thermodynamic cycle is delivered by the gas stream in the combustion chamber, created by the burning of kerosene. The 37F engine is equipped with annular combustion liners, made up of ten flame tubes. The flame tube heads are joined together by annular bars. The primary air needed to burn the fuel reaches the flame tubes by way of an atomizer and an opening in the head parts of the flame tube and is set into intensive rotation

and thrown against the walls of the flame tubes. The negative pressure created in the center of the flame tubes ensures the optimal mixing of air and fuel and stable combustion. The combustion chamber is ignited by two ignition systems, each between two flame tubes. The linking bars cause the flame to spread to the other tubes.

The main mass of the airstream, 70 percent of which is secondary air, passes through several rows of openings in the flame tubes, mixes with the hot combustion gases, cools them, and provides a temperature distribution, which under all conditions does not limit the strength of the turbine blades.

Through partial expansion of the gas stream, the turbine delivers the necessary torque to power the compressor and auxiliary equipment. The two-stage overpressure turbine consists of a guide device (stator) and one rotor per stage. The stator converts potential energy into kinetic energy and feeds the gas stream to the turbine blades. Pressure and temperature fall as the gases pass through the turbine, while the speed of the gas exiting the turbine rises. Air bled from the combustion chamber and compressor cools the turbine. To increase thrust without increasing the air throughput, the

View of the gear tray on the underside of the engine. The oil tank can be seen at the bottom left, while at the top right is the starter/DC generator.

equipment is mounted on the engine's accessory board, a hermetically sealed gearbox with several shafts and pairs of gear wheels with different rpm, and is powered by the high-pressure spool. This is true of the NR-21F main fuel pump, the NR-22F afterburner fuel pump, two NP 34-1T hydraulic pumps, the DZN 13-DT fuel booster pump, the lubrication unit, the centrifugal air separator, and the alternating (from the R11F2-300) and direct current generators. The low-pressure spool powers the rpm indicator and the centrifugal governor of the NR-21 pump.

Turning of the engine during start-up is accomplished by an electric starter, which after the conclusion of the engine start process functions as a DC generator that supplies power to the aircraft's electrical system. To enable this, the generator is connected to the high-pressure spool by a two-speed gearbox. A centrifugal claw coupling creates the frictional connection during starter operation. On reaching a speed of 4,200 to 4,800 rpm, the claw coupling is released and switched from starter to generator mode, so that the high-pressure spool, which is now rotating faster than the generator, picks it up by means of a clutch (similar to freewheeling on a bicycle). If the starter-generator is connected to an external power source, start time is about forty seconds, while on battery power it takes about eighty seconds. There is also a starter system with gasoline, which is delivered to the starter blocks by a PNR-10 starter pump.

The engine's automatic lubrication system provides pressure lubrication. It consists of one pressure pump and four suction pumps, the fuel-lubricant cooler, filters, and air and lubricant separators. Coming from the delivery tank, the fuel flows to the engine under the influence of gravity, low-pressure ventilation, and the extraction pump. The extraction pump is installed in an inverted flight container to deliver fuel for a short period even under negative load factors. From the extractor pump the fuel passes to the fuel booster pump, which increases fuel pressure and dampens pressure variations. While passing through the fuel-lubricant system, the fuel cools the lubricant and is warmed in the process.

The engine is designed for use with T-1, TS-1, T-2, and T-7 jet fuel, but it can also be driven by other types of approved fuel. The electromechanical fuel-regulating system ensures that the engine functions stably in all flight and engine regimes. Fuel regulation is achieved mainly by varying the amount of fuel in the main combustion chamber via the NR-21F fuel pump. Regulation of the afterburner is

engine is equipped with an afterburner behind the turbine. Additional fuel is sprayed into the afterburner, which is burned because of the surplus oxygen in the gas coming from the turbine. The afterburner consists of a diffuser, afterburner chamber, and variable thrust nozzle. The diffuser reduces the speed of the gas flow, and flame stabilizers with injection rings ensure stable combustion. A central flare igniter ignites the afterburner. The variable nozzle regulates the exhaust cross-section; the nozzle control system is electrohydraulic. The nozzle had its maximum diameter at maximum thrust without afterburning and varies between middle and maximum diameter with afterburning. The nozzle is fully open when the engine is at idle.

The energy necessary to operate the aircraft's systems is drawn mechanically from the engine's shaft system and converted into electrical or hydraulic energy. The necessary accomplished by the NR-22F afterburner pump in combination with the electrohydraulic nozzle control system.

The R11F2-300 (Product 37F2) engine is largely identical to its predecessor but is about 45 pounds lighter. It is designed for use with a larger intake, in which the shock cone operates continuously. The dimensions and flow areas of the compressor and turbine blades are also fractionally different. Because the main and afterburner combustion chambers are designed for higher gas temperatures and it has a fuel system with higher output and injection quantity, the 37F2 produces more thrust in maximum afterburner setting. The VK-21 height adjustor also improved acceleration times. Other devices, such as a metal-shaving detector and lubricant pressure–warning device, improve operational safety. The gasoline starter system has been deleted. Unlike the previous 37F and 37F2 modifications, the R11F2S-300 (Product 37F2S) and all subsequent derivatives can be operated with air bleed for the SPS flap-blowing system. Bleed air from the combustion chamber secondary stream is fed to the flaps, where it considerably improves the aircraft's low-speed handling and landing characteristics. The R11F2SK-300 (Product 37F2SK) is also equipped with a system to correct thrust nozzle diameter (SKDS). In case of inadequate fuel supply to the afterburner, the SKDS limits thrust loss by a pulsating reduction of the nozzle cross-section.

R13 (Product 95)

The greater weight of the third-generation MiG-21 and the need to improve performance required a redesign of the engine. The opportunities to improve the existing design had been largely exhausted with the 37F2SK. A new engine designated R13-300 was therefore created, while retaining the original's twin-shaft principal and external dimensions. Design differences compared to the R11 included redesigned, strengthened, and additional components and accessories; improved fuel supply; cooling and regulation; and new materials, in particular titanium alloys.

R11F-300 Specification

Parameters	Load Settings				
	AB max.	AB min.	Maximum	Nominal	Idle
Static Thrust (lb.)	12,905	10,790	8,678	≥6,834	≤382
Specific Fuel Consumption (lb./hr.)	≤524	≤389	215	209	164 gal./hr.
Low Pressure RPM (%)	100.5 ± 0.5	100.5 ± 0.5	100.5 ± 0.5	94 ± 0.5	33 ± 2
High Pressure RPM (%)	100.4	101	100.6	95.4	46.4
Gas Temperature (°F)	≤1,310	≤1,310	≤1,346	≤1,364	≤788
Thrust Nozzle Diameter (in.)	≤26.7	≥24	≥20.7	≥20.7	≤26.7

R11F2S-300 Specification

Parameters	Load Settings					
	AB max.	AB min.	Maximum	Max. SPS	Nominal	Idle
Static Thrust (lb.)	13,623	10,790	8,610	≥7,509	≥6,834	≤382
Specific Fuel Consumption (lb./hr.)	≤533	≤386	215		95	164 gal./hr.
Air Throughflow (lb./sec.) 144	144	144	144	144	136	33
Degree of Compression	8.9	8.9	8.6	8.6	7.9	1.5
Low Pressure RPM (%)	100.5 ± 0.5	100.5 ± 0.5	100.5 ± 0.5	100.5 ± 0.5	94 ± 0.5	33 ± 2
High Pressure RPM (%)	100.3	100.1	100.1	98.1	96	50 ± 2
Gas Temperature (°F)	≤1,364	≤1,364	≤1,364	≤1,364	≤1,382	≤788
Thrust Nozzle Diameter (in.) 26.7	≤26.7	≤25 ± 0.07	≥ 20.8	≥21.5	≥20.8	≤26.7

By enlarging the high-pressure compressor from three to five stages at the same pressure ratio, some of the load was taken off the compressor stages, and stability reserve and effectiveness were increased. A ribbed intake ring also contributes to an improvement in stability. The combustion chamber has a revised flame tube arrangement. The redesigned turbine has a higher entry temperature and therefore effectiveness, and also the turbine-compressor energy transfer and thus the compressor operating field are improved. Sturdier versions of the afterburner chamber and nozzle are used because of the increased heat and pressure load.

The new DZN-44DT fuel booster pump has a discharge socket, which results in additional delivery of fuel to the afterburner and a system to reduce pressure variations at high altitudes. The new NR-54 fuel pump has a mechanism for rpm overspeed in the second afterburner stage and a barometric height corrector. Thrust is thus improved in the maximum and afterburner thrust settings compared to the 37F2SK. A second afterburner thrust setting (NB-2) is available as an additional thrust setting from Mach 1.5. Thrust effectiveness and economy are improved through higher afterburner chamber pressure and fuel and air throughflow.

The R13F-300 (Product 95F) is a development of the R13-300 and is the first MiG-21 power plant to have a so-called special regime, which delivers a massive, short-term thrust increase at low level. The engine is equipped with an NR-54F2 main fuel pump, an NR-22F2M2 afterburner fuel pump, and an additional NR-44 afterburner pump, whose function is explained in the following description of the R25.

R25 (Product 25)

In keeping with the design of the MiG-21 for operation at high altitudes, the power plants used in its first- and second-

Outwardly, the R13 differed from its predecessor only in its grooved inlet ring.

R13-300 Specification

Parameters	Load Settings						
	AB 1	AB 2	AB min.	Maximum	Max. SPS	Nominal	Idle
Static Thrust (lb.)	14,972	14,545	11,690	9,037	7,508	7,508	382
Specific Fuel Consumption (lb./hr.)	505	143	216		205		
Air Throughflow (lb./sec.)	152	145–148	145–148	145–148	145–148		
Degree of Compression	8.75–8.9	8.75–8.9	8.75–8.9	8.75–8.9	8.75–8.9	8.75–8.9	8.75–8.9
Low Pressure RPM (%)	103.5 +1	100.5 ± 0.5	100.5 ± 0.5	100.5 ± 0.5	100.5 ± 0.5	95 ± 0.5	33.5 ± 1.5
High Pressure RPM (%)							
Gas Temperature (°F)	≤1,418	≤1,436	≤1,436	≤1,418	≤1,292		≤1,247
Thrust Nozzle Diameter (in.)	26.5 – 0.4	25.5 ± 0.4	24	21	21.8	≥21	26.5

R13F-300 Specification

Parameters	Load Settings						
	AB 1	AB 2	AB min.	Maximum	Max. SPS	Nominal	Idle
Thrust Nozzle Diameter (in.)	26 25 ±	0.12	23	20	21.25	21.6	25

generation versions had deficits in thrust in the lower altitude range. The R25-300, which had significantly greater thrust reserves in these areas compared to the previous design, with almost identical dimensions, was therefore created to power the MiG-21bis, which was optimized for operations at ground level and lower altitudes.

Development work focused on redesigning the low-pressure compressor, with the objective of achieving a greater mass flow rate and raising the turbine entry temperature. The afterburner fuel deficit that had formerly existed in certain regimes was eliminated.

The design of the R25-300 differs from that of its predecessors in having a redesigned low-pressure compressor with different blades, in particular in the first stage. The number of rotor blades is reduced from twenty-four to twenty-one, and the grooved intake ring is lengthened. To improve stability, when the weapons are being used, a air vent opens over the stator blades of the third compressor stage. Because of the 100 degree Kelvin (280 degree Fahrenheit) increase in turbine entry temperature, the rotor blades are also cooled for the first time. The afterburner has a variable convergent nozzle (previously a truncated cone), which minimizes power loss. The redesigned afterburner injectors are fed by two ring lines, of which one is supplied as

before by the NR-22 afterburner fuel pump, and one is supplied by the new additional NR-44 afterburner fuel pump. The flame stabilizer is now ring shaped, and the perforated cooling shell extends to the nozzle. The variable-nozzle-operating diagram has larger diameters to maximum power and smaller ones in the afterburner power settings. The equipment gearbox is expanded to include a fitting for the second afterburner fuel pump.

The aircraft's nose intake has revised dimensions and a modified operation diagram, resulting in greater air throughflow. The additional NR-44 afterburner fuel pump makes it possible for the engine to operate in the so-called special regime. This results in 21,800 pounds of thrust at Mach 1 at altitudes up to a maximum of 13,100 feet. Fuel consumption in this mode is very high, however, at 5,810 gallons per hour. The engine pumps deliver more fuel than the fuel tank pumps are capable of, and therefore additional quantities flow through a bypass. Use of this special regime is limited not just by the fact that the aircraft's fuel would be used up in less than ten minutes; because of thermal and mechanical loads, operating time is limited to three minutes. A thirty-second pause is required before the special regime can be engaged again.

The R25 had just twenty-one rotor blades in the first compressor stage, whereas the R13 had 24. The grooved inlet ring was made wider.

R25-300 Specification

Parameters	Load Settings						
	RATO	AB max.	AB min.	Maximum	Max. SPS	Nominal	Idle
Thrust (lb.)	21,829	15,647	15,107	9,037			
Air Throughflow (lb./sec.) 151	150						
Degree of Compression	9.6	9.1–9.5	9.1–9.5	9.1–9.5	9.1–9.5		
Low Pressure RPM (%)	102.5 + 1–0.5	100.5 + 1–0.5	100.5 + 1–0.5	100.5 + 1–0.5	100.5 + 1–0.5	100.5 + 1–0.5	100.5 + 1–0.5
High Pressure RPM (%)	<107.5						
Gas Temperature (°F)	1,418	1,436	1,436	1,418	1,292	788	
Thrust Nozzle Diameter (in.)	25±.11	25±.11	23	21	22	21	25±.11

Comparison of Engines

	R11F-300	R11F2-300	R11F2S-300	R13-300	R25-300
Overall Length with Afterburner Chamber and Nozzle (in.)	181	181	181	181	182
Maximum Diameter (in.)	35.6	35.6	35.6	35.7	35.7
Installation Weight (lb.)	2,615 + 2%	2,568 + 2%	2,632 + 2%	2,668 + 2%	2,844 + 2%
Turbine Inlet Temperature (°F)	1,634–1,696	1,651–1,714	1,688–1,742	1,723–1,904	
Afterburner Temperature (°F)			2,942	3,140	
Air Extraction during SPS Operation (lb./sec.)	–	–	5.5	5.5	5.5
Main Fuel Pump Maximum Performance (gal./hr.)	1,849 + 53		1,849 + 53 1	849 + 53 2	774 + 132
Afterburner Fuel Pump (1st) Maximum Performance (gal./hr.)	2,774-105	2,668-105	2,905-132	2,905-132	
Additional Afterburner Feed Maximum Performance (gal./hr.)	–	–	–	528 + 53	–
Afterburner Fuel Pump (2nd) Maximum Performance (gal./hr.)	–	–	–	–	2,905-132
Acceleration of Low-Speed RPM from 33% to 99% (sec.)	11.5–14.5	11.5–14.5 with WK-21	9–12	9–12	8–10
Acceleration of Low-Speed RPM from 85% to 99% (sec.)	8–11	8–11	5.5–7.5 2.5–4	2.5–4	
Acceleration of Low-Speed RPM from 50% to 99% with SPS (sec.)				> 5.5	> 4
100% Low Pressure RPM (1/min.)	11,150	11,150	11,156	11,156	
100% High Pressure RPM (1/min.)	11,425	11,412	11,362	11,362	

The SPRD-99 takeoff-assist rockets were supported by fuselage frame 28. The exit nozzles were canted downward, causing the thrust vector to pass through the aircraft's center of gravity, which made a safe takeoff possible even if one rocket failed.

A MiG-21M takes off with takeoff-assist rockets. This shortened the takeoff run by about 1,300 feet. The aircraft shown here crashed short after the picture was taken due to the hydraulic leakage visible on the tail. *Dirk Paatz Collection*

Chapter 4: Power Plants

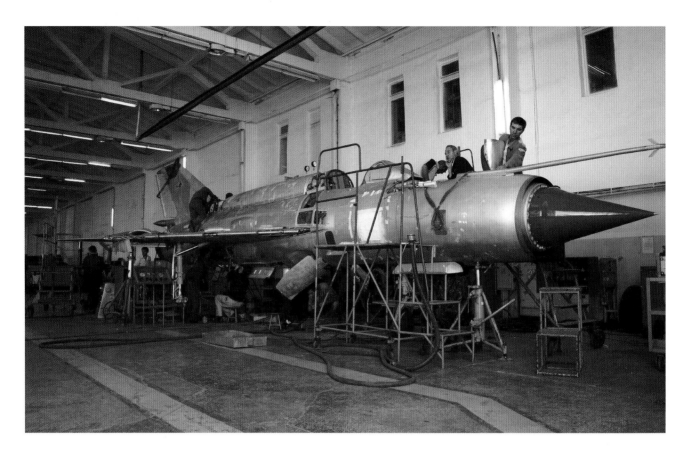

Though the R11/13/25 family of engines has overall good performance data, a decisive weakness—compared to Western engines—is their very short operating periods between overhauls. In the case of the first R11 engines, this was just 100 hours, while for the R13 it was 300 and the R25 it was 400 hours. The factory in Ufa now claims a time between major overhauls of 650 hours for the R13.

SPRD-99

To shorten takeoff distances or to increase payload, single-seat versions of the MiG-21 from the PF are capable of using two SPRD-99 takeoff-assist rockets. These solid-fuel rockets, developed in OKB-81 by a team under Ivan Ivanovich Kartukov, each produce 5,283 pounds of thrust with a burn duration of ten to eighteen seconds. The RATO units shorten takeoff distance by up to 1,200 feet.

The RATO units are attached to mounts on both sides of the fuselage between formers 22 and 28. After the afterburner is engaged, the pilot engages the DP 1-4 pyrocartridges, which ignite the ignition charges and thus the solid-fuel rockets.

The manufacturer delivers three nozzles with different diameters, with whose help thrust can be adjusted to suit various climatic zones. Once the solid-fuel rockets have burned out, they are jettisoned by the pilot. There are control surfaces on the RATO units that ensure that the airflow steers them away from the aircraft.

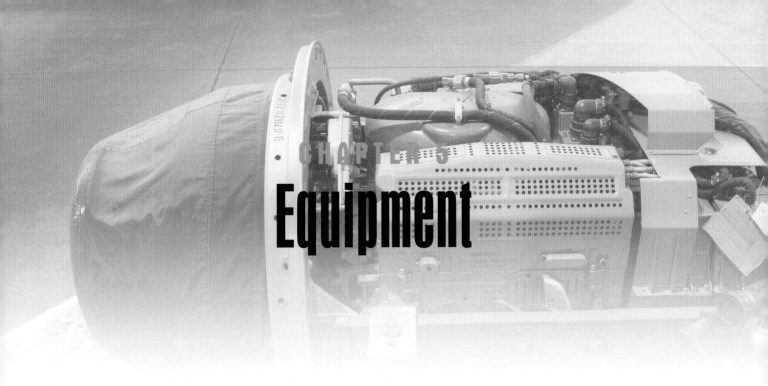

Equipment

Radar Range-Finder, and Radar SRD-5MK (Product Kvant)

The SRD-5MK radar range-finder measures the range to an aerial target by travel-time measurement of the reflected radar waves and determines the closure speed. Alternately, it can also determine the range from prominent ground targets. The radar range-finder radar has a fixed antenna in the intake shock cone, and therefore the target must be within the radar beam, which has a switchable aperture angle of 6 to 18 degrees. Maximum range is 4.35 miles. The range is displayed on the UD-1 indicator and is simultaneously coupled into the ASP optical sight to increase precision. Allowable missile-firing range is calculated in cooperation with the VRD-2A weapons computer. Optical and visual signals indicate when this range is reached or when the aircraft comes within minimum firing range. The MiG-21F and F-13 single-seaters and all two-seat versions are equipped with the SRD-5MK.

RP-21 (Product 830TK, Sapfir)

Originally developed as the RP-9 for the Su-9 fighter, the RP-21 (also designated RP-9-21) was adapted for use in the MiG-21. All essential components of the radar are located in a container in the intake shock cone. The RP-21 is fitted with a cassegrain antenna (parabolic antenna with an additional reflector). It is based on tube technology and a magnetron transmitter (vacuum electronic tubes to produce microwaves). Wavelength is approximately 1.25 inches; maximum range with a reflective target area of 10.75 square feet is 12 miles

in search mode and 6 miles in track mode (target identified and locked on). Locking on to a target is possible only from the rear hemisphere and only in the area of ±30 degrees azimuth and ±12 degrees in elevation.

The RP-21M and MA modifications (Product 830M/MA) have an additional rangefinder for use with cannon and can be linked to the PAK-21 testing complex. The measured range is used in the ASP optical gunsight for improved accuracy when the cannon is employed. The RP-21's lower operational altitude is limited to about 4,500 feet by ground reflections, which in this type of radar cannot be suppressed. The RP-21M has better protection against passive interference. Despite measures to reduce minimum operational altitude to 2,500 feet, locking onto a target below 3,500 feet is practically impossible. Target selection for the RS-2US missile is achieved by so-called glimmer tracking. The radar can be coupled with the SRZO-2 device to actively interrogate an aerial target.

The target is displayed on an indicator in the cockpit. The RP-21 is fitted in the MiG-21 versions PF, PFS, PFM, R, M, MF, and MT.

RP-22 (Product 010MA, Sapfir 21)

Semiconductors, subminiature tubes, a magnetron transmitter with selectable frequencies, and monopulse tracking are used by the more advanced RP-22 radar. The nonsynchronous signal processing prevents suppression of ground reflections. Compensation antennas and other circuit measures have enabled the minimum operational altitude to

The components of the radar are held in a container attached to the intake shock cone. The antenna fits into the cone itself.

be reduced to less than 2,500 feet. The RP-22 has a target illumination channel for the R-3R missile. The range of the radar is about 15.5 miles, and wavelength is about 0.9 inches. In practice, the result is strong reflections from cloud fronts and the danger of active radar jamming as the potential enemy was not operating in this frequency range and can therefore employ active jamming without affecting his own equipment. The RP-22 is found in the MiG-21 versions S, SM, SMT, and bis.

Autopilots

The purpose of an autopilot is to automatically control and stabilize an aircraft and thus improve safety in all flight regimes and reduce the pilot's workload. Two models with very different ranges of function were used in the MiG-21. The single-channel KAP-2 autopilot controlled the ailerons and thus operated exclusively about the aircraft's roll axis. It had operating modes to dampen brief oscillations and to hold predefined bank angles.

The AP-155 autopilot is a two-channel system with more capable leveling function and affects all three axes. The AP-155 returns the aircraft to horizontal flight from any starting position, can stabilize pitch and bank angles, and enables preset magnetic headings and altitudes to be maintained.

In the stabilization mode the aircraft is held at preset bank and pitch angles. These are maintained by the autopilot until the pilot's next control input. The stabilization mode is intended to make it easier for the pilot to control the aircraft in all flight modes from takeoff to landing.

Leveling mode, also known as "panic button" mode, returns the aircraft to level flight from any attitude should the pilot lose situational awareness. It subsequently stabilizes the aircraft's zero bank angle as well as altitude and heading. This mode can also be used on cross-country flights at constant speed to maintain altitude and heading.

Ground Control Interception (GCI) System

The Vozdukh/Lazur ground control interception system (Product 2000, ARL-S) enables a control site on the ground to guide an interceptor to a target without voice communications. The transmission of guidance information takes place automatically over a total of twenty radio channels, which can be alternated in the event of interference. Special indicators keep the pilot informed about altitude, speed, and heading; commands such as engage/disengage afterburner, turn, or abandon interception; and data on the position of the target. Use of the Vozdukh/Lazur fighter control system means that the fighter's radar does not have to be turned on until late in the interception or not at all, reducing the likelihood of detection.

Flight Data Recorder

The SARPP-12 flight data recorder records various operating parameters on a filmstrip during normal and emergency conditions and is able to safeguard the stored information even under great mechanical loads.

Sensors are installed in the aircraft's systems to record flight parameters, and these send signals to the flight data recorder. The flight data recorder is switched on manually or is activated by the SSA-120 speed sensor when the aircraft's speed is greater than 75 mph.

The flight data recorder records the following analog parameters: barometric height, speed, vertical and horizontal overload, stabilator pitch angle, and engine speed. In addition, binary signals record below-normal pressures in the main hydraulic and hydraulic booster systems, combat switch pressed, takeoff power selected, afterburner engaged, and autopilot active.

Data is recorded on a 35 mm filmstrip with a length of 35 feet and a feed rate of 0.04 or 0.1 inches per second. A time marker is saved every ten or four seconds.

Radio Equipment

The R-801 and R-802 radio sets were installed in the first-generation MiG-21s. Later aircraft used the R-832 VHF/UHF radio. While the R-802 operated in the VHF range (100 to 150 MHz), the R-832 had this and the UHF range (220 to 400 MHz). Both systems could be used for air-to-ground communications with air traffic control, ground-controlled interception (GCI), and command posts, as well as air-to-air communications with other aircraft.

Frequency settings on the R-802 were accomplished electromechanically with channel intervals of 83.33 kHz. Because of an electronic tuning system and new components,

Changing the SARPP-12 flight data recorder's cassette.

this was reduced to 25 kHz on the R-832. The SPU-7 and -9 intercom systems were installed for communications between cockpits of the two-seat MiG-21s and reception of acoustic signals—including from the compass and marker receiver—in the pilots' headsets.

For reception of commands from GCI stations (course, altitude, target range area [12, 7.5, 3 miles], and heading changes), the LAZUR system employed modified R-801 or R-802 receivers with corresponding decoders.

Depending on the version of the MiG-21, the radio antennas were located in the dorsal spine, atop the vertical tail, or forward in the false keel.

Radio Navigation Equipment

In all versions of the MiG-21, radio navigation was accomplished with the aid of the ARK-10 automatic direction finder, which constantly adjusts the aircraft's heading to signals received from medium-wave transmitters and

---

displays them on the course indicator. This can display the bearing of such a transmitter, the aircraft's position, or aircraft heading and correction. Thanks to coupling to distance-measuring equipment, the ARK-10 can constantly calculate and display the aircraft's distance from a transmitter. Directional determination is provided by a movable loop antenna.

The MRO-56 radio marker receiver signals overflight of a radio marker beacon, and it also functions as a radio aid during an instrument approach. It serves as a rough indication of the approach path by signaling passage over the outer and inner markers at the 2.5- and 0.6-mile points. The MRO-56's antenna is located beneath the aft fuselage.

The RK-UM radio altimeter measures and displays the aircraft's height above ground in the 0- to 350-foot range. So-called dangerous altitudes can be preset in fixed stages. If the aircraft goes below these altitudes, the pilot receives an acoustic and visual warning. This navigation aid serves both as a safety aid while on approach or in low-level flight and as an aid during air-to-ground gunnery. The radio altimeter's antennas are mounted beneath the wings.

The RSBN-5S system of the MiG-21bis (RSBN variants) represents a combination of navigation and instrument landing systems. The navigation system measures bearing and distance to a ground station, and using known initial values continuously computes the aircraft's position (automatic dead reckoning). The instrument landing system enables approaches, theoretically to ground level. Approaches are permitted to altitudes of 150 feet.

Identification Friend or Foe

The SRO-2 (Product 020 Chrome) and SRZO-2 (Product 023 Chrome-Nickel) are active interrogator-transponders and operate with the ground radar stations (ground-to-air interrogation) and with airborne radars (air-to-air interrogation) in the Kremniy identification system. With this, during the intercept process it is possible to identify friendly and hostile aircraft on the radar screens of GCI stations and interceptors and to select the most dangerous target.

Radar Illumination Warning Device

The SPO-2 Sirena-2, SPO-3 Sirena-3, and SPO-10 Sirena-3M warning devices alert the pilot acoustically and visually when his aircraft has been illuminated by radar, and indicate the general direction of the source of the illumination.

Transponder

The SOD-57M (Product 40) transponder receives signals from decimeter-wave radar stations, modifies and amplifies them, and transmits them back. This increases the radar detection range, minimizes the effects of jamming and weather, and enables transmission of altitude information and the aircraft's discrete code. The transponder has guidance modes (coarse/fine) in the Globus-2 radar guidance system and landing modes (individual/formation) in the RSP ground-controlled approach system. SOD-57M antennas are mounted on the tip and sides of the vertical tail and on the leading edges of the wings.

Ejection Seats

Ejection seats serve both to accommodate the pilot in the cockpit during flight and to leave the aircraft in emergency situations.

SK

The SK (*Sistema Katapultirovania*) ejection seat was developed by the MiG OKB and was first used in the E-50/2 prototype. It allows ejection between the altitudes of 360 feet and the aircraft's service ceiling at speeds of up to 680 mph. Some of the specific parameters differ considerably depending on whether the ejection process is shielded by the canopy. The F, F-13, PF, and FL versions of the MiG-21 have forward-opening canopies with integral windscreens, and these shield the pilot from the airflow during ejection. The canopy is engaged by the ejection seat and remains with it until approach velocity drops below a critical value. The MiG-21U two-seat version, which is also equipped with the SK seat, has side-opening canopy sections that do not offer this option. Depending on version, the maximum ejection speed without the shielding canopy is up to 530 mph. Minimum ejection height without the canopy shield is 360 feet (at speeds greater than 310 mph) or 425 feet (at speeds below 310 mph), and 490 feet with canopy. While integration of the canopy into the ejection process improves protection for the pilot, it also slows it.

The pilot begins the ejection process by tucking up his legs and then pulling the central ejection handle or the ejection handles on both sides of the seat (these were deleted during further development because of problems releasing the pilot from the seat). The leg restraints engage and the belts are tightened. The telescopic rods with the stabilization parachutes extend. At lower speeds and altitudes the canopy can be jettisoned, which shortens the process. At higher speeds and altitudes the canopy remains in position until the seat moves up the guide rails in the cockpit, engages pins in the rear canopy latches, and takes the canopy with it. The canopy folds forward to an angle of up to 70 degrees, then it separates from the airframe and the forward latches also engage the seat, so that it is positioned in front of the pilot, protecting his body. A pyrocartridge ignites and blasts the seat away from the aircraft with a maximum g-load of 18. The stabilized seat then drops until, on the basis of altitude or time after ejection, first the stabilizing chute and then the cockpit canopy separate from the seat. Harness buckles and leg restraints open, and the pilot separates from the seat and descends to the ground by parachute.

KM-1

The KM-1 (*Kreslo Mikoyana*) ejection seat was also designed by the MiG OKB, originally under the designation SK-3, after the crash of the E-50/3, when malfunction of the canopy prevented the test pilot from ejecting and he was killed in the subsequent crash. When the new seat was designed, incorporating the canopy into the ejection process was deleted. The KM-1 ensures the safe ejection from the aircraft through the combined KSM ejection mechanism at speeds up to 745 mph in level flight and at all altitudes, as well as during takeoff and landing at aircraft speeds of at least 80 mph. The seat's headrest, arm restraints, harness system to fix the pilot to the seat, and the system to stabilize the seat with the bottom facing forward protect the pilot from the airstream throughout the entire speed range.

The seat consists of the frame, which absorbs ejection forces, the adjustable seat pan, the ejection control system, the KSM combined ejection mechanism (ejection control system, solid-fuel rocket engine, parachute, and shoulder strap mechanism), the seat stabilization system, the pilot's NAS-7 emergency supply system (which includes food, tools, flare pistol, inflatable raft), and the automatic system to

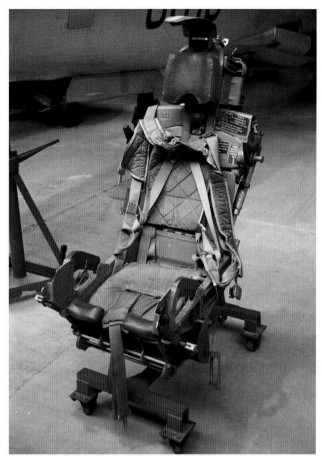

In its original version, the SK ejection seat had side-mounted ejection handles. To make it easier to operate, these were later replaced by a central handle.

separate the pilot from the seat. The pilot initiates ejection by pulling the double ejection handles on the seat pan. During the subsequent ejection process, all of the seat systems up to and including the opening of the pilot's parachute operate automatically, which results in a high degree of probability that the pilot will survive. First the shoulder belts are tightened and the arm restraints are folded down. Then the canopy is jettisoned and seat lock on the floor of the cockpit is released. The seat moves up the guide rails in the cockpit, the parachute mechanism's telescopic tubes extend, and the first stabilizing parachute is opened. When the seat begins to move, all connections between the seat and the aircraft are separated. When the height of the seat reaches about 32 inches, the solid-fuel rocket engine ignites and catapults the seat up to 145 feet high. The resulting load factors reach up to 20 g. After a maximum of 1.6 seconds of flight, the second stabilization parachute is opened and the seat descends to a preset altitude. On reaching this height, the pilot's restraints

The KM-1 ejection seat is a much more complex design than its predecessor, but it is also much more capable. A special crane is used to remove and install the seat.

For installation on the fuselage pylon, the SM jamming pod has the same attachment fixtures as the external fuel tanks. The receiving antennas are mounted in the "horns," and the transmitting antenna is beneath the nose fairing.

are released and the opening of his parachute separates him from the seat.

The KM-1 and KM-1M variants of the seat are used in the single-seat versions of the MiG-21, beginning with the late series PFS. The KM-1U/UM (for the student in the front seat) and the KM-1I/IM for the instructor in the rear seat) are installed in the MiG-21US and UM two-seaters.

SM Jamming Pod with SPS-41

The SM jamming pod is carried on the fuselage stores pylon of retrofitted MiG-21s. The SPS-141 jamming system produces and transmits active jamming signals against fire control radars and diverts missiles with radar seeker heads. The jamming signals are transmitted both in the forward and rear hemispheres.

The combination of various range and bearing deception methods protect the aircraft against surface-to-air missiles, guided air-to-air missiles, and radar-controlled antiaircraft guns.

In the receive mode the jamming pod receives signals beamed at the aircraft, analyzes them, and warns the pilot if the incoming signals are operating in the target-tracking mode. In transmit mode the jammer receives signals, enhances them, and beams them back.

There are four different programs that can be selected: self-defense of the carrier aircraft, protection against two or more aircraft with just one jammer pod, combined operation of two pods on two carrier aircraft, and irradiation of the surface of the earth to produce a false target. An ASO-2I chaff/flare dispenser is incorporated into the pod, and these flares are released when the aircraft is illuminated.

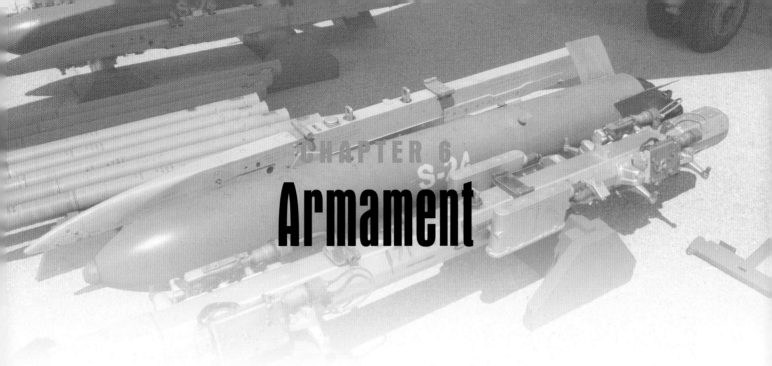

Armament

The MiG-21's armament reflects the aircraft's development from a day fighter into an all-weather multirole combat aircraft. At the same time, the Soviet design principle of not replacing systems and components unless absolutely necessary and retaining proven systems for long periods of time came into play. While the cannon and missile armament carried by the MiG-21 underwent numerous changes during the course of development, the final version, the MiG-21bis, can carry the same unguided rockets used by the first production version, the MiG-21F. Over the roughly fifteen years of ongoing MiG-21 development, the nature and extent of the weapons it carried underwent considerable changes.

Cannons and Machine Gun
NR-30 Cannon

The NR-30 is a single-barrel, automatic cannon with a caliber of 30 mm, in which recoil energy is used to open and slide back the breech and eject shell casings. The energy of the powder gases, which when the gun is fired is fed from the barrel into a gas collector and is compressed as it moves backward, serves to brake (a hydraulic buffer and a spring mechanism are also present) and move the barrel forward as well as to feed rounds. The powder gases are then vented into the atmosphere. Cocking is pneumatic, and firing is done electrically.

Seven different rounds were developed to enable the cannon to be used effectively against air and ground targets: these include high-explosive incendiary (OFZ) and armor-piercing high-explosive (BR) rounds, a round for engaging balloons, and a chaff round (PRL) for jamming enemy radars.

GSh-23 Cannon

The GSh-23 is a twin-barreled automatic cannon with a caliber of 23 mm, in which one automatic system feeds ammunition, locks, fires the weapon, and ejects the casings into a common housing, with the two barrels firing alternately. The mechanism is therefore compulsorily interlinked. The cannon uses the powder gas for operating the mechanism, with the gas first taken from one barrel and then the other. Ammunition is fed from a belt by way of a sprocket-like mechanism. The cannon has an electrically operated fire control and cocking mechanism. For engaging aerial targets, aiming is accomplished by using the radar or the optical sight, while the optical sight exclusively is used for attacking ground targets. The cannon is capable of firing AM-23 ammunition with high-explosive fragmentation, armor-piercing incendiary, high-explosive incendiary tracer, and radar-jamming projectiles with DOS-4 or DOS-15 chaff, and high-explosive incendiary projectiles with highly sensitive fuses for use against balloons. The standard belting consists of a one-to-one ratio of high-explosive fragmentation and armor-piercing incendiary rounds.

The MiG-21 versions FL, PFM, and S can carry the GSh-23 in a GP-9 gun pod under the fuselage. In addition to the cannon, the GP-9 contains 200 rounds of ammunition. Beginning with the SM (domestic) and M (export) versions, the cannon is permanently installed. Ammunition is stored in shafts directly under the fuselage skin, and on all versions with the exception of the MiG-21bis, it holds 200 rounds, while the latter has 250 rounds.

With an overall length of 84.75 inches, the NR-30 is comparatively large. Its rate of fire is 850 to 1,000 rounds per minute.

A-12.7 Machine Gun

The A-12.7 machine gun is a gas-operated weapon with a caliber of 12.7 mm. The ammunition belt can be fed from either side. The machine gun is cocked electropneumatically, and firing is electric. Rate of fire is 900 to 1,100 rounds per minute.

MiG-21U/US/UM two-seaters can carry the machine gun in a pod under the fuselage. Ammunition capacity is sixty rounds.

Air-to-Air Missiles
R-3S (K-13, Product 310A)

The first air-to-air missile in the MiG-21's arsenal was the infrared-guided R-3S, a copy of the American AIM-9 Sidewinder. The Soviet Union obtained the original via China, and since there were no domestic products that could match its effectiveness, the missile was copied.

The R-3S is of canard design, with cruciform control surfaces and trapezoidal tail fins. The missile consists of the following components: infrared seeker head, warhead with optical-proximity fuse, control element for vertical and horizontal flight control with rudder actuators, energy supply unit, and rocket motor. The infrared seeker head has an angle of view of 3.5 degrees at a maximum engagement range of 4.7 miles. The missile must have locked onto the target before launch, which because of the missile's limited engagement envelope requires the carrying aircraft to be pointed precisely at the target. After lock-on, the target can be pursued within a 25-degree cone; however, g-loads during launch cannot exceed 2 g, and the launching aircraft's speed must be greater than 480 mph. Depending on altitude, maximum firing range is between 0.9 and 2.15 miles. When firing in the direction of the sun, a minimum angle of 20 degrees to the sun must be maintained.

The delta-shaped, fully movable control surfaces with swept trailing edges are aligned with the tail fins. On the leading edge, there is an impact fuse to detonate the warhead in the event of a direct hit. The control engines are powered by powder gas bled from the rocket motor.

The rocket has a blast fragmentation warhead. The outer skin forms the warhead's fragmentation liner, so that it

With a rate of fire of 3,000 rounds per minute, the GSh-23's ammunition supply, consisting of 200 or 250 rounds, is expended in four to five seconds.

The A-12.7 machine gun is housed in a pod (behind) under the fuselage of the MiG-21 two-seat trainers. Its combat value is limited because of the gun's small caliber and its limited ammunition capacity of just sixty rounds. *Stefan Büttner*

produces a directed fragment pattern. Behind the warhead is the optical-proximity fuse with a range of 30 feet, which reacts to the target's thermal signature.

The solid-fuel rocket engine with its axisymmetric nozzle is in the tail of the rocket. At the end of the missile body are four trapezoidal fins with straight trailing edges, each at an angle of 45 degrees to the horizontal plane.

The solid fuel burns for just two seconds and accelerates the missile to a speed of about 2,300 feet per second. The missile's maneuverability is very limited, and in actuality only nonmaneuvering targets can be engaged. The warhead, which produces about 1,000 fragments, is effective, but the infrared-proximity fuse's sensitivity and resistance to countermeasures are limited. If the missile misses its target, it destroys itself after twenty-five or twenty-six seconds. Controlled flight lasts for a maximum of twenty-one seconds.

The R-3U inert version is an empty missile body with homing equipment and is used for training purposes. The inert training version delivers the same signals during target acquisition as the live missile, and it records data for subsequent evaluation.

RS-2US (K-5MS, Product IS)

The first radar-guided missile carried by the MiG-21 had been used in similar form and under the designations RS-1U and RS-2U by the earlier MiG-17PFU and MiG-19PM all-weather fighters. After it was adapted for use at higher speeds and altitudes, it also became part of the MiG-21's arsenal as the RS-2US, being used by versions equipped with the RP-21 radar.

Like the R-3, the RS-2-US was of canard configuration, with cruciform trapezoid-shaped control surfaces and tail fins. The missile body, with a diameter of 7.9 inches, housed the radio proximity fuse, the fragmentation warhead, the control system, control surface actuators, the roll stabilization system, and the rocket engine. The warhead has a weight of 28 pounds, and the range of the proximity fuse is 49 feet. Unlike most air-to-air missiles, the engine's gas jet is not ejected from a central nozzle in the tail, but instead through two channels in the side of the missile body at an angle of 15 degrees to its longitudinal axis. Ailerons were installed in the tail fins for roll stabilization.

The armament of a MiG-21MF, consisting of the radar-guided RS-2US on the inner APU-7 launch rail and the infrared-guided R-3S on the outer APU-13U. *Stefan Büttner*

The missile employed beam-riding radar guidance. The aircraft's radar illuminated the target, and after a relatively short independently stabilized phase of flight, the missile followed the radar beam. The missile had an operational range of 1.85 miles, and in the event of malfunction, it self-destructed after thirteen to twenty-three seconds of flight. Operational altitude was between 8,200 and 54,000 feet.

R-55 (Product 67)

The R-55 was based on the RS-2US, and the missile body, canard fins, and power plant were largely the same. New was the infrared seeker head with cooling and improved resistance to electronic countermeasures, thanks to which the missile could be used at all altitudes between sea level and 72,000 feet. Detection range is between 1 and 1.75 miles depending on the size of the target and its heat signature.

The second section of the missile houses an optical closing-in igniter and the forward part of the fragmentation warhead, the second part of which is in the tail section. An ignition mechanism in a fairing under the missile body ignites both. Despite the fact that its warhead is 25 percent smaller than that of the RS-2US, the R-55 is more effective, since the fragments spread in all directions. The missile's tail section is largely similar to that of the RS-2US, but it is longer and the tail fins are larger in area. Compared to its predecessor, the R-55 is 10.25 inches longer and 18.5 pounds heavier.

The R-55 is one part of a weapons system that also includes the RP-22 radar and the APU-68UM launcher. When the radar detects a target, the missile's seeker head turns in the corresponding direction. After it is fired, the missile pursues the target independently.

R-3R (K-13R, Product 320)

The beam-riding guidance of the RS-2US and the associated requirement to always have the entire aircraft pointed toward the target proved impractical against a maneuvering target. The result was development of the R-3R missile with semiactive radar homing, which enabled the missile to detect targets at an angle of 5 degrees from the longitudinal axis. The R-3R is based on the R-3S and shares its warhead, tail fins, and engine. New are the radar seeker head, the control surface actuators, and the radio proximity fuse.

Outwardly, the R-3R differs from the R-3S in the conical fairing over the radar seeker head, which replaces the hemispherical glass lens of the infrared seeker. The diameter of the radio proximity fuse is somewhat greater than that of the missile body, resulting in a thickening behind the control unit.

These modifications caused the missile's length to grow by 22.8 inches and its weight to increase by 15.65 pounds. Unlike the R-3S, which can be used only from the rear hemisphere, the R-3R can be fired at the target from any direction. While the R-3S can be used by all versions of the MiG-21, the R-3R can be used only by versions with the RP-22 radar. The inert training version of the R-3R is designated R-3RU and—unlike the R-3U—has tail surfaces; however, it is significantly shorter than the live R-3R.

R-13M (K-13M, Product 380)

The R-13M is a further development of the R-3S, with the same operational principle, meaning that is fired under visual conditions from the rear hemisphere. Similar in layout, the R-13M's inner workings and performance differ greatly from those of its predecessor. The infrared seeker head has a nitrogen cooling system, which doubles acquisition range and enables its use against ground targets with large heat signatures. The tail fins and control surfaces are larger in area and have a thicker profile for improved agility. A new proximity fuse is also fitted. The R-13M has a new warhead with a cylindrically shaped explosive core, around which there is a perforated steel sleeve. The steel sleeve consists of 144 forked steel rods, whose ends are welded to a continuous zigzag-shaped mantle. When the explosive core detonates, the steel rods expand radially to the missile's flight axis, causing the production of a zigzag-shaped steel chain with a diameter of approximately 30 feet. The highly ductile welded links prevent the chain from breaking apart prematurely. This warhead has a much-greater penetrative capability than a conventional fragmentation warhead. The expanding steel chain is capable of literally tearing apart an aerial target.

Despite its more compact design, the R-13M's rocket engine produces almost twice the thrust of the R-3R's engine. Burn duration is 3.3 to 5.4 seconds, and controlled flight duration is up to fifty-five seconds.

The second-generation infrared- and radar-guided air-to-air missiles—R-13M above and R-3R below—had clearly better performance parameters than their predecessors.

R-60 (K-60, Product 62)

The regional wars of the 1960s and 1970s demonstrated the basic unsuitability of existing air-to-air missiles against maneuvering targets, while the effectiveness of cannon armament was limited to a range of about 1,000 feet. At greater distances under air combat conditions, aiming errors and scatter were too great. At the same time, the minimum firing distances of the R-3S and R-13M missiles were between 0.56 and 0.8 miles. As well, allowable g-loads for launching the missiles were limited to 1.6 to 4 g. In dogfights, however, fighter aircraft were most frequently in the 1,300- to 3,280-foot distance range, with load coefficients greater than 5 g. Consequently there was an armaments gap precisely in the range and load coefficient areas in which air combat was played out. The R-60 air-to-air missile closed this gap for the first time.

The missile was of canard configuration and, with a length of 84.25 inches and weight of 97 pounds, was significantly more compact than its predecessors. In its forward section the R-60 has canards (destabilizers) in the nose and aerodynamic control surfaces and tail fins with gyroscopic rudders. It is made up of these components: infrared seeker head, warhead with radio proximity and contact fuse, control section with autopilot and control actuators, power supply unit, and rocket engine. The seeker head is electrically cooled by minus 351 degrees Fahrenheit below ambient air temperature. The missile can be employed against ground targets with heat contrast by turning off the radio fuze.

The guidance system consists of a passive infrared seeker head. In the first stage of active flight, the missile is stabilized for approximately 3.5 seconds, which means that guided flight begins only after this time. The missile has an adjustable arming time for combat use and for practice firing during combat training.

A radio proximity and contact fuse detonates the warhead. An explosive charge accelerates 104 unconnected rods, 4.7 inches long and 0.11 inches thick, to approximately 5,250 feet per second and a helical path, which up to a radius of approximately 15 feet impacts the target with almost the complete mass of the warhead.

Operational altitude is between 985 and 72,175 feet, while firing range from the rear hemisphere is between 0.18 and 5 miles. The allowable load coefficient on firing is -1.5 to +7 g. Burn duration is three to five seconds, with a controlled flight duration of twenty-three seconds. Self-destruct takes place after twenty-three to twenty-seven seconds.

Because of its considerably improved flight parameters compared to its predecessors, the R-60 made the MiG-21 a much more effective fighter, and older versions of the aircraft were retrofitted to use the R-60. The R-60 can be carried on the P-62-1M single launch rail and the P-62-2M twin launch rail.

The inert training version of the R-60 is called the UZR-60.

Air-to-Ground Missiles
Kh-66 (Product 66)

Although designed as a tactical fighter aircraft, from the PFM version onward the MiG-21 increasingly came to be seen by the Soviet air force as a multirole aircraft with a secondary role of fighter-bomber. Originally, however, the MiG-21 was capable only of employing nonguided air-to-surface weapons—cannon, bombs, and rockets.

This did not change until the Kh-66 tactical air-to-surface missile became available. Its design was based on the RS-2US air-to-air missile, and it used the latter's guidance system. The Kh-66 could thus be used by all variants of the MiG-21 capable of employing the RS-2US.

The missile, of canard configuration, was 11.9 feet long and weighed 613 pounds. It consisted of these components: high-explosive fragmentation warhead, guidance system, control actuators, roll stabilization system, and engine.

Operational altitude was between 1,640 and 16,400 feet, while maximum firing range was 6.2 miles. The warhead weighed 227 pounds and was equipped with an impact fuse. The missile has beam-riding guidance. The aircraft's radar (from the RP-21M onward) illuminates the target, and after a brief, self-stabilized flight phase, the missile independently rides the beam to the target.

The compact and agile R-60 is the most effective weapon against aerial targets in the arsenal of the classic MiG-21. The aircraft can carry up to six of these missiles.

S-21 (ARS-212)

A large-caliber unguided rocket was used by the first generation of MiG-21s, a weapon that had been used by its predecessors from the MiG-15: the S-21.

Two of these 8.35-inch rockets and the PU-21 launcher together formed the AS-21 weapons system. The S-21 can be used both against air and ground targets and is fired singly or in pairs. It consists of a blast fragmentation warhead, a solid-fuel rocket engine, and the rocket body itself, with a total of four stabilizing fins at the tail. The warhead is detonated by an impact-proximity fuse with adjustable time delay. The rocket is 5.8 feet long and weighs 258 pounds, 88 pounds of which make up the warhead. Range is 2,500 feet.

S-24 (ARS-240)

The S-24 is a development of the S-21 with increased caliber, improved range, and increased penetrative ability, and it can be employed by all MiG-21s after the first generation.

The rocket is spin stabilized and rotates at 450 revolutions per minute. Its construction is similar to that of the S-21. The warhead, which weighs 271 pounds, contains 51.8 pounds of explosives, which on detonation turns the metal casing into 4,000 fragments. To improve the fragmentation effect, the S-24N variant is equipped with a proximity fuse to detonate the explosive charge 100 feet above the target. Other versions of the S-24 are designed specially to penetrate concrete and metal armor. The standard version of the rocket is 7.3 feet long and weighs 518 pounds. The S-24 is fired from the PU-12-40U, APU-7, and APU-68 launchers.

S-5 (ARS-57)

The S-5 is an unguided rocket with a caliber of 57 mm (2.25 inches), used against single or area targets on the ground but also against aerial targets. It consists of a steel body with warhead and impact fuse in the nose, a solid-fuel rocket engine, and eight forward-folding stabilizing fins. These deploy when the rocket leaves the tube. Depending on the version, with fins folded the S-5 is between 2.7 and 2.5 feet long and weighs between 8 and 11 pounds, of which 1.75 to 4 pounds makes up the warhead. Range is 1.25 miles.

The rockets are available with explosive (S-5M), blast fragmentation (S-5MO), HEAT (S-5K), HEAT fragmentation (S-5KO), and HEAT blast fragmentation (S-5KBP) warheads.

S-5 rockets are fired from UB-16 pods, each carrying sixteen rounds, and UB-32 pods with thirty-two tubes. The UB-32 is 6.8 feet long, weighing 227 pounds empty and 562 pounds loaded. Up to the third-generation MiG-21, only the UB-16 could be used, but from the fourth generation of MiG-21s onward, two UB-32 rocket pods could be carried on the inner stores pylons.

Bombs

The bomb armament of the MiG-21 comprises free-falling bombs weighing 110, 220, 550, and 1,100 pounds, as well as incendiary bomb dispensers. The first- and second-generation MiG-21s and the two-seaters can carry two 550-pound bombs, while the third and fourth generations can carry four. All versions are capable of carrying two 1,100-pound bombs, which are mounted on BD3-60-21 universal pylons with the D3-57D bomb release mechanism (one bomb per pylon).

All MiG-21s can carry two 1,100-pound incendiary dispensers (SB-500), which are carried on BD3-60-21 universal pylons.

Nuclear Weapons

The MiG-21 is capable of delivering tactical nuclear weapons weighing approximately 990 pounds with an explosive force equivalent to 5.5 to 22 kilotons of TNT. The necessary equipment, which is installed only as needed, consists of a control panel, which is attached to the upper windscreen frame, a control unit mounted at the top right of the instrument panel, and the BD3-66-21N special pylon, which is mounted in place of the standard ventral pylon. The necessary wiring between the individual components is present in preprepared aircraft. The BD3-66-21N is only about half as deep as the fuselage pylon, to provide the necessary ground clearance while taxiing with the nuclear weapon in position. The special carrier's bomb lock protrudes from the top of the unit. An opening in the aircraft fuselage—usually covered by a metal cover—accepts the bomb carrier. The carrier has three pairs of sway braces, and its underside is shaped to match the shape of the nuclear device to provide further ground clearance. The wiring includes a special plug to supply the special bomb's systems. The plug is hermetically sealed to

The warhead accounts for almost half of the S-24 rocket's weight. Precision and range are limited, however.

The atomic bomb (practice round). The IAB-500, which externally was identical to the live round, was used to train pilots in the delivery of nuclear weapons.

The air-to-ground arsenal of this MiG-21 includes bombs of various calibers, which are carried on single-bomb or multibomb pylons, as well as UB-16 and UB-32 pods for unguided rockets.

Rack under the fuselage of a MiG-23 for carriage of nuclear weapons. The BD3-66-23N shown here was largely similar to the BD3-66-21N of the MiG-21.

prevent dirt and moisture from reaching the terminals, which thus improves the connection's reliability.

Before a nuclear weapon can be used, it must be armed by a coded radio signal that can be sent only by authorized headquarters. Without this the bomb can only be jettisoned unarmed.

Of the MiG-21s operated by the Soviet air forces, the S (some aircraft), SM, SMT, ST, and bis versions were capable of delivering nuclear weapons.

Export aircraft with this capability were special batches starting from the MiG-21PFM. The typical operational delivery method was so-called toss bombing, in which a low-flying aircraft released its bomb from various climb angles, after which the weapon followed a ballistic curve to its target. This method gave the crew a certain chance of survival. Because the MiG-21 did not have systems for the automated execution of this maneuver, the pilot had to be trained to carry it out with the required degree of precision.

Modernization: MiG-21s for the Twenty-First Century

The most-capable versions of the MiG-21 did not come to be until after the Soviet Union had come to an end. Several modernization programs addressed the MiG-21's deficits, especially its avionics in general and its radar in particular. All these measures made the MiG-21 capable of using many air-to-air missiles from all over the world, with the spectrum varying greatly between versions. Other additions to the aircraft's arsenal involved guided air-to-surface missiles in particular.

MiG-21-93

The centerpiece of the MiG-21-93 is the Kopyo radar by Phazotron, whose performance far exceeds that of the original RP-21/22. With a range of up to 35 miles, this pulse-doppler radar is capable of tracking eight targets and engaging two of them simultaneously. It has ground-mapping capability and can detect moving targets on the ground and measure the range of air and ground targets.

The MiG-21-93 program involves almost the complete replacement of the aircraft's avionics, the installation of a

Thanks to the medium-range R-77 AAM (inner) and the highly maneuverable R-73, the modernized MiG-21-93 had a much more effective armament.

The Kopjo radar, specially designed for the MiG-21, had three times the acquisition range of its predecessors and eliminated one of the significant weaknesses of the classic MiG-21 versions.

Derived from the MiG-21-93, the Indian MiG-21bis UPG differed from its predecessor in having Western avionic components. New to the aircraft's armament were S-8 (extreme left and right) unguided rockets and the KAB-500KR television-guided bomb (under the fuselage).

new bulged cockpit canopy with one-piece windscreen, and an improved energy supply and environmental system. In addition to the new radar, the avionics modernization includes heavily modified cockpit equipment, with a new head-up display, hands-on throttle and stick (HOTAS)–capable control elements and Shchel-3UM helmet-mounted sight, navigation computer, instrument landing system, IFF system, ground control interception system, and a BWP-30-26 chaff-and-flare dispenser coupled with an EWS-21 radar-warning receiver by Dassault Electronique, from France. The latter components are outwardly visible—the chaff-and-flare dispensers on the wing roots and the radar-warning receiver on the leading edge of the vertical stabilizer. The avionics are laid out as an open system, enabling the integration of foreign components.

Thanks to the radar and new avionics, in part based on those of the MiG-29, the aircraft can also use the R-3, R-13, and R-60 AAMs, as well as the medium-range, radar-guided R73 infrared AAM as well as the R-27 AAM, both with infrared and radar guidance. The type's air-to-ground armament of unguided rockets and bombs was supplemented by the KAB-500Kr television-guided bomb. The cannon armament is unchanged, consisting of the GSh-23.

The first and so far only customer for the MiG-21-93 program is India. The Indian version, called the MiG-21UPG or Bison, differs from the MiG-21-93 in various avionics components of non-Russian origin. These include a Totem 3000 inertial navigation system and the Topflight avionics suite by Sextant Avionique (now Thales), from France, consisting of head-up display; two multifunction displays and the Topsight helmet-mounted sight; Indian radio equipment, including radio, transponder, radio altimeter, and compass; and an Israeli chaff-flare dispenser. The avionics components are linked by an MIL-1553 data bus.

MiG-21 LanceR

The measures taken by the Romanian LanceR program (Lance + R for Romania) encompass the integration of new avionics and the ability to employ Soviet/Russian and Western weapons systems. The aircraft's airframe and engine remain largely unchanged. In the case of the LanceR C fighter version, the key component of the modernization is the EL/M-2032 radar from IAI ELTA. Compared to the original RP-21, this system represents a quantum leap, improving radar range from about 12.5 to 50 miles. Together with two multifunction displays and the DASH helmet-mounted sight by Elbit and a new head-up display from El-Op (also from Israel) in the cockpit, the EL/M-2032, which has been used in other modernization programs, gives the pilot a much more comprehensive overview of the aerial situation.

Instead of the EL/M-2032, the LanceR A air-to-ground version and the LanceR B two-seater have just an EL/M-2001-B radar rangefinder and one multifunction display in the cockpit. The MiG-21M and MiG-21MF form the preferred basis for the LanceR A, while the LanceR C aircraft are created exclusively from examples of the MiG-21MF-75—with the exception of one MiG-21MF, which was converted as a replacement for an aircraft that crashed during testing. As well, however, seven MiG-21MF-75 were converted into LanceR As.

Other Israeli components installed in the LanceR include the SPS-20 radar-warning receiver by Elisra, chaff-and-flare dispensers from IAI, and a radio-jamming pod from Elta, which can be mounted on the fuselage pylon. An MIL-STD-1553 data bus links the avionics components and the armament. Each run together in the Modular Multi-Role Computer (MMRC) from Elbit.

The navigation system consists of an inertial navigation system with accelerometers, which is coupled with a standard GPS receiver. Other standard components include the instrument landing system for VOR with DME from AlliedSignal Bendix (now Honeywell). Also new were two VHF/UHF radios, while many original components continued in use, such as the RK-UM radar altimeter, AP-155 autopilot, and ARK-10 radio compass.

Thanks to a newly developed universal carrier and corresponding interfaces, the LanceR is capable of employing both the original Soviet/Russian weapons as well as ones from Western nations. The spectrum of air-to-air missiles includes the R-60, the R-73, the Israeli Rafael Python 3, and the French Matra Magic 2. In addition to the original UB-16 and UB-32 pods for unguided S-5 rockets and conventional free-fall bombs, the LanceR can carry Elbit Opher and IAI MBT Griffin infrared- and laser-guided bombs.

The package also includes a flight simulator developed by SIMULTEC in Bucharest. A project called LanceR III (the LanceR A and B are combined under the designation LanceR I, while the C version is called LanceR II) based on the MiG-21bis did not go into production.

The Mozambiquan MiG-21bis, upgraded by Aerostar in 2013–14, received at least a few features of the LanceR III.

MiG-21bisD/UMD

In 2002, Croatia reached an agreement with AEROSTAR Bacău for the modernization of eight MiG-21bis plus four additionally procured MiG-21UM. In addition to the overhauling of the engines and airframes, the contract, worth 8.2 million US dollars, called for the installation of new IFF equipment, radio, and navigation aids (GPS, ILS, VOR, DME), but unlike the Romanian MiG-21 LanceR, not radar or weapons systems. These steps ensured that the aircraft could remain in service for a number of years and would have limited NATO compatibility. After the modernization, the single-seaters were designated MiG-21bisD; the two-seaters, MiG-21UMD.

MiG-21 2000

Key components of the MiG-21 2000 are a central mission and indicator processor, ergonomic cockpit based on the HOTAS principle, and the EL/M-2032 radar by Elta Systems, a subsidiary of IAI, which is also used in the LanceR. As an option, the IAI avionics package can also include the DASH helmet sight from Elbit. The MiG-21 2000's armament includes the Python 3 air-to-air guided missile, of which up to four can be carried, and the Griffin, a laser-guided bomb developed by IAI. The MiG-21 2000 can carry three of the 530-pound Mk.82 variants and one of the 1,985-pound Mk.84. The Litening pod by Rafael is used for targeting. In contrast to the MiG-21-93, the MiG-21 2000's arsenal does not include any medium-range AAMs. Further equipment options include two different electronic warfare pods and a reconnaissance pod.

Part of IAI's original concept was the Martin-Baker Mk.16 LHS ejection seat and a one-piece windscreen. No customers opted for these modifications, however; in the case of the ejection seat, undoubtedly because of the capabilities of the original KM-1M, but in the case of the windscreen, probably because of cost. The options of a 343-gallon external fuel tank or aerodynamic improvements were not realized. Most

---

The EL/M-2032 multifunction radar and an extensive avionics package made the LanceR C the top model of the Romanian-Israeli MiG-21 modernization program. In keeping with its role, this aircraft is finished in a gray-white camouflage scheme.

customers who chose modernization by IAI selected the most basic of the original variants for budgetary reasons. Only the MiG-21bis fighters for Uganda underwent a comprehensive modernization process.

At the end of the 1990s, the price for the complete package was set at about 1.5 million US dollars and was thus roughly equivalent to the other programs.

MiG-21MFN

In parallel with the country's entry into NATO, the Czech Republic put ten of its MiG-21MF fighters through a limited avionics upgrade to ensure compatibility with its new allies. Components that were no longer needed or were obsolete, such as the LAZUR system, the SRZO-2 IFF system, the SOD-57 transponder, the ARK-10 radio compass, and the RK-UM radio altimeter, were supplemented or replaced by more-modern, mainly Western equipment. Among the new systems was a Trimble 2001 I/O Plus GPS receiver, Raytheon AN/APX-100 IFF, Bendix/King KXP-756 transponder, Rockwell-Collins DME-42 distance-measuring equipment, and anticollision

beacons by Hella. The modernization was carried out by LOK Kbely. The aircraft's radar and armament remained unchanged, however, and consequently the operational capabilities of these aircraft, which were designated MiG-21MFN (N=NATO) or MiG-21MF/RNAV, were not increased.

MiG-21MU

OdesAviaRemServis, based in Odessa in the Ukraine, offered different upgrades for the MiG-21: the so-called complete modernization, with a maximum exchange of avionics components, and a partial upgrade, whose most attractive feature was low cost. To reduce costs, even the complete modernization—called the MiG-21MU—retained the original RP-21/22 Sapfir radar and equipped it with new components for improved performance.

Other measures included a new avionics suite, with glass cockpit, head-up display, multifunctional color displays (MFCD), and HOTAS-capable cockpit equipment, as well as a single-piece windscreen and a SPO-15 Beresa radar-warning receiver. OdesAviaRemService also offered the Sura-K

The LanceR A wears a typical fighter-bomber camouflage scheme of brown and green. Aircraft converted from MiG-21Ms have three-digit serial numbers. LanceRs created from the MiG-21MF/MF-75 have four-digit numbers.

In terms of equipment, the LanceR B two-seat trainers are equivalent to the A version and are the result of conversions of the MiG-21UM. Several of these aircraft are fitted with rear canopies without periscopes.

Chapter 7: Modernization: MiG-21s for the Twenty-First Century

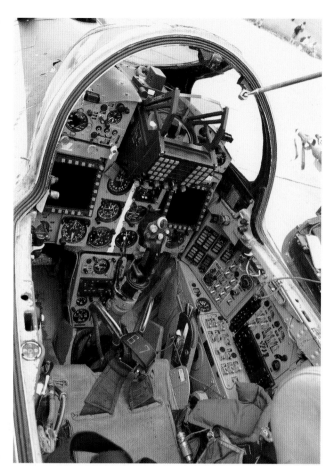

Side-by-side view of the cockpits of the LanceR A and C: while the A version has just one multifunction display, the C has two.

The EL/M-2001-B radar used by the fighter-bomber and two-seat trainer variants is much more compact than the radar of the fighter version.

Based on the MiG-21bis, the LanceR III was displayed at the Aerosalon Le Bourget but attracted no customers.

The entire armament spectrum of the MiG-21 LanceR at one glance. In addition to several types of air-to-air missiles, this includes guided bombs, electronic jamming pods, and laser target designators.

Externally, the MiG-21UMD differs from its predecessor only in having two additional antennas under the fuselage and on the vertical tail.

A Croatian MiG-21bisD after its acceptance flight at AEROSTAR at Bacău. The modernization measures undertaken were much less extensive than those incorporated in the Romanian LanceR.

Chapter 7: Modernization: MiG-21s for the Twenty-First Century

MiG-21s modernized by IAI for specific customers—such as these former Polish aircraft for Uganda—exhibited far-fewer external changes than the prototype aircraft.

helmet-mounted sight, which is also used in the Su-30. The helmet sight and the associated R-60 and R-73 air-to-air missiles are also key elements of the partial modernization, in which the majority of the original avionics are retained. In contrast, the MiG-21MU is capable of using Western weapons systems such as the Magic 2 and Python 3/4 AAMs, Mk.82 laser-guided bombs, and Russian R-77 medium-range missiles.

Obviously, OdesAviaRemServis failed to find customers for its own modernization programme. Instead, between 2013 and 2015, the company overhauled and upgraded Croatian MiG-21bis and UM to the bisD and UMD standard (see MiG-21bisD/UMD) respectively.

Egyptian Modernization Programs

After the breakup of the Soviet Union, Egypt's large MiG-21 fleet was brought up to Western standards with the help of western European and American partners, especially British Aerospace. The equipment components included a navigation system and IFF by Teledyne, a head-up display by GEC-Marconi, and an AN/ALE-40 chaff-and-flare dispenser by Tracor. Another modernization stage took place in the late 1980s, in the course of which electronic warfare pods were acquired from Elettronica (Italy), while from the United States came AIM-9P3 and AIM-9L Sidewinder AAMs.

Like the MiG-21-93, catalogue of measures for the MiG-21 2000 by IAI—one of the prototypes is seen here—included the one-piece windscreen. The Israeli company failed to find any customers for this modified variant, however.

The EL/M-2032 radar used in the LanceR C is a product of the IAI subsidiary Elta Systems and is installed in the MiG-21 2000. *Stefan Büttner*

Chapter 7: Modernization: MiG-21s for the Twenty-First Century

The MiG-21MFN differs from its predecessor in having a plethora of new antennas—such as those on the nose, the fuselage spine, and the vertical tail.

In the cockpit of this disassembled Egyptian MiG-21MF can be seen the head-up display, which is of Western origin.

CHAPTER 8

The Chinese MiG-21s: From Copy to Independent Aircraft Family

In preparation for Communist China's second five-year plan (1958–62), the Chinese aviation industry was given the task of preparing, with Soviet help, to build the MiG-19, MiG-21, and Tu-16 plus the Mi-4 helicopter under license. A contract with the Soviet Union was signed in the fourth quarter of 1957, at a time when no MiG-21 from series production had yet flown, not even in its country of origin. China itself had just begun producing the MiG-17. When Soviet-Chinese relations soured in mid-July 1960, and Soviet specialists were withdrawn, preparations for license production were not very far advanced and would probably have foundered had not the USSR announced its willingness to assist in February 1961. A contract covering this was signed in Moscow on March 30, 1961. It provided for the delivery to China of MiG-21F-13 fighters, R11F-300 engines, and R-3S air-to-air missiles.

In April 1962, Aircraft Factory No. 112 in Shenyang began receiving components for fifteen MiG-21F-13s and three pattern aircraft from Gorki. The deliveries also included twenty R11F-300 power plants. Assembly of the fighter aircraft, which were designated type 62 by the Chinese, began on November 23, 1962, and the first flight took place on April 30, 1964. Another ten sets of components were assembled that same year, and the remaining four were completed in 1965. With the introduction of the new designation system in November 1964, the type received the designation Jian Qi (Fighter) 7.

License production of the MiG-21F-13 as the J-7 began the same month. On January 17, 1966, test pilot Ge Wenjong made the first flight in one of the prototypes. At the same time, the Shenyang Engine Works began working on a copy of the R11F-300 power plant. The engine was placed in production as the WoPen-7 in December 1966. Series production of the J-7 began at Shenyang on December 28, 1966. A total of thirty-nine aircraft—one prototype, fifteen MiG-21F-13s assembled from Russian components, and twenty-three J-7s—were delivered before the temporary halt in production resulting from the Cultural Revolution. Twelve MiG-21F-13s delivered to Albania were given the export designation F-7A (F = Fighter).

Preparations for the redesign of the J-7 began in April 1969, at Aircraft Factory No. 132 in Chengdu and in the later Lijang Engine Works in Guijang, Guizhou Province. As a first step, going back to the technology of the MiG-21F, the port NR-30 cannon was again installed, increasing the aircraft's firepower. The intake shock cone was made continuously adjustable instead of retaining the three positions of the F-13's cone, and some geometric changes were made to the intake, improving its performance at low and high speeds. The first J-7 thus modified flew for the first time in June 1973. Flight testing was concluded by June 1975, and 154 of these aircraft, which were given the designation J-7I Three Improvements, were produced.

In a second development phase, the engine's thrust was increased by adopting hollow, cooled turbine blades that made possible higher intake temperatures. The modified engine was called the WP-7B, and it produced thrust levels comparable to those of the Soviet R11F2-300. The engine's time between overhaul rose in stages from 100 to 300 hours.

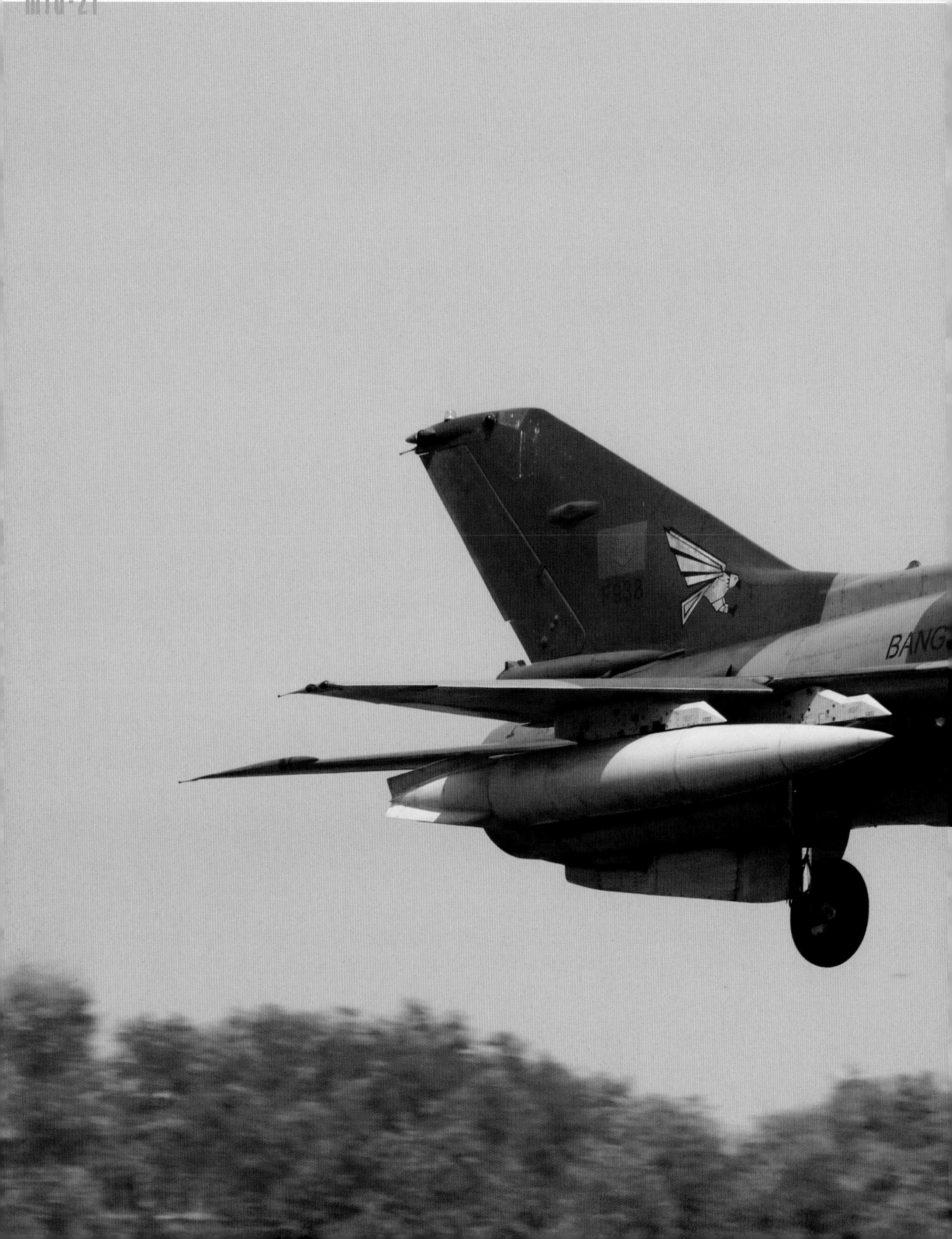
BANG

Except for the retrofitted braking-parachute container, the J-7 is an exact copy of the MiG-21F-13. *Guido E. Bühlmann*

The new type II ejection seat, later designated HTY-2, was adopted while retaining the forward-hinged canopy. The wings now had two integral fuel tanks. Production of the resulting J-7I Six Improvements continued until 1981, and a total of thirty-four examples were built.

Work on the new J-7II version, which saw the integration of several Chinese solutions into the J-7, which had been built so far completely according to Soviet pattern, began at the factory in Chengdu in July 1975. The new ejection seat used by the last production J-7I aircraft was combined with a new canopy hinged at the rear. Unlike the previous system, the new combination ensured a safe departure from the aircraft in an emergency at speeds from 155 to 550 mph and between 0 feet and the aircraft's service ceiling.

The new braking-parachute container at the base of the vertical stabilizer, with a single, upward-opening cover, also differed from the Soviet original, with two sideways-opening doors. By placing the container at the base of the vertical stabilizer, the braking chute could be released at 1.5 to 3 feet above the ground, like the later Soviet MiG-21s. Older J-7s

were retrofitted with this braking-chute container, and it cannot therefore be used as an identifying feature. This is also true of the external fuel tank carried under the fuselage. Unlike the larger Soviet tank, with a capacity of 210 gallons, the J-7II's tank could hold just 190 gallons of jet fuel. The J-7II is equipped with a WP-7B engine without the earlier gasoline starter system.

On December 30, 1978, Yu Mingwen made the first test flight in the J-7II. A total of 375 of these aircraft were produced between 1979 and 1986. The majority were delivered by the Chengdu aircraft factory, while about 100 were made by Factory 011 in Guizhou.

Whereas the armament carried by the previous versions of the J-7 had consisted exclusively of copies of Soviet systems (cannon, unguided rockets, and PL-2 guided missiles), on the J-7IIH—later designated J-7H—which was designed solely for internal use, the Chinese for the first time used Western technology in the shape of the Israeli-made Rafael Python 3, which was built under license in China as the PL-8. The new version of the J-7 had wing pylons for

The aircraft delivered to Albania as the F-7A were very probably MiG-21F-13s assembled in China from Soviet-supplied components.

The installation of an additional cannon on the port side of the fuselage is one of the first of a long series of modifications that ultimately led to an independent Chinese line of MiG-21 development.

Chapter 8: The Chinese MiG-21s: From Copy to Independent Aircraft Family

carriage of the PL-8, but these could also be used with the PL-2 and PL-5. Combined with weight reductions in the forward fuselage, the modifications resulted in the center of gravity shifting to the rear, which necessitated the trim weight in the nose having to be increased to 440 pounds. A chaff/flare dispenser—probably of Israeli origin—is located beneath the aft fuselage of the J-7IIH. The aircraft is powered by a WP-7B engine. A version for the navy called the J-7IIHH (J-7HH) has improved anticorrosion features to better protect components made of aluminum and titanium alloys from the effects of sea salt.

An aircraft with all these modifications took to the air on its first flight in March 1985, with Yu Mingwen at the controls. Deliveries began in February 1986, and 221 examples were produced by 1993.

Work on a special export version of the J-7II began in the late 1970s. It was intended for export to nations allied with China, and also to bring in export revenues for Chinese companies. Since the required technology was not available in China, it was acquired from the West. This resulted in versions of the F-7 that were technically superior to the J-7s operated by the Chinese military and that incorporated technical innovations before they were integrated into domestic versions.

The first export version, which was sold to Egypt and Iraq beginning in 1980, was still built to the Chinese production standard. Aircraft later delivered to Zimbabwe and Myanmar had wings with two pylons, which had long been standard on Soviet versions of the MiG-21 and were present on the J-7III/IV and the later F-7M. These wing stations could accommodate external fuel tanks or armament. These aircraft were the first representatives of the J-7 development line based on the MiG-21F-13 to have this feature as standard. The forward-hinged canopy was replaced by one hinged at the rear. Beginning in the mid-1980s, Egypt and Iraq received this aircraft, along with Zimbabwe, Myanmar, and the United States—the latter for realistic adversary training.

The various export versions based on the J-7I and J-7II received the designation F-7B, with technical differences and the various recipient nations indicated by additional letters; for example, F-7BE for Egypt and F-7BS for Sri Lanka. Like the Soviet original, new features flowed into series production. Some early J-7II/F-7B subvariants were retrofitted with the additional wing stores pylons—most likely by replacing the entire wing.

In 1975, the decision was made to produce the MiG-21MF under the designation J-7III. In preparation for copying the aircraft, the Chinese traveled actively to friendly nations to gain the required know-how. In 1978, Chinese delegations visited Romania, Bangladesh, and Egypt to examine the MiG-21MF. One example—nonflyable—was obtained from Egypt, and it arrived in China in January 1979.

Building on this knowledge, replication began in the Chengdu aircraft factory. Production drawings were completed by January 1982. Meanwhile, China had obtained a flyable MiG-21MF from Egypt for a price of 5.5 million US dollars. On March 25, 1984, Yu Mingwen made the first flight in the machine, which in China was designated J-7III (later J-7C). Three prototypes of this type, which externally and in terms of equipment was essentially an exact copy of the MiG-21MF, were completed by May 1984.

Subsequent production of the J-7C was limited to just seventeen examples, which were completed by 1996. The air force had already lost interest in this variant, which was less maneuverable than the J-7I/II. Despite this, on August 20, 1991, the improved J-7IIIA (also designated J-7IV and J-7D) made its first flight with Liu Qingli at the controls. The J-7IIIA was characterized by further development of the copied Soviet technology of its predecessor, especially avionics and weapons systems. This included an inertial navigation system and a complex for electronic warfare. The aircraft was capable of using the PL-5, PL-7 (for a planned F-7D export version), PL-8, and PL-9 AAMs. Once again, however, the new aircraft failed to find favor with the air force, and just thirty-two examples were produced by 1999.

With the Egyptian delivery of January 1979, the Chinese also received a flyable MiG-21 two-seater. The Guizhou aircraft factory subsequently began preparations to replicate the aircraft. For technological simplification and standardization, airframe components in which the Chinese model differed considerably from the Soviet original were replaced with domestic designs. The larger vertical stabilizer of the MiG-21US was dispensed with, and the tail section of the J-7II was used instead. The SPS flap-blowing system was also deleted. To improve stability, two large fins replaced the central false keel under the fuselage. The JJ-7 was powered by the WP-7 engine. The construction of five prototypes began in 1983. Yan Xiufu made the first flight on July 5, 1985, and after testing was concluded, the aircraft entered production on February 4, 1988.

Several of the F-7B export aircraft—based on the J-7I—differed from the prototype in having two stores pylons under each wing. Among these were the F-7BS aircraft delivered to Sri Lanka. The aircraft illustrated here has also been retrofitted with chaff/flare dispensers.

In parallel to the J-7C/D, modernization of the classic version was pushed ahead for the export market. After the previous expansion of the type's armament spectrum, further development of the J/F-7 concentrated on modernization of the aircraft's avionics. Because there were no suitable domestic products, the choice fell on British equipment, which, because of China's closer ties to the West (which began in the late 1970s), was available.

At the 1987 Paris Air Salon, China exhibited the F-7M, a version—externally identifiable by its high-mounted pitot tube—that had numerous innovations and little in common with domestic versions of the aircraft. The F-7M was based on the airframe of the J-7II, but it was equipped with Western avionics and new armament. The central elements of the avionics upgrade were the GEC-Marconi 226 Skyranger radar rangefinder and the type 956 head-up display from the same manufacturer. Other new components included radio, navigation, and IFF equipment. Externally, the F-7M differed from earlier models in having a broad antenna aft of the cockpit and a pitot tube mounted atop the forward fuselage, as well as an angle-of-attack sensor on the nose. The WP-

7BM engine was also new and weighed less than the WP-7 while producing the same amount of thrust. Armament consisted of PL-2 and PL-7 AAMs. Variants of the F-7M were sold to Bangladesh, Iran, and Iraq; the Iranian aircraft are compatible with Western ground equipment.

The F-7P for Pakistan, which was originally called the Skybolt, differed from the J-7M in having numerous modifications affecting armament and equipment. The aircraft used Western air-to-air missiles—AIM-9D Sidewinder or Matra 550 Magic—exclusively and was equipped with the British Martin-Baker Mk.10L ejection seat and head-up display from GEC, identification friend or foe (IFF), chaff/flare dispenser, and radar-warning receiver, also from Western sources. In place of the Skyranger radar, the F-7MP, also developed specially for the Pakistani air force, had the more capable Italian FIAR (now SELEX Galileo) Grifo 7 and numerous other changes to its avionics. The new radar was also later retrofitted in the F-7P.

Variants of the F-7M were given the internal designations J-7IIA and J-7IIM, but only a few examples were used for trials, and the types did not enter Chinese service.

Chapter 8: The Chinese MiG-21s: From Copy to Independent Aircraft Family

The FT-7 was one of the first aircraft displayed by China at international air shows. Most of the two-seat trainers that were exported, however, were based on the FT-7P with the longer fuselage. *Guido E. Bühlmann*

After the negative experience with the J-7 versions based on the MiG-21MF, the J-7E was the first representative of a third generation of Chinese MiG-21s. Once again the designers used the original fuselage design. At the same time, a considerable aerodynamic improvement was achieved by using a new double-delta wing. The inner wing retained the MiG-21's sweep angle of 57 degrees, while the outer wing sweep was reduced to 42 degrees and the trailing edge of the wing now had a negative sweep angle of 9.5 degrees. Aerodynamic advantages resulted from increasing wing area from 248 to 268 square feet and aspect ratio from 2.2 to 2.8, as well as maneuvering flaps on the outer wing with a maximum deflection angle of 25 degrees and new flaps. The aircraft's power plant is the more powerful WP-13. The J-7E is the first version of the MiG-21 or J-7 with a pressure-fueling system.

Most of the avionics are copies of Western systems used in the export models. This is true of the ranging radar—a copy of the GEC-Marconi 226 Skyranger—as well as the head-up display (HUD), radio equipment, TACAN, air data computer, radar-warning device, and chaff/flare dispenser. Distinctive features from earlier versions include the encapsulated angle-of-attack sensor, lack of nosewheel braking, deletion of the portside cannon, which is replaced by a 26.4-gallon fuel tank, and a powered trim tab on the rudder. The performance of the J-7E is significantly improved compared to earlier versions, but unlike the J-7D, which was developed at the same time, the J-7E lacks a radar gunsight. The installed ranging radar allows target detection and range measurement only to 8.7 miles.

The first prototype made its maiden flight on May 18, 1990. Production began in 1993, and more than 200 examples of the J-7E were completed by 2005. Versions for the Chinese naval air arm with special anticorrosion protection measures on the airframe and engine were designated J-7EH.

Developed especially for Pakistan, the F-7P was based on the F-7M, which was first exhibited in 1987; however, it was equipped with avionics and armament specified by the customer.

Recently, an number of J-E was upgraded to J-7L standard, receiving the fire control radar of the J-7G and also components from the J-10. Externally, it can be distiguished from the J-7E by new antennas behind and underneath the cockpit and on the tail.

GAIC developed a two-seat version to meet the requirements of the Pakistani air force. With a fuselage lengthened by 2 feet compared to the JJ-7, it was designated FT-7P. An additional section added aft of the cockpit enabled fuel volume to be increased to 740 gallons, while at the same time a type 23-II cannon was installed beneath the fuselage. Like those of the single-seater, each of the wings of the FT-7P has two stores pylons, of which the outer is capable of carrying an external fuel tank. This brings fuel volume and range to the level of the single-seater. Because of the first fire control radar in a two-seat MiG-21—the same Grifo 7M as in the F-7P—and the HK-03E head-up display, the FT-7P has the same operational capabilities as the single-seater.

The rear seat position is slightly raised to give the instructor a better view. The aircraft is powered by a WP-7B engine. Flight testing began in November 1990, and fifteen examples were delivered to the Pakistani air force.

Additional two-seat versions were developed from the FT-7P—the FT-7PG for Pakistan, the FT-7BG for Bangladesh, the FT-7NG for Namibia, and the FT-7NI for Nigeria. All were powered by the WP-13F.

For Chinese use, the JJ-7A (J-7LA) was derived from the JJ-7, with the standard fuselage and avionics adapted for the single-seater. The aircraft had the head-up display used by the J-7E. The first flight took place in May 1995, and deliveries of the production aircraft to the air force and navy began in 1997. More than 100 JJ-7s were built for domestic use.

An export version of the J-7E was crated, once again using Western avionics, essentially from GEC-Marconi (now BAE Systems) and AlliedSignal (now Honeywell). The key element was the Super Skyranger radar. The type 956 WAC-

The J-7E marked the first time that Chinese designers deviated from the aerodynamic scheme of the MiG-21 and adopted their own solution, the double-delta wing.

HUD (Wide-Angle Conventional Head-Up Display) also comes from this manufacturer. Additional avionics components include a Chinese electronic-warfare system, a radar-warning receiver, a chaff/flare dispenser, color displays, and a Chinese or an American radio. The cockpit is laid out according to the HOTAS principle and is equipped with a Chinese ejection seat. The F-7MG variant was exhibited at Airshow China in Zhuhai in 1996.

In the F-7PG version for Pakistan, the more capable Grifo MG radar replaced the Skyranger of the J-7E. Outwardly, the F-7PG differs from the Chinese original only in the additional 30 mm cannon on the portside of the fuselage and the one-piece windscreen analogous to the J-7G developed at the same time. Other changes included an external-loads management system, a voice alert system, and an electronic flight instrument system (EFIS) with two color screens and radio compass, a VOR receiver, TACAN, and an instrument landing system (ILS). The first aircraft arrived in Pakistan in 2001.

The new windscreen is the most obvious external feature of the J-7G, which is the final version, making its first flight on June 28, 2002. The one-piece unbraced windscreen not only offers the pilot a better view, it also optimizes the capabilities of the head-up display and the helmet-mounted sight. The combination of these components with the new SWL-2 pulse-Doppler radar (with a search range of twenty miles), the cockpit designed to the HOTAS principle, and the PL-9C air-to-air missile make this a much more effective combat aircraft.

Thanks to integrated satellite navigation and a precision bombing regime, the aircraft can employ fall-retarded and precision-guided bombs, such as the laser-guided LT-2.

Also new is the HTY-6 zero-zero ejection seat. The aircraft is powered by the WP-13F. Deliveries to four different air

Because of its lengthened fuselage and greater fuel capacity, plus four wing pylons and radar, the FT-7P was the first MiG-21 two-seat trainer to have the same combat capabilities as the single-seat aircraft.

The final two-seat version—the FT-7NI is seen here—had a new avionics and antenna suite but retained the classic delta wing.

Chapter 8: The Chinese MiG-21s: From Copy to Independent Aircraft Family

forces began in November 2004; a total of 110 aircraft have been produced. Export versions have been built for Bangladesh (F-7BG), Nigeria (F-7NI), and Sri Lanka (F-7GS); and again for Bangladesh (F-7BGI)—the latter having only one cannon. With delivery of the latter in May 2013, production of the single seaters at Chengdu ends.

Though many new types are rolling off the production lines in China's aircraft factories in considerable numbers; procurement of the J-7 for the Chinese Air Force went on until September 2016, when the last JJ-7A were delivered. With these aircraft production of the MiG-21 ended after fifty-seven years. Completion of the last JJ-7A was reported on October 31, 2010. Since then, the JL-9, alias FTC-2000, considerable parts of which are based on the MiG-21U/FT-7, has been built at Guizhou. Despite this, it is a new design with side air intakes and a double-delta wing.

Power Plants

In 1963, the Institute for Engine Development No. 606 in Shenyang began preliminary work for the replication of the R11F-300 turbojet. Production was the responsibility of the Shenyang Liming Aero Engine Factory. The first engine was assembled there in October 1965, and ground tests began in March 1966. These continued until the engine was accepted in December 1966.

The power plant was subsequently given the designation WoPen 7 (Turbojet Engine 7), or WP-7 for short. The first production model came off the line in June 1967, but it was not until a year later that it completed a fifty-hour run. It was another year until flight testing of the WP-7 and its derivative (the WP-7A) for the twin-engine J-8 began. In 1969–70, production was moved to the Guizhou Lijang Aero Engine Factory.

In 1998, the F-7MG export version derived from the J-7E was displayed with a one-piece windscreen. This became standard beginning with the F-7PG fighter for Pakistan.

In addition to the new windscreen, external features of the J-7G include modified antennas and the deletion of the port cannon.

Double-delta J/F-7 E/G were the only MiG-21 versions that featured a pressure refueling.

Chapter 8: The Chinese MiG-21s: From Copy to Independent Aircraft Family

The WP-7 was identical in design to the R11F-300; however, the early Chinese engines exhibited more-serious design and production shortcomings than the Soviet original. To overcome these, in 1969 an intensive development program was launched, with thousands of hours of test runs on the ground and in the air. After dedicating enormous resources for ten years, in 1979 the Chinese finally had an operational engine, though it still had a limited operating life of 300 hours and a time between overhaul of just 100 hours.

During preparations for production, the turbine inlet temperature was successively increased by 100 degrees Kelvin (280 degrees Fahrenheit), resulting in an increase in maximum thrust. The WP-7B(M) export engine was first installed in the F-7M. By 1992 the WP-7B engine's service life had been increased to 900 hours.

Development of a successor to the WP-7, the WP-13, began in 1978. Both the Guizhou Lijang Aero Engine Factory and the one in Chengdu played leading roles. The work was advanced and significantly influenced by the acquisition of a Soviet R13-300 engine from Egypt in 1979.

Consequently, the WP-13 was based on the Soviet R13-300 but also included elements from the development of the WP-7B, especially with respect to the compressor, combustion chamber, turbine, and afterburner. As of the development stage of the WP-13F, the Chinese engine surpassed the Soviet original in maximum thrust but could not match it in afterburner. The operating life of the last variant, the WP-13FI, reached 900 hours, the same as the WP-7B. Different variants of this engine were also produced for the J-7 and the twin-engine J-8II. While the WP-13 destined for the J-7C entered production in 1988, the WP-13F for the J-7E was not ready for production until 1992. Production of the WP-13FI, a developed version, finally began in 1995.

Armament

Since the first Chinese air-to-air missile, the PL-1 (that is, PiLi = Thunder), was built only in small numbers for the J-6 (MiG-19), the missile armament of the J-7 consists of the infrared-guided PL-2. It is a copy of the Soviet R-3S, which is itself a copy of the early Sidewinder.

Like the R11, the WP-7—cutaway model shown here—has five compressor stages. The WP-13, which appears in the schematic behind the model, has eight, like the engine from which it was derived, the Soviet R13.

For a long time, Soviet power plants were built in China unchanged. Ultimately, however, changes were incorporated, such as the flame stabilizer on the WP-13F shown here.

Production drawings and pattern parts were provided by the Soviets, together with other equipment needed to begin production, in 1961. The air-to-air missile, designated PiLi-2 by the Chinese, entered production in November 1967. Like the J-7, it took several years before a noteworthy production output was achieved.

In the late 1970s, the Chinese produced an improved version designated PL-2A with an improved seeker and greater resistance to countermeasures. Outwardly, the PL-2A resembled the American AIM-9D Sidewinder or the Soviet R-13M; however, its seeker was much smaller and was not cooled. The control and tail surfaces were unchanged from the PL-2, while the missile body was slightly longer.

The final version of the missile was the PL-2B, which was heavier than its predecessor and had a larger warhead. The triangular control surfaces were moved farther forward, and the infrared-proximity fuse was improved.

All variants of the PL-2 could be carried by all first- and second-generation J-7s as well as by the two-seat version.

Power Plants Compared

	WP-7	WP-7B	WP-13	WP-13F	WP-13FI
Aircraft	J-7/7I	J-7I/II	J-7C	J-7E	J-7D/G
Compressor Stages Low Pressure + High Pressure	3 + 3	3 + 3	3 + 5	3 + 5	3 + 5
Max. Static Thrust (lb.)	8,610	9,712	8,812	9,712	10,139
Max. Static Thrust AB (lb.)	12,679	13,444	14,118	14,230	14,995
Specific Fuel Consumption at Max. Static Thrust (lb./hr.)	218	227	216	222	222
Specific Fuel Consumption at Max. Static Thrust AB (lb./hr.)	516	450	505	460	460
Maximum Compression	8.9	8.9	8.8	8.8	9.2
Turbine Inlet Temperature (°F)	1,679	1,859	1,778	1,859	1,859
Air Throughflow (lb./sec.)	141	143	145–148	145–148	150–152

The PL-5 was the first short-range missile that—according to official sources—was developed on the basis of Chinese technology; however, the outward similarity to the American AIM-9G Sidewinder suggests that the missile, including its launch rail, that is also very close to the American original, is a copy of captured technology. The target seeker head is cooled by compressed air to improve sensitivity. The further developed PL-5B also has larger tail fins and double-delta control surfaces, causing it to resemble the AIM-9L.

Using the technology employed by the PL-7, a significantly much more capable version, the PL-5E (see below), appeared in the late 1980s. It differed from its predecessors in having a more pointed seeker head. The seeker behind it has a greater boresight angle of 25 degrees before and 40 degrees after firing. The missile's control surfaces were moved farther forward for better maneuverability, and the warhead is detonated by a laser-proximity fuse. The B and C versions of the PL-5 can be used only from the rear hemisphere, while the PL-5E can be fired from any direction. Though not officially confirmed, the PL-7 air-to-air missile, which was first shown in 1987, is identical to the French Matra 550 Magic. It is unclear if it is a license-built version, an unlicensed copy, or simply a relabeling of the original. The PL-7 is used exclusively to arm the export variants of the J-7 and is not used by the Chinese military.

Also originally a foreign product is the Chinese PL-8 air-to-air missile, a version of the Israeli Python 3 built under license, which at the time of its introduction at the end of the 1980s was the most capable Chinese AAM. This highly agile, infrared-guided missile is used against aerial targets of all kinds from any direction, against any background, and against maneuvering targets. The missile has a canard configuration, as well as large aerodynamic control surfaces mounted forward and four large fins on its tail. The warhead

The PL-5E is a development of the PL-5—itself a copy of the AIM-9G Sidewinder AAM—using the technology of the PL-7 alias Matra 550 Magic.

The PL-7—here a model on the wing of the F-7MG—was produced exclusively for export.

Pakistani F-7s are largely equipped with Western weapons systems such as the AIM-9 Sidewinder AAM.

Chapter 8: The Chinese MiG-21s: From Copy to Independent Aircraft Family

is detonated by an active proximity fuse. Originally made by using imported components, the PL-8 was subsequently produced entirely in China. Target selection can be made by using radar or a helmet-mounted sight. The Pythons received from Israel were designated PL-8 in China, while the PL-8A and PL-8B are versions produced in China from Israeli components or entirely from Chinese-made parts. Parallel to the PL-8, the PL-9 is being developed. The reason for the parallel development of two air-to-air missiles for identical purposes is suspected to have been export restrictions on the PL-8. The PL-9 combines the seeker technology of the PL-8 or Python 3 with a missile body developed in China. Production in small numbers began in 1989.

Outwardly, the PL-9 resembles the PL-8, but its range is significantly less. Unlike the PL-8, the PL-9 has trapezoid-shaped guide fins. The missile has a liquid-nitrogen-cooled infrared seeker head with a boresight angle of ±40 degrees. The PL-9's performance can be enhanced through the use of a helmet-mounted sight. The system is a copy of the Soviet-Ukrainian Shchel-3 and for the F-7 was available from the MG version.

The American Sidewinder, which equips the F-7s for Pakistan, is based on the first guided air-to-air missile to be built in large numbers. The first version entered service in 1956. The missile has been in continuous development since then and is still in production today—albeit in completely redesigned form. The construction and operation of the infrared-guided missile are identical to those described for the R-3S and R-13M. The AIM-9L and AIM-9P3 versions are used by the F-7 (and MiG-21). The AIM-9L is a much-improved version of the Sidewinder that entered production in 1977. For the first time, a cooled seeker head allows the detection of targets from the forward hemisphere. The control surfaces have a double-delta configuration, and the warhead is detonated by an active laser-proximity fuse. The AIM-9P3

is a less capable export version of the AIM-9L. It has a low-smoke engine and the same proximity fuse as the AIM-9L but has a less capable seeker head.

The J-7/F-7's cannon armament consists of copies of the Soviet NR-30 and GSh-23. Unguided air-to-surface rockets were also developed in the USSR. The bombs carried by the J-7 cover the spectrum from free-fall to guided to cluster bombs, both of Chinese and Western origin.

Equipment

Significant elements of the equipment carried by the J-7/F-7 are based on original Soviet components and are described there. Decisive technological advances did not take place until the integration of radars, described in the following chapter, which were a key element of the new avionics.

The GEC-Marconi Super Skyranger pulse-Doppler radar has two main modes of operation for the use of missiles or cannon, and a maximum range of 9 miles in the first mode and 3 miles in the second. Minimum range in this mode of operation is 492 to 984 feet. The radar operates in the frequency range of about 10 GHz, with a maximum scan deflection of ±30 degrees, but because of the installation configuration in the F-7MG, this is limited to ±20 degrees. Operating modes include search in the HUD's range of vision, vertical search, fixed beam, pursuit of a target, and range measurement—the latter during the search as well. The Super Skyranger has look-down shoot-down capability and is coupled with the onboard computer by an ARINC 429 data bus. It can track eight targets simultaneously and engage one of them.

The FIAR Grifo pulse-Doppler radar was originally developed in the early 1990s to equip the modernized F-5, and different-shaped antennas allowed it to be fitted in many aircraft types with limited installation space. The radar

Armament

	PL-5	PL-5E	PL-7	PL-8	PL-9	AIM-9L	AIM-9P
Length (ft.)	10.2	9.5	9.0	9.7	9.5	9.35	10
Weight (lb.)	326	183	198	265	253	188	172
Firing Range (mi.)	0.8–10	0.3–8.7	0.3–9.2	0.3–3.1	11	11	
Allowable G-Load	20	40	35	35			

A copy of the GSh-23 cannon is installed in different new variants of the FT-7. Unlike those in the Soviet MiG-21s, this cannon is fitted with a muzzle brake.

The HF-5A and HF-18S pods for unguided 57 mm (0.19-inch) rockets, which are analogous to the S-5, are similar to Soviet designs.

As the model shows, the Grifo radar was originally designed for use in the F-5 but was subsequently adapted for installation in the J-7/F-7.

operates in the 10 GHz frequency range and has modes for search, target tracking, aerial combat, and use against ground targets. Up to eight targets can be tracked in the air-to-air mode. In the version for the F-7, designated Grifo 7 and Grifo 7 PG, because of its small antenna its weight is just 121 pounds. Cooling of the radar is independent of the aircraft's systems, which simplifies installation. The two versions differ in vertical scan deflection, which for the Grifo 7 is limited to ±10 degrees, while for the Grifo 7 PG it is ±30 degrees. The radar is connected to the aircraft's onboard system by the MIL-STD-1553B bus. Stated range is approximately 34 miles.

The most-modern variants of the J-7/F-7 make use of head-up displays and multifunction screens. Otherwise the cockpit layout is still straight out of the 1950s.

In Action on the Front Lines of the Cold War

Soviet MiG-21s in European Nations outside the USSR

After the end of the Second World War, the Soviet air forces continued using hundreds of German airfields located in the territory of the Soviet Occupation Zone, the German Democratic Republic (GDR, founded in 1949), and Poland. There were also bases in Hungary and, after the suppression of the Prague Spring in 1968, in Czechoslovakia as well. The units stationed in Poland were organized into the Northern Group of Troops (SGV); those in the GDR, into the Western Group (ZGV). The aviation units belonged to the 4th (for a time the 37th) and 24th Air Armies (VA), and later the 16th Air Army. The troop contingents in Hungary formed a group of troops initially called the Central group and later the Southern Group of Troops (YuGV). Part of the SGT was the 36th Air Army. Stationed in the ČSSR (and ultimately in the ČSFR) was the Central Group of Troops (TsGV), and with it, the 131st Mixed Aviation Division.

The MiG-21 entered service in 1960, and initially only selected regiments were equipped with it. Among the first ones outside the border of the Soviet Union are: the 833rd Fighter Regiment (IAP) at Jüterbog-Altes Lager and the 73rd Guards Fighter Regiment (GvIAP) at Köthen. Not until the MiG-21F-13, which was produced from 1960 to 1962, became available could the large-scale reequipping of VVS units with the new type begin. In addition to the two named units, the 25th IAP at Zerbst and the 33rd IAP at Wittstock also received the aircraft. The career of the first-generation MiG-21s was quite brief, however. The MiG-21F and F-13

left service by the start of the 1970s. All the subsequent variants, however, were at least still in use by flying schools when the Soviet Union collapsed. The introduction of the MiG-21PF began a process that was to continue until the end of quantity production. The elite units of the first strategic echelon received the latest versions of the MiG-21 and passed on their older aircraft to units in peripheral regions and to flying schools. The 16th WA was equipped with the MiG-21PF and PFS, which it flew until 1965. These versions were subsequently flown by the 33rd IAP, the 35th IAP, the 85th GvIAP at Merseburg, the 31st GvIAP at Falkenberg, the 787th IAP at Templin, and the 833rd IAP. According to reports by the US Military Liaison Mission, by 1963 there were 105 MiG-21s of the F-13, PF, and PFS versions stationed in East Germany, and 126 by 1964.

The two-seat MiG-21U became available for training and instrument flights in 1963. Prior to this, pilot training had been done on the MiG-15UTI, whose flight characteristics were completely different than those of the MiG-21, which was twice as fast and much larger.

Industrial-level overhauls of the MiG-21 began at Soviet aircraft maintenance facilities in about 1963. The reason this happened so soon after the type entered service was the extremely low authorized airframe-, system-, and engine-operating times of the early versions of the MiG-21. The 152nd Aircraft Repair Center (ARS) at Jüterbog-Altes Lager took over this role in the 24th Air Army. In addition, a large

As a rule, Soviet combat aircraft, such as the MiG-21PF seen here, carried a two-digit serial number that served only to identify an aircraft within a squadron. *Popsuyevich Collection*

number of units were kept busy repairing aircraft components (engines, electronic equipment, etc.). Among these was the 307th ARS in Jüterbog-Damm. Overall, Soviet MiG-21s underwent fewer major overhauls than those of its allies because, as a rule, the operating lives of individual aircraft were lower due to their early replacement by new types.

The first MiG-21PFM fighters arrived in Wittstock in the summer of 1965, and within a year they were also received by the 773rd IAP at Damgarten, the 31st GvIAP, the 296th IAP, and the 787th and 833rd IAP. With the arrival of the MiG-21PFM, which was built in large numbers, the MiG-21 now formed the backbone of the frontal aviation forces. In keeping with the multirole character of this new version, for the first time fighter-bombers and close-support regiments were also among the recipients. The MiG-21 was not pushed out of its central role until the arrival of massive numbers of MiG-23s in the mid-1970s.

With the MiG-21PFM also came the introduction of the MiG-21US, the second trainer version. This enabled two-

seaters to be provided to every regiment. The first reconnaissance version, the MiG-21R, was initially sighted in Germany in 1966—flown by the 294th Independent Reconnaissance Regiment (ORAP), stationed at Altenburg. One year this unit and its aircraft moved closer to the border—to Allstedt. From there it regularly flew reconnaissance flights to Damgarten and back.

Almost every version of the MiG-21 to have entered service so far took part in the invasion of Czechoslovakia by Soviet and Warsaw Pact troops in 1968. As part of "Operation Danube," about 300 MiG-21s, which took off from bases in the Ukraine, Byelorussia, the GDR, Poland, and Hungary, landed almost simultaneously at every important Czechoslovak airfield. Between the end of August and the end of October, four regiments moved from the area of the 4th VA to Czechoslovak airfields.

Conversion to third-generation MiG-21s began with the arrival of the MiG-21SM at the 787th IAP at Templin (from 1970 onward, Finow) and Köthen in the summer of 1969.

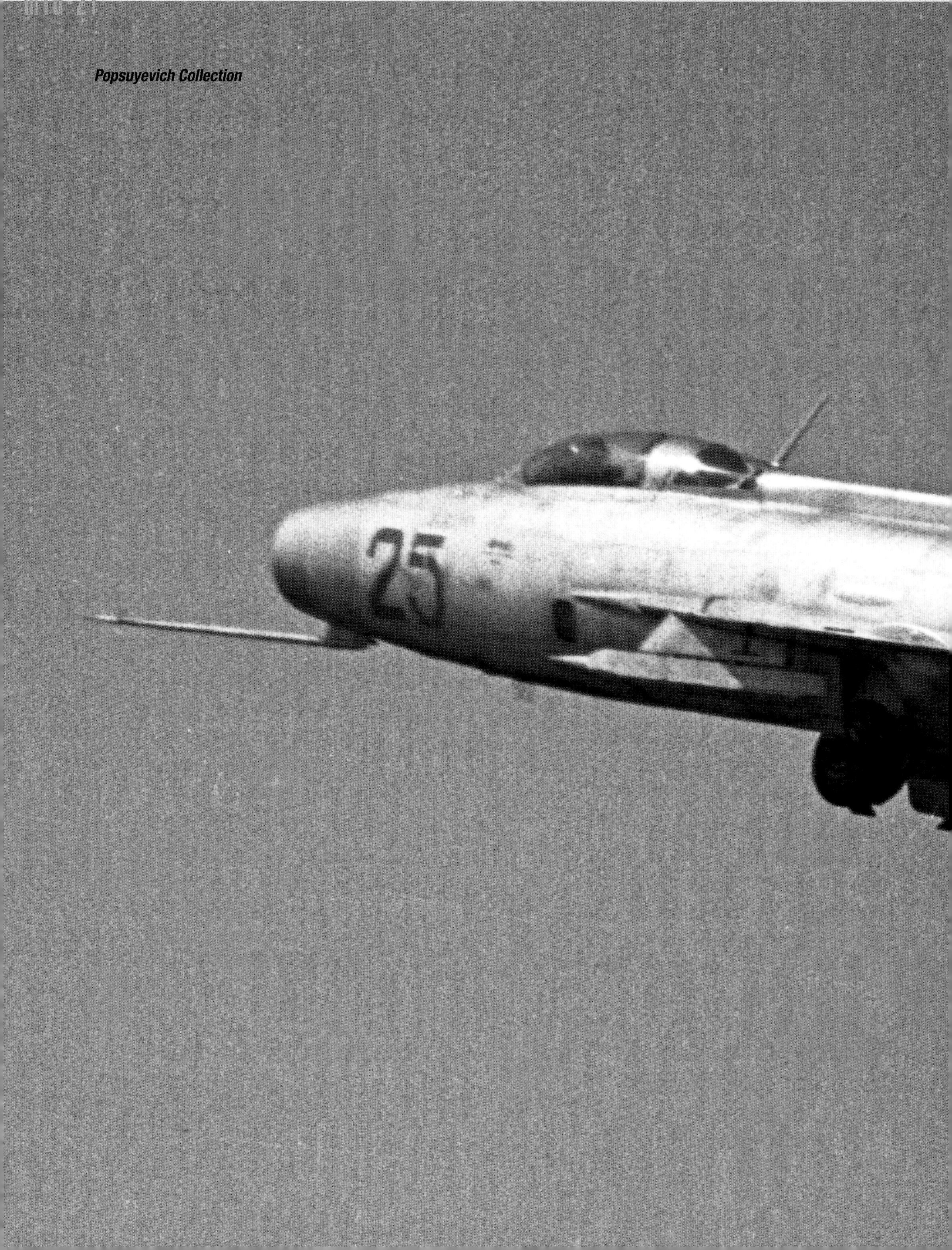

Popsuyevich Collection

From 1971 onward, this version also flew from Merseburg. These aircraft were also used for nuclear weapons training—a practice that was carried out even more intensely with the following versions. At the same time, after evaluating the lessons of the Six-Day War in the Middle East, the erection of type AU-11 shelters tailored for the MiG-21 began on Soviet airfields in Germany.

In 1971, the Soviet aviation regiments in the GDR began receiving the MiG-21UM two-seater and the MiG-21SMT, which within a year completely equipped the units at Merseburg, Altenburg, and Wittstock. Others went to Zerbst, where, in 1973, the first camouflaged examples were seen—including a number of MiG-21MT aircraft. Previously all MiG-21s had flown "naked." The first MiG-21bis LAZUR also arrived at Damgarten and Jüterbog that year, while the older MiG-21PF/PFM aircraft were sent back to the Soviet Union. The introduction of the MiG-23 into service also began in 1973, first at Falkenberg, where it flew alongside the MiG-21PF/PFM. New MiG-21s continued to be delivered, however:

new MiG-21bis SAUs also flew from Jüterbog; these aircraft had been given a pale-gray finish at the factory. At about the same time, the MiG-23 began replacing the MiG-21 at Zerbst and Finow. In 1975, the 730th Fighter-Bomber Regiment (IBAP; from 1976 onward, the 730th APIB) at Neuruppin, which had previously flown the MiG-17, received MiG-21s—first the PF and PFM versions, but within six months the SM as well. It was thus not only the last Soviet aviation regiment stationed in East Germany to receive the MiG-21, but also the one with the shortest time of use: the MiG-21's replacement, the Su-17M, began arriving in 1979.

That same year, the Su-17M3 also replaced the MiG-21R in the 294th ORAP at Allstedt. By that time, the regiments at Köthen and Wittstock had also received new technology in the MiG-23ML and sent their old equipment to the Soviet Union. According to American observations, the number of MiG-21s had fallen from 243 to 91 between the end of 1979 and the end of 1980, while the number of MiG-23s and Su-17s had grown to a similar degree. Finally, in 1984, the 296th

Like all MiG-21s until the third generation, the MiG-21PFM was delivered without camouflage. This was later applied at the unit level, however. *Popsuyevich Collection*

Soviet units in Europe were given priority with regard to the receipt of new technology. In 1969 this included the MiG-21SM. After it was replaced by newer versions, this aircraft remained at Wünsdorf as a monument. *Guido E. Bühlmann*

Two-seat trainers such as this UM were retained by the regiments following the retirement of the MiG-21. They were used by staff officers who were not trained on the new types to maintain proficiency. *Alexander Golz*

Chapter 9: In Action on the Front Lines of the Cold War

APIB at Altenburg reequipped on the MiG-27, the regiments at Jüterbog and Merseburg having received different versions of the MiG-23. Probably the last Soviet MiG-21 unit in the GDR, however, was the 773rd IAP at Damgarten, where according to unconfirmed sources a MiG-21bis squadron operated until 1986.

In Czechoslovakia, from 1968 onward, the MiG-21PF, PFS, and PFM were stationed at Sliač with the 159th IAP and with the 192nd IAP at Hradčany. There were also the MiG-21R reconnaissance aircraft of the 390th Independent Mixed Aviation Regiment (OSAP) and later the 100th Independent Reconnaissance Squadron (ORAE), first at Mladá and then at Sliač. In the mid-1970s, the reformed 159th IAP reequipped on the MiG-23 as the 114th IAP, while the 192nd IAP switched to the MiG-21bis. It was still equipped with that version when it left Czechoslovakia in 1984.

Of the Soviet regiments stationed in Poland, the 582nd IAP, based at Chojna, received the first examples of the MiG-

21F in 1960, followed in 1961 by the 159th GvIAP, which was then at Żagań airfield and received several MiG-21Fs as its initial equipment. A short time later, both regiments received the MiG-21F-13. In 1963, the 159th GvIAP had two squadrons with that version. After the unit was moved to Kluczewo in 1964, the regiment still had one squadron flying the MiG-21F-13, while the other was already flying the MiG-21PF. The first MiG-21PFM fighters arrived simultaneously with the first MiG-21U two-seaters. These versions also operated from Chojna. At the same time, the 871st IAP at Bagicz near Kołobrzeg (Kolberg) also began equipping on the MiG-21PFM. The regiment flew this version until 1973, when it reequipped on the MiG-23M.

The 159th GvIAP began equipping on the MiG-21R in 1967, and the conversion process was completed a year later. Why the regiment, which operated in the fighter role, was equipped with the reconnaissance version of the MiG-21 remains unexplained. It is known for certain, however, that

Only a few MiG-21s remain flyable in Russia as company aircraft. This MiG-21bis, seen in formation with a MiG-29 and a MiG-31 flying over Zhukovski, belongs to NAZ Sokol at Nizhni Novgorod. *Alexander Golz*

the unit was still operating the MiG-21R when the invasion of Czechoslovakia took place in 1968. Two years later the regiment converted onto the MiG-21SM—a process that was again completed within a year. The two-seat MiG-21UM now served alongside the new SM. The 582nd IAP received the MiG-21SMT in 1972. From about that time, the 215th Independent Tactical Reconnaissance Squadron (OAETR) at Brzeg also had the MiG-21R, which remained in action there until the early 1980s. Not until 1976 did the 42nd Guards Fighter-Bomber Regiment (GvAPIB) begin the MiG-21 era with the assignment of the MiG-21PF, having previously flown the MiG-17. Also in the mid-1970s, the 159th GvIAP and the 42nd GvIAP converted onto the MiG-21SMT. While the Su-24 replaced the latter unit's MiG-21SMTs in 1984, the 159th GvIAP retained the type until 1987, when it was replaced by the Su-27. The 582nd IAP kept its MiG-21SMTs until 1989, when it also converted onto the Su-27.

The MiG-21 began flying with the Soviet aviation forces in Hungary in 1962, when a complete regimental complement of MiG-21F-13s arrived at the 515th IAP at Tököl, near Budapest. Interestingly, the Hungarian air force had received its first MiG-21s one year earlier. Also in 1962, MiG-21F-13s were delivered for one squadron of the 5th GvIAP at Sármellék, as well as for one of the 14th GvIAP at Kiskunlacháza. In 1964–65, the 515th IAP was completely reequipped with the MiG-21PF. The 14th GvIAP followed in 1965 and the 5th GvIAP did likewise in 1966, the aircraft obviously having been relinquished by other regiments. Finally, this version also entered service with the staff flight of the 11th Guards Fighter Division (GvIAD) at Tököl. All three regiments were flying the MiG-21PF when they took part in the invasion of Czechoslovakia. The 315th OGRAE at Kunmadaras received MiG-21Rs and MiG-21U and UM two-seaters in 1967. The unit was subsequently reformed as the 328th ORGRAP and

Several Soviet MiG-21s got a second career abroad like this MiG-21bis that found its way to North Korea via Kazakhstan.

The last two still-flyable Albanian F-7A fighters were kept at readiness at Tirana-Rinas.

After the 2005 decision to phase out all aircraft, the ongoing maintenance work was suspended, and these F-7As remain in semicompleted condition in the aircraft tunnel at Gjadër.

The marks left by decades of underground storage are clearly evident on the stored Albanian F-7As. Unless funds are found for use of these aircraft as museum displays, they will probably never again see the light of day.

Chapter 9: In Action on the Front Lines of the Cold War

continued operating these types until they were replaced by the Su-17 in 1984–85.

Not until after the MiG-21R did the MiG-21PFM enter service with the fighter regiments of the southern group. From 1968 onward this version was flown by the 515th IAP; from 1970 onward, by the 14th and 5th GvIAP. The latter exchanged its aircraft for MiG-21SM and a few SMT fighters in 1972, and then in 1975 and 1976 these were replaced by MiG-23M aircraft. The 515th IAP received MiG-21SM and SMT aircraft in 1972–73 and retained them until 1982. Used MiG-21bis arrived as replacements and remained in service until the MiG-29 arrived in 1987. By the time of the withdrawal of Soviet and Russian aviation regiments from the countries of central and eastern Europe at the beginning of the 1990s, no MiG-21s were left in service. In the Soviet Union itself and its successor states, the MiG-21 had also been replaced by new types. Only the flying schools retained MiG-21s, which continued in service for a short time. Today in the entire Commonwealth of Independent States (CIS, a.k.a. the Russian Commonwealth) there are only a few MiG-21s still flying as factory aircraft.

Albania

Established at Tirana on April 24, 1951, the *Forcat Ushtarake Ajrore Shqipetare* (FASh, or Albanian air force) literally had to be created from the ground up, since there had not previously been any Albanian military aviation. At first, its buildup was supported by the Soviet Union, but after the break in relations in 1961, China assumed this role.

From the Chinese period of recent Albanian history came the twelve F-7A (J-7) fighters produced by the Shenyang aircraft factory. The aircraft, which had been broken down into subassemblies, arrived in the port of Durres in November 1970. They were probably used aircraft that had some hours on them and had briefly served with the Chinese air forces. Chinese technicians assembled the aircraft, and a Chinese pilot test-flew the first aircraft in December 1970. One month later, an Albanian pilot made the first flight in an F-7A. Originally stationed at Tirana-Rinas with the 7594th Regiment, the F-7s served with the 1st Squadron of the 5646th Regiment, which also had two squadrons of F-6s (MiG-19s). The base at Gjadër, about 40 miles north of Tirana, was built in 1969 especially for this regiment, whose primary role was to defend against Albania's archenemy, Yugoslavia. The first

Bulgaria received part of its fleet of MiG-21s as used aircraft from the Soviet Union. This Gorki-built MiG-21PFM is one such aircraft.

Numerous examples of the MiG-21bis were also delivered free of charge in 1990. They differed from the aircraft previously purchased in having second-generation IFF antennas (above and below the nose).

A MiG-21bis undergoes maintenance in an aircraft shelter. These protective structures, the result of an analysis of the Six-Day War between the Israelis and Arabs in 1967, were built everywhere in the Warsaw Pact states.

A view of the flight line at Graf Ignatievo. The MiG-21 and MiG-29 have been operated side by side for years and also share QRA (quick reaction alert) duty.

F-7 landed on its runway on July 10, 1973. After the MiG-19PMs originally obtained from the Soviet Union were exchanged for Chinese aircraft, the F-7A, which was armed with the PL-2, was the only missile-armed fighter in the Albanian arsenal. It is interesting that the Albanians always used the designation MiG-21 for the aircraft—an indication that the aircraft had been built from Soviet parts.

After Albania's breakaway from China in 1978, the FASh did not obtain any new systems. Since the People's Republic was also the main supplier of spares, the fleet could be kept serviceable only because of extensive self-sufficiency. In the 1970s, the maintenance facility in Kucova achieved the capability of completely overhauling the most-important types, and at the same time took over the overhauling of power plants, which had previously been done in China.

By secretly obtaining technology on the world market (including from Sweden), Albania achieved the capability to manufacture spares and engine components for most aircraft types, but not for the F-7. This resulted in the F-7As being flown significantly less than the rest of the fleet. The aircraft logged between only 300 and 600 hours in the air before they were retired.

Prior to the break with Peking, the Albanian F-7 pilots received training in China. Between 1978 and 1990, training was done by the regiment at Gjadër. Two aircraft were lost while in service. One crashed in 1974—prior to the move to Gjadër—as a result of pilot error, while a second machine fell victim to a bird strike during takeoff. The remaining ten aircraft survived both the end of communism and the revolts akin to civil war in the years that followed.

The political shift, which began in Albania with the death of dictator Enver Hoxha in 1985, opened new markets for the procurement of military equipment; however, the country lacked the means with which to purchase even the most-basic components. Cutbacks were required even to maintain the status quo. The training of new pilots on the F-7A was stopped in 1990, since the available resources were barely sufficient to maintain the proficiency of the pilots who had already been trained. The Federal Republic of Germany delivered numerous MiG-21 engines to Albania in the early 1990s and it was because of this that its F-7As were able to keep flying. The engines from East German stocks replaced the unreliable Chinese power plants.

The FASh's aircraft fleet suffered massive cuts during the unrest in 1997, from which it was never to recover. Many airfields, including Gjadër, were stormed by mobs, and the installations and aircraft there were destroyed.

Only by mobilizing all available resources were the F-7s of the FASh able, in 1998, to carry out a number of flights to deter airspace violations by Yugoslavian aircraft and take part in the air display marking the ninetieth anniversary of the Albanian army in 2002. The Albanian F-7As were probably the last machines of the first J/F-7 generation active anywhere in the world. As part of the restructuring of the Albanian air force that began in 2002, all operational Albanian aircraft, including the F-7As, were concentrated at Rinas near Tirana. On December 2 of that same year, an F-7A took off for the last time on a brief flight.

Reports that Albania planned to form a second squadron of MiG-21s and was procuring ten MiG-21bis from the Ukraine proved to be false. Likewise, an alleged agreement with Romania for the modernization of the F-7As had no basis in fact. At the end of 2005, after making a realistic appraisal of its own possibilities, the Albanian government grounded all fixed-wing aircraft and thus killed the hopes of its pilots and technicians for a second life for its Mach 2 fighters. The ministry of defense even refused to grant a request from military personnel to stage a farewell flight on Air Force Day on April 24, 2006. At that time, just one pilot still had a valid type rating. The last two operational aircraft are today parked at Rinas, while the other eight nonflyable aircraft are at Gjadër. It is hoped that at least a few of the F-7As, whose origins and numbers make them among the most exotic combat aircraft in Europe, will survive for posterity.

Bulgaria

In the People's Republic of Bulgaria, formed in 1946, Soviet aircraft replaced the existing German, Polish, and Czech technology. This later founding member of the Warsaw Pact was equipped by the Soviet Union with more or less current aircraft—often in the form of gifts of used machines.

The introduction of the MiG-21 by the *Bulgarski Woennowzdushni Sili* (BWWS, or Bulgarian air force) began in the summer of 1963, when the first pilots and technicians of the BWWS received familiarization training on the new type at the Soviet training center in Krasnodar. In September of that year, eleven MiG-21F-13s arrived at the 19th *Istrebitelen Awiazionen Polk* (IAP = fighter regiment) at Graf Ignatievo Airfield, where they relieved the MiG-19s of the 3rd IAE

Technical personnel attend to a MiG-21UM after a sortie.

(*Istrebitelna Awioeskadrila*, or fighter squadron). A twelfth machine followed a short time later. In 1974, the nine surviving aircraft of that version were handed over to the 26th Reconnaissance Aviation Regiment (*Rasusnavatelen Awiazionen Polk*, RAP) at Tolbuchin (Dobrich), where they served as reconnaissance aircraft until 1988. In 1976, the aircraft were fitted with an AFA-39 camera for their new role. Air-to-ground missions were envisaged as a secondary role.

From 1968 onward, airframes and engines of Bulgarian MiG-21F-13s and all subsequent versions were maintained and overhauled in the country. The work was carried out by the Georgi Benkovski (until 1993, Georgi Dimitrov) VRZ (*Voenno Remonten Zavod*, or military repair operation) at the Graf Ignatievo base. The latter has been active since 1939, when it was established to maintain German technology in use by Bulgaria, and it was subsequently active in providing industry-level maintenance for aircraft types from the Yak-17 to MiG-19. In addition to Bulgarian aircraft, the facility has also overhauled foreign MiG-21s, including those from Syria. In 1990, there was talk of modernizing Bulgarian as well as Indian and Arabian MiG-21s at the facility. These plans were

never realized, however. The Khan Asparuch MRZ in Dobrich—like the facility at Graf Ignatievo part of the TEREM Company, which was operated by the Bulgarian defense ministry—also carried out maintenance on the MF and UM variants of the MiG-21.

On February 12, 1965, Soviet pilots flew twelve MiG-21PF fighters to the base at Gabrovnitsa. One week later, the 2nd IAE of the 18th Fighter Regiment commenced flight operations on these machines, and in July of the same year the unit went to the Soviet base in Astrakhan for gunnery practice. The pilots had previously received training on the new type in the Soviet Union. MiG-23s arrived in 1983, and nine surviving MiG-21s were transferred to the 21st Fighter Regiment at Uzundzhovo and from there to the reconnaissance regiment at Dobrich, where they remained in service until 1991.

In 1966, the 1st IAE of the 15th Fighter Regiment at Rawnez received twelve examples of the MiG-21PFM from the factory in Gorki. In 1977–78, the Soviet Union provided, free of charge, another thirty-six used aircraft of the MiG-21PFS/PFM versions, also built in Gorki, to Bulgaria. These

Night-flying operations at Count Ignatievo. Because of economic difficulties and low flying hours in the 1990s, most eastern European air forces restricted themselves to "fair-weather flying," but night and bad-weather flying are now once again a part of normal operations.

A pair of MiG-21bis photographed during a low pass. Almost every Bulgarian MiG-21 has a unique camouflage scheme.

aircraft were used to replace the MiG-17s and were issued to elements of the 15th Fighter Regiment stationed at Ravnets and Balchik and to the 18th IAP at Gabrovnitsa. From 1985 until they were retired in 1992, the MiG-21PFMs were flown by the 2nd Training Regiment (UBAP = *Utschebno-Bojen Awiazionen Polk*) at Kamenets, alongside the MiG-21US/UM two-seat trainers delivered later. Two more training versions were procured in 1986, one of which served at Kamenets.

In 1966, after three versions of the MiG-21 had already entered service, the Bulgarian air force received its first two seater, a MiG-21U. This aircraft was used in rotation by all MiG-21 regiments, and in 1969 it was supplemented by two MiG-21US trainers. Three more examples followed in 1970.

Six MiG-21R reconnaissance aircraft arrived at Dobrich in 1969. This version remained in service with the 26th Reconnaissance Regiment until it was retired in 1996. Three aircraft were lost during operations.

Twelve examples of the next version, the MiG-21M, were delivered to the 19th Fighter Regiment at Graf Ignatievo between August and December 1969, replacing MiG-19s of the 2nd IAE. The 2nd Squadron of the 18th Fighter Regiment at Gabrovnitsa received three more aircraft in August of the following year. The MiG-21Ms of the 2nd and 19th IAE were equipped to deliver nuclear weapons. As in other states of the Warsaw Pact, in the event of war these weapons would have been made available by Soviet troops. The units regularly trained on the delivery methods for the so-called special bombs. The service life of the Bulgarian MiG-21M was shorter than any other version of the MiG-21, and these machines were retired in 1990.

Deliveries of a total of twenty-nine MiG-21UM trainers began in 1974 and continued until 1982. The 18th Fighter Regiment at Dobroslavtsi received the first two aircraft, and the rest were divided among the MiG-21 regiments. In 1990,

Since the MiG-21F-13 was produced in large numbers under license in Czechoslovakia and remained in production for a decade, sufficient resources were available to keep this version in service until the early 1990s. *Guido E. Bühlmann*

the Soviet Union delivered another six used MiG-21UM trainers.

At the same time as the first MiG-21UM trainers, the 1st and 18th Fighter Regiments also received nine MiG-21MF fighters, replacing MiG-19s. Another eleven examples of the MiG-21MF-75 went to Graf Ignatievo (19th IAP). All MiG-21M and MF aircraft were later transferred to the 21st IAP at Uzundzhovo as replacements for the last MiG-17Fs still in service in Europe. After its disbandment, the aircraft remained in service with the 2nd RAE of the 26th RAP, until it too ceased flying operations in 2001. During the period when the MiG-21MF was entering service, there was a special training program at Krasnodar in the Soviet Union in which experienced Bulgarian MiG-21 pilots took part. The program was called Exercise 500, and the pilots received special dogfighting training based on the evaluation of aerial combat in the Middle East a year earlier.

Not until much later, between 1983 and 1985, in parallel to deliveries of the MiG-23, did the Bulgarians receive the last and numerically most important version, the MiG-21bis.

Initially, thirty-six new examples of this type were delivered to the 19th IAP at Graf Ignatievo, where they replaced the MiG-21M/MF. The Soviet Union subsequently provided another thirty-six used aircraft, which were divided among the 15th IAP at Balchik and the 21st IAP at Uzundzhovo, free of charge, along with the previously mentioned MiG-21UM trainers in 1990. At Balchik these replaced the last operational aircraft of the PFM version. While the newly purchased MiG-21bis were equipped with the RSBN navigation system, the used examples had the LAZUR ground control interception system. At least some of the MiG-21bis and MiG-21UM aircraft from the last delivery were equipped with the Parol IFF set, which was not installed in export aircraft until the MiG-29. Some MiG-21bis from this delivery also had a gun camera, which was installed just behind the pitot tube and was recognizable by its prominent fairing.

Bulgaria received a total of 226 MiG-21s of various versions, of which about 150 were in service during the Bulgarian air force's heyday in the mid-1980s.

Chapter 9: In Action on the Front Lines of the Cold War

Bulgaria was also affected by the political changes that took place in November 1989. Disarmament measures and economic problems subsequently led to massive reductions in the Bulgarian MiG-21 force. In 1990, MiG-21s were still stationed at five bases: thirty-six MiG-21bis and five two-seaters at Graf Ignatievo, thirty-five MiG-21bis and three two-seaters at Uzundzhovo, thirty-eight single-seat and four two-seat MiG-21s at Balchik, thirteen MiG-21s of various versions at Dobrich, and thirteen MiG-21PFM and eight MiG-21UM at Kamenets. At that time, an additional fifty-two MiG-21s (six MiG-21PFs, eight MiG-21Ms, thirty-six MiG-21PFMs, and two MiG-21UMs) were at Military Repair Facility No. 1 (WARR-1) at Graf Ignatievo.

The 21st IAP at Uzundzhovo was disbanded in 1991. The 3rd Squadron of the 19th IAP at Graf Ignatievo (3/19 IAE) continued operating its MiG-21bis and MiG-21UM aircraft at the same airfield. In 1992, the 1/2 UBAE (UBAE = *Utschebno-*

Bojen Awioeskadrila = training squadron) ceased MiG-21 operations at Kamenets and retired all of its PFM, US (the last active machines of this version), and UM versions of the MiG-21.

After all the MiG-21PF and M aircraft were grounded between 1990 and 1992 (the MiG-21F-13s were already worn out by the end of the 1980s and, as previously mentioned, were retired), the fleet was reduced further. The MiG-21bis lost their nuclear capability. To avoid the limitations of the treaty concerning conventional forces in Europe (CFE), in 1995, the wing pylons and gunsights were removed from nineteen of the twenty-five MiG-21UM trainers, and they were operated as unarmed training aircraft under the designation MiG-21UM-2. To comply with the treaty, a total of sixteen MiG-21s of the PF, PFM, US, R, and M versions were scrapped (according to other sources, two MiG-21F-13s, seventeen MiG-21PFMs, and ten MiG-21MFs), while another

As of the MiG-21PF, Czechoslovakia—like all of the "brother nations"—received Soviet-built MiG-21s. *Guido E. Bühlmann*

two dozen were displayed at museums or became gate guardians.

Efforts to sell the remaining nine MiG-21M aircraft were unsuccessful. The transfer of twelve MiG-21bis to Macedonia in late 1999 also came to nothing, since the recipient country was unable to come up with the funds for overhaul of the aircraft by TEREM, a Bulgarian condition for the sale. Bulgaria hoped to be able to sell up to forty more aircraft. In 2007–2008, several ex-Bulgarian MiG-21s were undergoing overhaul at OdesAviaRemServis for unidentified customers.

In 1995–96, several MiG-21MF were converted as replacements for the MiG-21R, which had been retired. Their GSh-23 cannon were removed and reconnaissance pods from the MiG-21R were installed. The machines thus modified were designated MiG-21MFR. Some MiG-21MFs had previously carried reconnaissance pods that were UB-16 pods with an AFA-39 camera installed.

Of the numerous MiG-21 bases, in the end only Graf Ignatievo remained. Uzundzhovo and Balchik were closed in 1998 and Dobrich followed in 2001. The aircraft there were sent to Graf Ignatievo and continued in use or were mothballed. The number of aircraft on strength was to be reduced from 118 single-seaters and eighteen trainers (as of January 1, 2000) to thirty-six MiG-21bis and eight MiG-21UMs in 2004. In reality, the number of serviceable aircraft was well below this mark. In March 2006, there were still eighteen serviceable MiG-21s. The modernization of these aircraft was repeatedly considered during the 1990s, with both RAC MiG and IAI making proposals. The only work that was actually done, however, was the equipping of several machines with GPS receivers.

Finally, the MiG-21 was planned for retirement in 2012. But due to technical problems of the MiG-29s, a small fleet of one MiG-21UM and three MiG-21bis—the latter still fullfilling the QRA role—remained in service. On December 18, 2015, the last three operational MiG-21 of the BVVS—one MiG-21UM and two MiG-21bis—were retired in a small ceremony.

In fifty-two years of service, forty-two Bulgarian MiG-21s were lost in accidents, killing twenty-five pilots

ČSSR/ČSFR and Successor States

With the military coup on February 25, 1948, the Czechoslovakian communists took power in the country. From then on, the air force, which in addition to domestic types operated a mix of German, British, and Soviet aircraft types, imported equipment exclusively from the latter. At the same time, the air force underwent a period of expansion. With a long tradition behind it, the Czechoslovak aviation industry was able to produce modern Soviet aircraft types, beginning with the MiG-15 for domestic use and export. Preparations for introduction of the MiG-21 by the *Protivzdušna Obrana Státu* (PVOS; national air defense) of the ČSSR began in the early 1960s. This type was also to be built in Czechoslovakia. In May 1961, ten pilots were sent on a conversion course in the USSR, where on July 15 the first flight in a MiG-21F by a Czechoslovak pilot took place. It was more than a year, however, until the *Výcvikova letka* (training squadron; later, *Výcvikova střediska letectva* [VSL], training center) of the PVOS at Milovice-Mladá received the first three MiG-21F-13s—two aircraft built under license and the pattern aircraft delivered from the Soviet Union—for familiarization. These were followed by another thirty-three aircraft by August 1969. The successor unit, the 1st Flight Training Regiment (*letecký školní pluk* or *lšp*) at Přerov, received six more aircraft in 1971–72.

The MiG-21s were officially unveiled during the Liberation Day parade in Prague on May 9, 1963. Unlike most socialist countries, such public displays were common practice in the ČSSR. For example, the 1st Fighter Regiment (*stíhací letecký pluk* or *slp*) performed at public displays in two four-aircraft formations, while the 11th Fighter Regiment gave demonstrations at official functions with a group of six aircraft; the 4th Fighter Regiment, a group of four. The occupation of Czechoslovakia by Warsaw Pact troops in August 1968 and the resulting so-called normalization led to the cessation of such activities.

The first four operational aircraft, which like all other aircraft of the PVOS wore the last four digits of their construction numbers as serial numbers (0002–0005), went to the 1st Squadron of the 11th Fighter Regiment at Žatec in November 1963. Seven aircraft followed in 1964, four in 1965, and twelve in 1966, and these replaced the MiG-19s of the regiment's 3rd Squadron. The same year, MiG-21s of the 11th Fighter Regiment took part in "Operation October Storm" in the German Democratic Republic. In May 1964, the 1st Fighter Regiment at České Budějovice received a MiG-21F-13. Significant numbers followed half a year later: nine aircraft for the 2nd Squadron between January and December

The MiG-21M was designated MiG-21MA by the air force of the ČSSR. The periscope and FOD deflectors were added during overhaul. *Guido E. Bühlmann*

Czech air force MiG-21MF on approach to land. The aircraft has been updated to use the R-60 air-to-air missile and carries the necessary launch rails on the inner wing pylons. *Guido E. Bühlmann*

1965, twelve in 1966, and five more in 1971–72. The 4th Fighter Regiment at Pardubice began reequipping on the MiG-21F-13 in 1965, when six aircraft arrived for the 1st Squadron. Ten and seven aircraft followed in 1966–67. The regiment meanwhile continued flying the MiG-19. Finally, between October and December 1965, the 2nd Squadron of the 9th Fighter Regiment converted to the new type at Bechyně. It received three aircraft from the factory and ten from VSL and the 4th Fighter Regiment. Eight more followed in 1967, plus seven aircraft between 1969 and 1972. In 1967, the MiG-19s of the 8th Fighter Regiment at Mošnov were replaced by sixteen MiG-21F-13s, and three more of this type followed between 1969 and 1972. The last regiment to receive the MiG-21F-13 as a replacement for the MiG-19 was the 5th Fighter Regiment at Plzeň-Líně. In addition to twelve aircraft from the factory, machines were received from other regiments, and by 1972 the 5th Fighter Regiment had forty-six MiG-21s of this version. The last MiG-21F-13 built in the ČSSR was received by the 9th Fighter Regiment at

Bechyně, aircraft 1114 arriving there on July 14, 1972.

Eleven MiG-21F-13s, including three assembled from Soviet parts, were delivered to Syria in 1973 as part of a Warsaw Pact aid program.

The 11th Fighter Regiment operated the MiG-21F-13 until the end of the 1970s, though in the end only the 1st Squadron was flying the type. At the same time, the 1st Fighter Regiment's F-13s were replaced by MiG-21MFs and MiG-23s. The MiG-21F-13s of the 8th Fighter Regiment's 3rd Squadron were transferred to the 1st Flight Training Regiment at Přerov after the arrival of the MiG-21PFM in 1983. The 9th Fighter Regiment continued flying the MiG-21F-13 until the beginning of the 1980s. From 1983 to 1989, a total of nine aircraft were handed over to the 4th and 5th Fighter Regiments. Between 1985 and 1988, the 4th Fighter Regiment received MiG-21F-13s from the 5th Fighter Regiment. When it was disbanded as part of the Warsaw Pact's disarmament initiative on July 31, 1989, the regiment still included one squadron with fourteen MiG-21F-13s. Six

A MiG-21MF-75 is towed to the flight line. The colorful markings identify the aircraft as part of the Delta F display team, which appeared at numerous air shows in the 1990s. *Guido E. Bühlmann*

of these went to the 1st Flight Training Regiment, and four went to the 5th Fighter Regiment . The MiG-21F-13 remained in service there until 1990. The remaining thirty-five MiG-21F-13s were retired by the 1st Flight Training Regiment in March 1990. On May 20, 1991, aircraft 1104 was ferried from Kbely to Vodochody, the last flight by a Czechoslovakian MiG-21F-13. In keeping with the terms of the Treaty on Conventional Armed Forces in Europe, ninety-eight combat aircraft, including seventy-eight MiG-21s, were retired in the early 1990s and placed in storage at Vodochody and Přerov. Most of these aircraft were scrapped by 1995, but several were given to museums or sold. Of the 168 MiG-21F-13s operated by the PVOS, forty-four were destroyed in crashes or accidents. Two of these were lost while being flown by students from Libya who were training with the 1st Flight Training Regiment at Přerov. Another was mistakenly shot down by Soviet fighter aircraft over East Germany in 1964.

From the beginning, industry-level maintenance of Czechoslovak MiG-21s was carried out by the *Letecké opravny Kbely* (LOK; an aircraft maintenance facility), which had previously gained experience maintaining the MiG-15/17/19. Many of the two-seat trainers, but also MiG-21MF fighters, were also overhauled at the aircraft maintenance facility *Flugzeugwerft Dresden*.

New versions of the MiG-21 were delivered from the USSR while production was still under way at Aero Vodochody. The first version imported from the Soviet Union was the MiG-21PF, which was produced in Moscow; however, it was not acquired in the same numbers as its predecessor. A conversion course was carried out at Žatec from July to September 1964. The sixteen MiG-21PFs delivered from then until the end of the year were divided among the 1st Fighter Regiment (1st Squadron) and the 8th Fighter Regiment at Mošnov, where this type initiated the Mach 2 era. The 3rd Squadron of the 11th Fighter Regiment was the third unit to receive the MiG-21PF—as replacements for the MiG-19PM. Ten aircraft arrived there between February and April 1965, while at the same time the 1st Fighter Regiment received six more aircraft and the 8th Fighter Regiment received seven. The MiG-21PFs of the 1st and 4th Fighter

The aluminum paint on this MiG-21UM has partially worn away, revealing the yellow primer coat. *Guido E. Bühlmann*

Czech MiG-21MFs from the later production batches flew until the millennium wearing the green-brown camouflage scheme in which they were delivered.

Regiments received their baptism of fire in Exercise Vltava (Danube) in September 1966. The 9th Fighter Regiment at Bechyně did not receive its MiG-21PFs until 1985, in the form of nine aircraft made available when the 8th Fighter Regiment received the MiG-21MF.

The 1st Fighter Regiment's MiG-21PFs were replaced by MiG-23s beginning in 1977 and were transferred to the 8th Fighter Regiment. This version remained in service with the 11th Fighter Regiment until the mid-1980s. In 1988 the 8th Fighter Regiment—then based at Brno-Tuřany—still had twenty MiG-21PFs on strength in two squadrons. The 9th Fighter Regiment operated the PF until May 1989. Once retired, the aircraft, like the MiG-21F-13s before them, were gathered at Přerov or Vodochody. Three aircraft went to museums, and three were sent back to the 8th Fighter Regiment. This unit retired its last four MiG-21PFs in 1990 and flew them to Přerov. In September 1990, MiG-21PF 1304 was flown to Great Britain and handed over to the RAF Benevolent Fund. Eight MiG-21PFs were destroyed in accidents.

Simultaneous with the MiG-21PF, the PVOS received its first two-seat trainers, all of which were concentrated at the training center at Milovice-Mladá (later the 1st Flight Training Regiment at Přerov). The first three MiG-21U-400s built in Moscow arrived in April 1965, followed by a second batch of four aircraft in spring 1966, and a third and final delivery of four MiG-21U-600s between June and September 1967. Three MiG-21U trainers were later issued to operational units (1st, 4th, and 9th Fighter Regiments). Retirement of the MiG-21U began in the early 1990s. The last flight by a PVOS aircraft of this type took place on May 2, 1990, by the 1st Flight Training Regiment at Přerov. One aircraft continued flying with VZLÚ at Kleby as a testbed for ejection seats. After retirement, seven MiG-21Us were ferried to the training regiment at Vodochody and placed in storage. One of the eleven MiG-21Us delivered was lost in a crash.

Introduction of the MiG-21PFM began in 1966, with a conversion course given by the 1st Fighter Regiment at České Budějovice. The regiment's 3rd Squadron was equipped with seven aircraft of this type in August of that

Toward the end of their service lives, the Czech MiG-21MFs were finished in a modern scheme consisting of two shades of gray and conducted up to three scrambles per day—in all kinds of weather, day and night.

year. In November 1966, ten MiG-21PFMs were delivered to the 3rd Squadron of the 9th Fighter Regiment at Bechyně, and three more were sent to the 1st Fighter Regiment. The 1st and 9th Fighter Regiments shared the six aircraft delivered in July 1967 (four and two, respectively). In June–July 1968, the 1st Squadron of the 11th Fighter Regiment at Žatec converted onto the MiG-21PFM, having received twelve examples of this type beginning in April. Finally, in July–August 1968, the 9th Fighter Regiment introduced twelve MiG-21PFMN aircraft, capable of carrying nuclear weapons, into service. Its older MiG-21PFM aircraft were handed over to the 8th Fighter Regiment, and consequently, from spring 1969 onward, this regiment had one squadron each equipped with the MiG-21F-13, PF, and PFM.

The MiG-21PFMNs remained at Bechyně until April 1973 and were then transferred to the 1st Fighter Regiment. After the arrival of the MiG-23ML in late 1981, the 11th Fighter Regiment received the remaining aircraft at České Budějovice, after which there were two squadrons equipped with the type there. The conversion of one squadron of the 11th Fighter

Regiment to MiG-23s in 1983 made its MiG-21PFMs available, and they were given to the 8th Fighter Regiment. With the arrival of the aircraft from the 11th Fighter Regiment in 1983, two squadrons of the 8th Fighter Regiment were entirely or partly equipped with the MiG-21PFM. In 1989, several of these machines were given back to the 11th Fighter Regiment in Žatec, and the rest were placed in storage at Brno. In April 1991, these last five MiG-21PFM flew to the collection site at Vodochody, where they were to be destroyed in keeping with the Treaty on Conventional Armed Forces in Europe (CFE). Their fate was shared by twenty-eight MiG-21PFMs of the 11th Fighter Regiment from Žatec, which had received the MiG-21MFs of the disbanded 5th Fighter Regiment at Plzeň-Líně. Of the fifty MiG-21PFMs delivered to Czechoslovakia, twelve were lost while in service.

In May 1968, selected pilots from the 47th PZLP (*pruzkumný letecký pluk* = reconnaissance aviation regiment) underwent conversion training on the MiG-21 at Milovice-Mladá. At first, their only aircraft were six MiG-21FR taken over from the 8th Fighter Regiment, which could be fitted

Landing with a unique silhouette in the background: a MiG-21MFN in the QRA configuration of its final years of operations, with two external fuel tanks and two R-60 AAMs, about to touch down on the road at Cáslav.

Preparations on the flight line. While the Czech MiG-21UMs were given a new finish toward the end of the service lives, the aircraft themselves were not updated.

Chapter 9: In Action on the Front Lines of the Cold War

An aircraft is towed to the flight line. Typical ground equipment, consisting of a tool box, a protective mat to guard the surface of the wing, wheel chocks, and the unavoidable bucket are transported on and in the aircraft.

The MiG's replacement taxis in. A Saab JAS-39 Gripen, the Czech Republic's new combat aircraft, rolls past MiG-21MFs lined up on the flight line for the type's farewell flight.

The Czech MiG-21 made its last flight on July 12, 2005. Five aircraft, flown by Col. Jirí Verner; Lt. Col. Libor Štefánik; Majors Petr Lanci, Luboš Bechnye, and Roman Svoboda; and Capt. Jirí Kapitán, took off from Cáslav and overflew several former MiG-21 bases before landing for the last time at Přerov.

with two reconnaissance pods, each housing four AFA-39 cameras. The first two MiG-21R reconnaissance aircraft from Gorki arrived at Paradubice, to where the regiment was being moved after Soviet units took over its original base in January 1969. Other deliveries included six aircraft in June–July 1969, and ten from February to June 1970. Seven more aircraft were delivered between October and December 1971. The 2nd Squadron of the 47th Reconnaissance Regiment was equipped with MiG-21R aircraft. In 1985, the 47th Reconnaissance Regiment moved to Hradec Králové, where it remained until its disbandment. Parallel to the MiG-21R, the MiG-21US was delivered between November 1968 and July 1970. Unlike the MiG-21U, the new two-seat trainers were shared among the operational regiments exclusively. Of the four aircraft delivered in 1968, five in 1969, and four in 1970, the 47th Reconnaissance Regiment received four; the 9th Fighter Regiment, three; and the 1st, 8th, and 11th Fighter Regiments, two examples each, the majority of which remained with their units for many years.

The first fourteen MiG-21M (called MiG-21MA by the PVOS) arrived at the 4th Fighter Regiment's base at Pardubice in July 1969. One year later, deliveries of this version concluded with ten more aircraft, which were also assigned to the 4th Fighter Regiment. Between October and December 1974, the 4th Fighter Regiment received the MiG-21MF, whereupon eight MiG-21Ms were given to the 47th Reconnaissance Regiment, also at Pardubice. After the 47th Reconnaissance Regiment began operating the Su-22 in 1984, several of these aircraft returned to the 4th Fighter Regiment. When the 4th Fighter Regiment was disbanded as part of the Warsaw Pact's disarmament initiative in 1989, one squadron was completely equipped and another was partially equipped with a total of eighteen MiG-21Ms, of which twelve were transferred to the 5th Fighter Regiment and six went to the 9th Fighter Regiment.

From 1971 to 1975, the PVOS received the MiG-21MF, which was to remain the main subtype until it stopped using the MiG-21. The first twelve MiG-21MFs, built in Moscow, reached the 4th Fighter Regiment at Pardubice in August 1971. Twelve MiG-21MFs destined for the 5th Fighter Regiment arrived at Pardubice in March 1972. After conversion training, the pilots of the 1st Squadron of the 5th

The very last landing: after several flights carrying selected passengers, at 1520 on July 13, 2005, a MiG-21 wearing Czech markings landed for the last time, touching down at Přerov.

Aircraft 5026 was the only Slovak two-seat trainer to fly in a two-color camouflage scheme. All others were unpainted. The code HL on the vertical tail identifies the machine's home base, Sliač.

Fighter Regiment flew their aircraft to their home base at Plzeň-Líně. In November 1974, four more aircraft were delivered directly to Plzeň. The introduction of the MiG-21MF resulted in the greatest technological leap forward for the 6th SBOLP (*stíhací bombardovací letecký pluk* = fighter-bomber regiment) at Přerov, which transitioned from the MiG-15bisSB directly to the new type. The first five MiG-21MFs arrived there on June 27, 1973, directly from the factory. A total of twenty-five aircraft were delivered by October, followed by another sixteen aircraft between July and November 1974.

In March 1973, the 9th Fighter Regiment at Bechyně received the 4th Fighter Regiment's entire complement of MiG-21MF fighters. The aircraft released by the 4th Fighter Regiment were replaced by thirteen new MiG-21MFs between October and December 1974. The regiment thus consisted of one squadron with thirteen MiG-21MFs, one squadron with fourteen MiG-21Ms, and one squadron with MiG-21F-13s. In June 1975, the 1st Fighter Regiment at České Budějovice received the first four MiG-21MF-75s made at Gorki, and these were followed by another group of sixteen aircraft in September. At the beginning of 1976, the 9th Fighter Regiment took over four of these machines by way of the 4th and 5th Fighter Regiments. After this, strength levels remained constant for some time. In the mid- to late 1980s, the 5th Fighter Regiment received five MiG-21MFs each from the 4th and 6th Fighter Regiments and two from the 9th Fighter-Bomber Regiment. In turn, various units received aircraft from the 5th Fighter Regiment. When all MiG-23s were concentrated in the 1st Fighter Regiment in May 1989, the twenty-two MiG-21s of that regiment's 2nd and 3rd Squadrons were passed on to the 8th Fighter Regiment. Among the thirteen MiG-21MFs were eight MF-75s that had been retrofitted with the SM jamming pod.

When, in 1989, it was decided to disband the 4th Fighter Regiment, its 2nd Squadron still had six MiG-21MFs, which were assigned to the 8th (two aircraft) and 9th Fighter Regiments. After the first Su-22s were delivered to the 6th Fighter-Bomber Regiment in 1988, twelve MiG-21MFs were passed on to other regiments. Ten alone went to the 9th Fighter Regiment, which also received two aircraft from the 1st Fighter Regiment and four from the 4th Fighter Regiment. The arrival of additional Su-22s at the 6th Fighter-Bomber Regiment resulted in the transfer of five MiG-21MFs to the 8th Fighter Regiment in December 1989. The 8th Fighter Regiment was thus fully equipped with the MiG-21MF.

The procurement of MiG-21UM two-seat trainers began immediately after the introduction of the MiG-21MF. The first three aircraft went to the 4th Fighter Regiment beginning in

Slovakian MiG-21MFs flew both in camouflage and unpainted. The camouflage scheme on 9713 is not original and was obviously applied during overhaul.

For years, aircraft 7713, known as "Milka" because of its characteristic three-tone camouflage scheme, was the Slovakian MiG-21 demonstration aircraft.

In addition to squadron markings, the Slovakian MiG-21s wore a variety of nonstandard markings.

June 1972. These were later followed by three more. By 1982 the MiG-21UM was also received by the 1st Fighter Regiment (three), the 5th Fighter Regiment (three), the 6th Fighter-Bomber Regiment (five), the 9th Fighter Regiment (five), and the 47th Reconnaissance Regiment (one). One other aircraft cannot be linked to any unit. The last aircraft was delivered to the 1st Flight Training Regiment (which had previously received seven other examples), and it ended deliveries of the MiG-21 to the PVOS, since the MiG-21bis was not provided to the ČSSR. Finally, the 8th Fighter Regiment received a MiG-21UM from the disbanded 4th Fighter Regiment; thus, all MiG-21 units flew this two-seat training version.

As the main type flown by the PVOS, the MiG-21 took part in all major Warsaw Pact maneuvers. During one of the biggest exercises of this type, Shield 84, the rapid evacuation of an airfield before an enemy attack was demonstrated to representatives of the supreme staffs of the Warsaw Pact states. Twelve MiG-23MLDs and twelve MiG-21MFs of the 1st Fighter Regiment, twelve MiG-23MFs, twelve MiG-21PFMs, and twelve MiG-21PFs of the 11th Fighter Regiment and twelve MiG-21F-13s of the 9th Fighter Regiment,

seventy-two aircraft in total, took off from Žatec airfield in less than five minutes! Aircraft took off from the runway at intervals in opposite directions (!), both from taxiways and from the grass strip. That there were no collisions demonstrates the professionalism and high level of training of all who took part.

After the so-called "Velvet Revolution" in Czechoslovakia and the renaming of the country as the Czech and Slovak Federative Republic (ČSFR), massive cuts to the air force, now called *Vojenske Letectvo a Protivzdušna Obrana* (VL a PVO; air force / air defense), were not long in coming. In 1991, the strength of all regiments was reduced to two squadrons, entire command structures and many units were disbanded, and all MiG-21F-13, PF, PFM, and U aircraft were retired.

The first MiG-21 regiments to be affected were the 5th and 8th Fighter Regiments and the 6th Fighter-Bomber Regiment, which ceased operations on April 30, July 31, and August 31, 1999, respectively. Sixteen MiG-21MF/MF-75 plus two MiG-21USs and two MiG-21UMs of the 8th Fighter Regiment went to Ostrava-Mošnov, where they formed the basis of the 81st and 82nd SSLT (*samostatná stíhací letka* =

independent squadron), established on May 1, 1991. The 81st Independent Squadron's aircraft were subsequently stationed at the former Soviet airfield of Sliač in Slovakia and thus became the first Czechoslovakian combat aircraft stationed in that part of the country since 1968. Thirteen MiG-21MFs and two MiG-21UMs of the 6th Fighter-Bomber Regiment, two MiG-21UMs of the 6th Fighter-Bomber Regiment, and two MiG-21Ms of the 9th Fighter-Bomber Regiment were also flown there in May–June 1991.

Ten MiG-21Ms of the 5th Fighter Regiment and six MiG-21MFs of the 6th Fighter-Bomber Regiment went to the 1st Flight Training Regiment at Přerov in March–April 1991. Of the twenty-three MiG-21MFs of the 5th Fighter Regiment, eleven were passed on to the 11th Fighter Regiment at Žatec, which became the last unit to receive the MiG-21MF. The 1st Flight Training Regiment at Přerov received eight more aircraft. One MiG-21MF, together with a MiG-21UM and an L-29, remained at Plzeň, where these aircraft formed the basis of the 1st LZS (*letecké zkušební středisko* = flight test center) of the LZO (*letecké zkušební odbor* = flight testing department). Three MiG-21MFs of the 8th Fighter Regiment

went to the 11th Fighter Regiment. Also, as the 11th Fighter Regiment, the 9th Fighter-Bomber Regiment (the unit was renamed in 1991) also profited from reductions by other regiments—by 1992 its strength had risen to thirty-three MiG-21MF/MF-75s in two squadrons.

Slovakian efforts to achieve independence resulted in the division of Czechoslovakia and its armed forces in 1992. With the exception of the MiG-29s, which were divided equally, and the MiG-23s, all of which remained in the Czech Republic, the arsenal was divided between the Czechs and Slovaks in a two-to-one ratio. By then, five of twenty-five MiG-21Rs, four of thirteen MiG-21USs, eight of twenty-four MiG-21Ms, three of thirty-two MiG-21UMs, and sixteen of 102 MiG-21MFs had been lost in accidents, two of the latter while being flown by Algerian students with the 1st Flight Training Regiment. Altogether, of the 464 Czechoslovakian MiG-21s, twenty-seven single-seaters and six two-seat trainers had been destroyed in crashes, in which thirty-nine pilots lost their lives. Another sixty-four single-seat and one two-seat MiG-21s were written off after accidents. The total number of aircraft lost was thus ninety-seven.

Guido E. Bühlmann

The NVA's last MiG-21F-13s were retired in 1985, after which they served as mock targets on MiG-21 airfields. *Guido E. Bühlmann*

The Czech Republic received ninety-two of the total of 162 remaining MiG-21s (four MiG-21Ms, fifty-two MiG-21MFs, twelve MiG-21Rs, five MiG-21USs, and nineteen MiG-21UMs) from the divided ČSFR.

The *Letectvo Armády Česke Republiky* (air forces of the army of the Czech Republic) began another phase of massive reductions and reorganizations immediately after the countries separated on January 1, 1993. The bases at Bechyně (9th Fighter-Bomber Regiment) and Hradec Králové (47th Reconnaissance Regiment) were shut down on May 31, 1993.

In November 1992, during the division of air force assets, Slovakian pilots flew eight MiG-21Rs to Malacky-Kuchyňa. The twelve MiG-21Rs and five MiG-21USs that remained at Hradec Králové were transferred to Čáslav, where they formed the 3rd (Reconnaissance) Squadron of the 28th Fighter-Bomber Regiment. Fourteen MiG-21MFs, three MiG-21Ms, and three MiG-21UMs of the 9th Fighter-Bomber Regiment were flown to Sliač and Malacky, and the remaining aircraft were divided between the 11th Fighter Regiment

(three), the 82nd Independent Squadron (two), and the 28th Fighter-Bomber Regiment (one).

In 1991–92, the 82nd Independent Squadron received nine MiG-21Ms from the 1st Flight Training Regiment and the 5th Fighter Regiment. Six of these, together with one MiG-21US and one MiG-21UM, were given to Slovakia at the end of 1992. One MiG-21M, two MiG-21MFs, and four MiG-21UMs of the 1st Flight Training Regiment went the same way, being flown to Sliač and Malacky airfields of the future Slovakian air force. After general overhaul by LOK at Kleby in 1993, four MiG-21MFs and one MiG-21UM from the holdings of the 9th Fighter-Bomber Regiment were ferried to Slovakia.

A short time later the disbandment order also reached the 11th Fighter Regiment. After the cessation of flight operations on December 31, 1993, ten MiG-21MFs were moved from Žatec to the 28th Fighter-Bomber Regiment at Čáslav, where they were used to form the 43rd SLT (*stíhací letka* = aviation squadron). Seven others went to the 82nd Independent Squadron at Mošnov. The 82nd Independent Squadron operated from Mošnov until October 1993. Then the squadron

MiG-21PFM 717 is prepared for an afterburner test run at *FAG* 15's base at Rothenburg. To prevent the aircraft from sliding with the engine at full thrust, in addition to the wheel chocks it was fixed in place with steel cables. *Guido E. Bühlmann*

was moved to Přerov and with elements of the disbanded 1st Flight Training Regiment was reformed into the 4th Independent Squadron. When flying at Přerov had to be halted on February 1, 1994, under pressure from the communal authorities, there were thirty-three MiG-21MFs and MiG-21UMs of the 4th Independent Squadron and the 1st Flight Training Regiment there. At the same time there were thirty-four MiG-21s of the R, M, MF, US, and UM versions at Čáslav, including the LZO, with ten MiG-21MFs, two MiG-21Rs, and three MiG-21UM/US trainers, which were subsequently stationed at Plzeň-Líně and finally at Ceské-Budějovice. After the airfield at Přerov was finally closed, the 4th Independent Squadron also moved to Čáslav.

As part of a fundamental reorganization, all remaining regiments and squadrons of the PVO were disbanded by December 31, 1994. In its place, the 4th ZSL (*základna stíhacího letectva* = fighter base) was established on January 1, 1995. The 1st Fighter Regiment with its MiG-23s had already moved to Čáslav in November 1994, and there it formed the 41st Aviation Squadron. From the 28th Fighter-

Bomber Regiment and the 4th Independent Squadron were formed the 42nd and 43rd Aviation Squadrons, equipped with twelve and fourteen MiG-21MFs and four and five MiG-21UMs, respectively. Thus all fighter forces were concentrated at this base. At the same time, the MiG-21R and MiG-21US aircraft were taken out of service and flown to Plzeň-Líně. Together with six MiG-21MFs and one MiG-21UM of the LZO (flight testing department), the total number of aircraft was forty-two. Surplus aircraft were placed in storage at Ceské-Budějovice, many were scrapped, and some went to museums.

In the course of a further round of reorganization in the Letectvo a PVO in 1997, the 4th Fighter Base was renamed the 4th ZTL (*základna taktického letectva* = tactical fighter base), the 43rd Aviation Squadron was disbanded, all MiG-21s were concentrated in the 42nd Aviation Squadron, and the last MiG-21Ms were retired. The LZO was also disbanded in 1998. At the same time, for economic reasons, all modern MiG-23 and MiG-29 fighter aircraft were taken out of service. At the beginning of 1999, therefore, just thirty-one MiG-

21MFs and seven MiG-21UMs remained in service with the unit, which was renamed the 41st Aviation Squadron.

In preparation for the joining of NATO, the Czechs had to adapt the role, technology, and organization of their air force to the new structure. Instead of a planned but never realized modernization of the MiG-21, a decision was made to procure the Czech-designed L-159 ALCA and a modern multirole combat aircraft. In order to be able to provide even a symbolic number of compatible aircraft to NATO's NATINEADS (NATO integrated and extended air defense system), since early 2000 ten MiG-21MFs have undergone a limited avionics modernization program, resulting in the designated MiG-21MFN. Two others were prepared for modernization, but their conversion fell victim to austerity measures. To meet its numerical commitments to NATO, aircraft that had not been modernized also had to remain in service. Since the beginning of the new millennium, the 41st Aviation Squadron has been flying eight MiG-21MFs, eight MiG-21MFNs, and three MiG-21UMs. By the end of 2004, just two MiG-21MFs, six MiG-21MFNs, and two MiG-21UMs remain in service.

At the end of 2003, the decision was made to procure the JAS-39 Gripen as a replacement for the MiG-21. After these took over the air defense role in early July 2005, the MiG-21 was officially retired on the twelfth of the same month. On their farewell flight the last five aircraft overflew their home base at Čáslav and other Czech bases before landing at Přerov and being placed in storage. The three very last flights by a MiG-21 in the Czech Republic were made by two-seater 9341 from Přerov on July 13, 2005.

This aircraft and the nonmodernized MiG-21MFs 5508 and 5512 were exported to Mali in September 2005. With the exception of one museum aircraft, the MFNs were scrapped. Until the MiG-21 was retired by the air force of the Czech Republic, it lost eight MiG-21MF/MFNs and two MiG-21UMs in accidents. Four pilots were killed.

From the assets of the ČSSR, Slovakia received seventy MiG-21s—eight MiG-21Rs, thirteen MiG-21Ms, thirty-six MiG-21MFs, two MiG-21USs, and eleven MiG-21UMs. As well, at the time the land was divided, there were twelve MiG-

A number of the NVA's MiG-21PFs were supposed to be exported to Iran, but the political changes in Europe prevented this from happening. Most of the aircraft were scrapped. *Guido E. Bühlmann*

TAFS 87's flight line at Drewitz in the summer of 1990. The reconnaissance *Staffel*, which was still in the formation process, never reached full operational status in the short time that remained in the MiG-21's service life. *Guido E. Bühlmann*

21F-13s, eleven MiG-21PFMs, and two MiG-21Us stored on Slovakian airfields, and these were subsequently scrapped.

The main problem in forming the *Vojenskí Letectvo a Protivzdušná Obrana Slovenskej Republiky* (VL a PVO: air forces / air defense of the Slovakian Republic), which originally consisted of five regiments on January 1, 1993, was the lack of suitable airfields for these aircraft. Extensive measures were taken to prepare the former Soviet airfield at Sliač and the base at Malacky-Kuchyňa for continuous flight operations by entire units.

On January 1, 1993, the 81st Independent Squadron of the Czechoslovak Air Force, with two MiG-21M and 15 MiG-21MF fighters plus one MiG-21US and two MiG-21UMs, became the 1st *letecky pluk* (fighter regiment) of the VL a PVO. The aircraft's pilots belonged to the 2nd and 3rd *stíhacia letka* (s.let. = fighter squadrons), while the 2nd, 3rd, and later also the 4th *techniká letka* (technical squadrons) were responsible for maintaining the aircraft. The base itself was given the title 1st *letecká základňa* (air base). All other aircraft—eleven MiG-21Ms, twenty-one MiG-21MFs, eight MiG-21Rs, one MiG-21US, and nine MiG-21UMs—were assigned to the 2nd and 3rd *stíhací bombardovací* (fighter-bomber squadrons) and the 4th *prieskumní letka* (reconnaissance squadron) of the 3rd *stíhací bombardovací pluk* (fighter-bomber regiment) at Malacky (3rd *letecká základňa*). The 2nd Technical Squadron was responsible for maintenance. With the basing of additional assets at Sliač, the MiG-21s were assigned to the 3rd and 4th Fighter Squadrons. In September 1994, the Su-25s based at Trenčín moved to Malacky, where they formed the 3rd Fighter-Bomber Squadron. In return, all excess MiG-21s went to Sliač. Two MiG-21Ms, three MiG-21MFs, eight MiG-21Rs, and five MiG-21UMs were flown there in several groups. As a result of the CFE agreement, five MiG-21Ms still at Malacky were placed in storage. This fate was shared by all the MiG-21Rs at Sliač, whose responsibilities were taken over by suitably equipped Su-22s, plus several MiG-21M and MiG-21UM aircraft. A total of twenty-one MiG-21s were affected, several of which were either scrapped or demilitarized and put on display. One MiG-21MF had previously been donated to the RAF Benevolent Fund.

In 1995, there was a restructuring—as in the Czech Republic—of the Slovakian service, now called *Vzdušné Sily Armády Slovenskej Republiky* (air forces of the army of the Slovakian Republic), which placed all aviation units under the command of the 3rd *zbor letectva a protivzdušna obrana* (corps) of the air forces / air defense. The 1st and 3rd Air Bases became the 31st and 33rd Air Bases, the 1st Fighter Regiment and the 3rd Fighter-Bomber Regiment became the 1st *stíhací letecké krídlo* (fighter wing), and the 3rd *stíhací bombardovaci letecké krídlo* (fighter-bomber wing).

At the end of 1995, after logging more than 4,500 flying hours, the MiG-21s still active at Malacky-Kuchyňa—seven MiG-21MFs and two MiG-21UMs—were moved to Sliač. Prior to this, two aircraft were equipped with new navigation equipment at LOT Trenčín, where they also underwent industry-level maintenance. At Sliač the MiG-21s were flown by pilots of the 4th Fighter Squadron, and maintenance was provided by the 4th Technical Squadron. Since the Slovaks, unlike the Czechs, decided on the procurement of new aircraft from the beginning, the MiG-29 was procured from Russia between 1993 and 1995, instead of pursuing a fundamental modernization of the MiG-21. From that point on, the numbers and serviceability levels of the MiG-21 fleet dropped steadily. In 1998, there were still thirty-eight aircraft in service, but this number fell to twenty-six in 1999, sixteen in 2000, and thirteen in 2001.

On December 23, 2002, the Slovakian air forces, now the *Vzdušné Sily Ozbrojených Síl Slovenskej Republiky*, retired its last six MiG-21s. The last flight by a MiG-21 wearing Slovakian markings had taken place on December 12, 2002, by MiG-21MF 7704. The Slovakian MiG-21 fleet suffered no losses.

German Democratic Republic

A modern air force was created in the GDR when the *National Volksarmee* (NVA; National People's Army) was founded on March 1, 1956. Within just six years it transitioned from the piston-engined Yak-11 to the MiG-21, capable of Mach 2—a development that pushed the new air force to the limits of its capabilities and resulted in heavy losses in men and aircraft.

The MiG-21 entered service with the air forces / air defense (LSK/LV) of the NVA on June 20, 1962, when *Jagdfliegergeschwader* (*JG*) 8 first flew a MiG-21F-13 bearing the emblem of the GDR in Marxwalde. This had been preceded by a conversion course for a number of pilots and members of the technical-engineering personnel (ITP) of *JG* 8 at Krasnodar in the extreme south of Russia, which lasted from January to April 1962. The first MiG-21 flight by a pilot of the NVA took place there on April 11 of the same year. After returning to East Germany, the course participants, who had trained on the MiG-21F and F-13, trained the remaining personnel. The first five MiG-21s arrived at Marxwalde in May 1962, and on June 20 a MiG-21 wearing East German markings took to the air for the first time. Between June and September 1962, *JG* 8 took delivery of twenty more MiG-21F-13s from the Gorki production Line, and the available aircraft were sufficient to equip the 1st and 2nd *Jagdfliegerstaffel* (*JS*). The first MiG-21 *Geschwader* (wing) of the NVA was made operational on August 1. In April 1963, aircraft of the unit took part in the Warsaw Pact exercise Zenith 63. In October 1963, twenty-five MiG-21F-13s, this time from the Moscow production facility, were delivered to Preschen. *JG* 3, which was based there, received seven aircraft with which to equip its 3rd *Staffel*. *JG* 3's personnel had previously undergone a three-month conversion course at Krasnodar. Of the remaining aircraft, six went to *JG* 9 at Peenemünde, and twelve went to *JG* 8, which in return released twelve aircraft from the first delivery batch. Deliveries were concluded with twenty-five MiG-21F-13s, which were assigned to *JG* 8 and *JG* 3 between May and July 1964. Likewise, with aircraft passed on from *JG* 8—as mentioned—and *JG* 3, in 1964, *JG* 9 and fighter training wing *Jagdfliegerausbildungsgeschwader* (*JAG*) 15 at Rothenburg were also equipped with the MiG-21F-13.

With the arrival of the MiG-21F-13 in *JAG* 15, a new training program was introduced in which student officers went straight from the L-29 jet trainer to the MiG-21 without using other types. The first course using the new method was held in 1966–67. In the years that followed, the student officers logged about seventy hours in the MiG-21 in their third and fourth years of study.

The experience gained by other regiments accelerated the acceptance rate: just about a month after beginning theoretical conversion training in April 1964, *JG* 9 began flight training on the new type. This was done at *JG* 3's bases at Preschen and at Trollenhagen. The MiG-21F-13 served with *JG* 9 for just a short time: in 1966–67, they all were transferred to *JG* 3 and *JAG* 15.

A MiG-21M of *TAFS* 47 carrying a CLA-87/III reconnaissance pod. The pod was developed in the GDR and consisted of cameras installed in a standard UB-16 rocket pod. *Guido E. Bühlmann*

A MiG-21MF of *JG* 3 taxis out for takeoff at Preschen. The *Geschwader* retained just one *Staffel* of MiG-21s after delivery of the MiG-29 in 1988. *Guido E. Bühlmann*

Chapter 9: In Action on the Front Lines of the Cold War

Periodic checks on a MiG-21M at the check-and-repair *Staffel* (KRS). The aircraft has been placed on jacks, the nose hatch has been opened, and the ejection seat has been removed. *Guido E. Bühlmann*

The crew of a MiG-21UM board their aircraft. Delivered in 1978, this machine was originally painted pale gray. Earlier examples were in natural metal or two-tone camouflage finish. *Guido E. Bühlmann*

Since the NVA did not receive the MiG-21R reconnaissance version, within a year, beginning in November 1974, the 3rd *Staffel* of *JG* 3 at Preschen, which flew the MiG-21F-13, became *Aufklärungsstaffel* 31 (*AFS* 31, later *AFS* 47 or tactical reconnaissance squadron *TAFS* 47). An AFA-39 camera was fitted in place of the starboard landing light, and the aircraft received a camouflage scheme consisting of two colors (prior to this, the MiG-21 had flown unpainted). Thus modified, the aircraft flew with the reconnaissance *Staffel* until retired in 1985. The first planned retirement of a total of nineteen MiG-21F-13s took place in November 1978. *JAG* 15's use of the MiG-21F-13 also ended at that time. Several of its aircraft were passed to *TAFS* 47. A second and final withdrawal from service phase took place in October 1985, when the last fourteen MiG-21F-13s were retired. More than twenty MiG-21F-13s were set up as decoys at the bases of *Jagdfliegergeschwader* 1, 2, 3, 8, and 9 and were still there when the NVA was disbanded. Others were used as instructional airframes or were destroyed as ground targets or in firefighting training. Twenty-four of the seventy-five aircraft delivered fell victim to what were called special incidents (crashes); forty-eight were scrapped.

In November 1962, just five months after entering service, the MiG-21F-13s of one *Staffel* of *JG* 8 were taken into the LSK/LV's *Diensthabende System* (*DHS* or integrated warning and air defense system). This was a role the MiG-21 was to retain until the NVA was disbanded. Armament varied on the basis of the capabilities of the various versions, but also the

actual threat assessment. While the cannon—in those variants that carried it—was always armed with a full load of sixty rounds of ammunition (NR-30 of the MiG-21F-13), 200 rounds (GSh-23 from the MiG-21M), or 250 rounds (GSh-23 of the MiG-21bis), the MiG-21F-13 was kept at readiness armed with two R-3S AAMs; the MiG-21PFM, with two RS-2US or two R-3S AAMs; and the MiG-21M/MF, with two RS-2US and two R-3S AAMs. The MiG-21bis carried various combinations of R-3S, R-3R, R-13M, and R-60M air-to-air missiles.

Soon after the MiG-21F-13 entered service, industry-level maintenance became necessary. The interval between medium-level overhauls was just 200 hours. Preparations began at the VEB *Flugzeugwerft* (Aircraft Maintenance Facility) in Dresden, which was responsible for airframes and associated equipment, and the VEB Industriewerke in Ludwigsfelde, which was responsible for power plants, in 1963. After the production of aircraft in East Germany ended, both facilities had been restructured as pure maintenance facilities. The first medium-level overhaul of a MiG-21F-13 took place in 1964. All subsequent versions of the MiG-21 used by the NVA were overhauled in Dresden, as were aircraft from Poland, the ČSSR, Egypt, Syria, and Iraq.

From the end of the 1950s onward, each year some East German fighter wings went to the Soviet base at Astrakhan on the Volga for live firing. Initially, air-to-air missiles were fired at R-3M decoy rockets, but later, radio-controlled La-17 drones were used as targets. MiG-21 pilots from *JG* 3 took

The author in front of "his" MiG-21bis in the summer of 1990. Like all aircraft of the 3rd *Staffel* of *JG* 8 at Marxwalde, 879 spent the entire year outdoors. *Marco Hanisch*

part in such an exercise for the first time in 1964. While for a long time the Soviet Union provided the aircraft and equipment, in 1968 *JG* 1 became the first unit to send its own aircraft: twelve MiG-21PFMs and one MiG-21UM two-seat trainer from the 2nd *Staffel*. The next year, *JG* 8 sent its 1st *Jagdstaffel* with MiG-21bis aircraft. While trips to the USSR remained the exception because of costs, from 1973 onward, regular training in intercepting target aircraft was augmented by the firing of infrared AAMs at decoy missiles and parachute flares in Air Firing Zone II (LSZ II) over the Baltic Sea. Then, in the 1980s, gunnery training was begun in which the aircraft fired their cannon at KT-04-towed targets. LSZ II was used by Soviet, Polish, Czechoslovakian, and East German fighter pilots. Immediately after delivery of the MiG-21F-13 in November 1968, *JG* 8 received the first thirteen examples of the MiG-21PF, which, because of modifications to the radar, the NVA referred to inaccurately as the MiG-21PFM. This delivery was again preceded by flights by German pilots on MiG-21s of this type in the Soviet Union, the first of which took place on August 17, 1964. The first MiG-21PF flew in the GDR on December 10 of the same year. An additional sixteen aircraft arrived at Marxwalde in April–

May 1965. All subsequent MiG-21PFs—twenty-four in number—were delivered to *JG* 1 at Cottbus between February and June 1965. The aircraft were flown by pilots of *JG* 8 and a Soviet unit. For the first time, the MiG-21U two-seat trainer was available for conversion training.

In 1965, five pilots of *JG* 8 took part in one of the most spectacular actions in the history of the LSK/LV: together with Soviet aircraft, they flew over the congress hall in West Berlin to disrupt a sitting by the West German *Bundestag* (parliament).

In 1966, some of *JG* 8's aircraft were passed on to the 2nd and 3rd Fighter Squadrons of *JG* 9. After the MiG-21PFM was delivered in 1968, these were transferred to *JG* 2 at Neubrandenburg-Trollenhagen. *JG* 2 received additional aircraft directly from *JG* 8. After *JG* 1 also gave up its aircraft, all MiG-21PF aircraft were concentrated in *JG* 2, where they were given a two-color camouflage scheme, having previously flown unpainted. To improve the MiG-21PF's operational capability, they were modified to use the Polish Monsun double stores launcher, which enabled them to carry four R-3S air-to-air missiles. The MiG-21PF remained with *JG* 2 until it was retired from service in 1987–88. Twenty-three

A MiG-21bis SAU of *JG* 8 at Marxwalde is towed from its aircraft shelter (GDF) prior to the start of daily flight operations. Ladder, tools, and wheel chocks are loaded on the tow vehicle as per regulations. The tarpaulins are being carried on the aircraft's wing. *Guido E. Bühlmann*

MiG-21bis SAU taxiing out for takeoff. Aircraft 978 had obviously undergone a major overhaul in Dresden, where it received a new paint job. *Guido E. Bühlmann*

Chapter 9: In Action on the Front Lines of the Cold War

MiG-21PFs were lost while in service, and forty were scrapped after the end of the GDR.

Until the mid-1960s, the MiG-21 wings used the MiG-15UTI for training, certification, and weather flights. This did not change until April 1965, when the first five Moscow-built MiG-21U two-seat trainers arrived at *JAG* 15 at Rothenburg. These aircraft were examples of the MiG-21U-400 subvariant, as were nine others delivered to the 1st, 3rd, 8th, and 9th Fighter Wings in May and June of the same year. Ten examples of the subsequent MiG-21U-600 arrived between March and September 1966, again going to *JAG* 15 first. These and all subsequent aircraft were delivered in natural metal finish but were later painted in green-brown camouflage. Unlike the combat aircraft, which wore red serial numbers, the two-seat trainers wore black codes. The remaining twenty-one examples of the MiG-21U, which entered service between December 1966 and July 1967, were again shared by *JG* 1, 3, 8, and 9, and *JAG* 15. *JG* 2 and *JG* 7 at Drewitz also later received this version, all of which were finally transferred to Rothenburg in the late 1970s. *JG* 3 and *TAFS* 47 were the last operational units, each turning over one aircraft in 1985. Retirement of the MiG-21U began in spring 1988, and the last flight by a German MiG-21U took place on March 8, 1989, by what was now *Fliegerausbildungsgeschwader* 15. By that time, six MiG-21-400 and four MiG-21U-600 trainers had been lost in accidents, and eighteen had been scrapped.

Twelve MiG-21PFs and four MiG-21U-600s were to have been exported to Iran, and in 1989 they were overhauled by the VEB Flugzeugwerft Dresden. Two MiG-21U-600s were flown to Isfahan in an Iranian Boeing 747 and there were assembled by technicians from the Dresden facility. One of these aircraft is now on display in the Museum of the Revolutionary Guard in Teheran. The end of the GDR prevented the delivery of the other aircraft.

JG 8 was again the first East German unit to receive the next single-seat version, the MiG-21PFM (called the MiG-21SPS by the NVA). Between April 1966 and February 1967, the *Geschwader* received a complete complement of forty-eight aircraft from the Moscow production line. The second large delivery of this type, thirty-four aircraft, was made to *JG* 1 between March 1967 and March 1968. The MiG-21PFM was eventually also passed on to *JG* 3 and *JAG* 15, and then to *JG* 2. The MiG-21SPS-K, the NVA designation for a subvariant with the ability to carry the GP-9 cannon pod, was

delivered to the 1st, 3rd, 8th, and 9th Fighter Regiments between March and June 1968. A total of fifty-two were delivered, making the MiG-21PFM numerically the most important combat aircraft in the LSK/LV. In *JG* 9 the MiG-21PFM first replaced the MiG-21F-13s and MiG-21PFs of the 2nd and 3rd Fighter Squadrons. By the end of 1969, the MiG-21PFM also replaced the MiG-17PFs of the 1st Fighter Squadron, and thus the *Geschwader* was completely equipped with forty-two MiG-21s of this version. Following delivery of the MiG-21PFM and MiG-21U, *JG* 1 was also completely equipped with the MiG-21. At the end of 1968, *JG* 3 received fourteen MiG-21PFMs from *JG* 8, and these replaced the last MiG-19s of the 1st Fighter Squadron. At the end of 1970, the 2nd Fighter Squadron exchanged its MiG-21F-13s for thirteen MiG-21PFMs from *JG* 1. From 1969 onward, after receiving aircraft from other wings, *JG* 7 also operated the MiG-21PFM. In 1968, *JG* 8 made one of the few public appearances by NVA combat aircraft. During the world aerobatics championship at Magdeburg, the MiGs demonstrated a RATO takeoff, gave displays by single aircraft and formations, and made a flyby with a Tu-124.

In 1978, *JAG* 15 received MiG-21PFMs from the stocks of *JG* 1 and *JG* 3. Then, in 1982, *JG* 3 handed the last of this version over to the training regiment (seven), while *JG* 1 transferred four and *JG* 2 sent one. That same year, a MiG-21PFM was modified to carry the R-60 short-range AAM. The experiment was a success, and by 1985 a total of twenty-four aircraft had received this modification, which significantly improved the aircraft's combat capabilities. After its first MiG-21PFs were retired in November 1987, *JG* 2 received MiG-21PFMs from *JG* 1, which in turn took over MiG-21MFs from *JG* 3. This process was repeated in 1988–89. The MiG-21PFM remained in service until the end of the NVA. Delivered in natural metal finish and later painted pale gray, the aircraft were ultimately given a two-color camouflage scheme. As part of the disarmament initiative by the Warsaw Pact, in 1989 fifty aircraft were taken out of service and used as sources of spare parts or for training purposes, while some were held in reserve. Nineteen MiG-21SPS and sixteen MiG-21SPS-K aircraft were lost in accidents.

When the MiG-21 first entered service, combat aircraft were usually parked on the flight line or dispersals right on the circular taxiways, but in response to the severe losses sustained by the Arab air forces in the Six-Day War in 1967, that same year construction of open aircraft shelters (blast

Many NVA aircraft were flown to WTD-61 at Manching for evaluation. Little interest was shown in the MiG-21, however, and evaluations concentrated on the MiG-23 (in the background), MiG-29, and Su-22. *Guido E. Bühlmann*

walls or ODF) began at airfields used by fighter and fighter-bombers units of the NVA. Then, in response to the Yom Kippur War of 1973, which was almost as costly to the Arab air forces, the construction of closed aircraft shelters (GDF) began. Requiring one to one and a half years to construct, *JG* 9's airfield at Peenemünde was the first to have the hardened aircraft shelters, although there were never enough for all combat aircraft. Exercises were regularly carried out from

these open and closed shelters, but as a rule, most flight operations were carried out from the *Geschwader* flight line.

Between September 1968 and August 1970, seventeen MiG-21US two-seat trainers built in Tbilisi were issued to Fighter Wings 1, 2, 3, 7, and 9 to increase the number of two-seaters in these units. This trainer version was also delivered in natural metal and later painted in a two-color camouflage scheme. In 1975, *JG* 7 gave its four MiG-21US trainers to *JG* 2, which in 1973 had received one of these aircraft from *JG* 9. In 1978, *JG* 1 transferred seven aircraft of this type to *JAG* 15; a MiG-21US still at Cottbus followed in 1981. The last operational *Geschwader* with the MiG-21US were thus *JG* 2 and *JG* 3, which had four and two examples, respectively, at the end of 1987. The remaining thirteen aircraft all were concentrated in *FAG* 15 until 1989, by which time four had crashed.

The LSK/LV carried out takeoffs and landings from sections of the autobahn by using the PFM and US versions of the MiG-21, which had reduced landing speeds because of the SPS flap-blowing system. In July 1970, aircraft of *JG* 3 landed on the autobahn near Forst for the first time. Later, all fighter and fighter-bomber wings regularly practiced this type of deployment. Prior to this, flight operations from grass strips (e.g., *JG* 8 from Müncheberg airfield and *JG* 9 from Gross-Mohrdorf) had become a regular element of combat training.

The LSK/LV was the first air force worldwide to place the MiG-21M, representative of the third generation of MiG-21s, into service. Introduction into service began with thirty aircraft delivered direct from the factory in Moscow to *JG* 9 in July and August 1969. *JG* 7 and *JG* 8 received another fourteen aircraft at almost the same time. Twelve of the MiG-21Ms delivered in 1969 were capable of carrying nuclear weapons.

Deliveries ended the following year, with ten aircraft for *JG* 8 in March and thirty-three for *JG* 7 between March and November, bringing the total number in service to eighty-seven aircraft. In October 1973, twelve of *JG* 8's MiG-21Ms were disassembled and transported to Syria in An-12 transports. There they were reassembled by NVA personnel, test-flown, and handed over to the Syrian air force. The purpose of this aid effort, which was carried out in similar form by other socialist countries, was to make good the losses suffered by the Arab countries in the Yom Kippur War. East Germany, however, was the only country to provide a current combat type. At that time the MiG-21M was still flying in natural metal finish as delivered. Later, all aircraft received a two-color camouflage finish. In 1977–78, *JG* 9 transferred its remaining MiG-21Ms to *JG* 7, which as a result was completely equipped with this type. In the mid-1980s, *JG* 7 had forty MiG-21Ms and six MiG-21UM two-seat trainers. *JG* 2 subsequently received the MiG-21M and, after the disbandment of *JG* 7 in 1989, operated this type exclusively, as did the 2nd Fighter Squadron of *JG* 3 as of March 1978 and, from 1985 onward, *TAFS* 47 (sixteen aircraft). As well, in October 1988, formation began at Drewitz of *TAFS* 87 with twelve MiG-21Ms (and two MiG-21UM two-seat trainers). While these aircraft had no reconnaissance equipment, the

This reconnaissance pod was produced in Finland and was used by the MiG-21F-13.

MiG-21Ms of *TAFS* 47—like the MiG-21F-13s before them—were fitted with an AFA-39 camera. In addition, in cooperation with NVA offices and facilities of the East German armaments industry, several types of reconnaissance pods were introduced that were capable of taking vertical and oblique photos and video. The following reconnaissance pods, all based on the UB-16 rocket pod, were developed: the CLA-87/1 for vertical photos, the CLA-87/II for video, and the CLA-87/III for vertical and oblique photos. A total of nineteen MiG-21Ms fell victim to "special incidents."

Completion of the complement of two-seat trainers began in July–August 1971, with the introduction of the MiG-21UM. *JG* 8 and *JG* 2 received the first nine aircraft. In 1972, nine more were delivered to *JG* 3 and *JG* 9. The three aircraft delivered in 1973 also entered service with *JG* 9, as did the first four delivered in 1974. That same year, another four went to *JG* 7, which also received four in the 1975 delivery year. The procurement of MiG-21UMs ended with four aircraft for *JG* 8 in March 1978. These aircraft had the more powerful R13 engine, which was later installed in other MiG-21UM two-seat trainers. The last aircraft received were finished in pale gray, while the earlier aircraft were delivered in natural

metal or two-color camouflage finish. With a total of thirty-seven aircraft, the MiG-21UM became the most important two-seat trainer version. Eventually, *TAFS* 47 and *TAFS* 87, as well as *JG* 1 and *JG* 2, received aircraft of this type, transferred from other units. The last recipient was *FAG* 15 in 1990. With the exception of one lost in a crash, all of the MiG-21UMs survived.

From April to November 1975, *JG* 3 became the first *Geschwader* to receive the MiG-21MF to equip its 2nd and 3rd Fighter Squadrons—a total of twenty-six aircraft. This was, as usual, preceded by conversion training for pilots and technicians in the USSR. The acquisition of the MiG-21MF followed the transfer of *JG* 3's MiG-21PFMs to *JG* 2. All subsequent deliveries of the MiG-21MF—twelve machines in July 1973, ten in January–February 1974, and two in April 1974—went, some after a brief stop at Preschen, to *JG* 9, which in the process received the NVA's last MiG-21s from the Moscow production line. Whereas the first fourteen MiG-21MFs were delivered in natural metal finish, the rest arrived from the factory painted in a green-brown camouflage scheme. In July 1975, the *Geschwader* at Peenemünde also received twelve MiG-21MF-75 fighters that had originally

MK-103, the only Finnish MiG-21U still extant, flew for the last time on May 29, 1981. It was then used for braking-parachute trials and is now on display in the Finnish Air Force Museum at Tikkakoski.

been destined for North Vietnam. These aircraft, painted pale gray and, according to some sources, with North Vietnamese markings, were the first of this type to be built. To replace the MiG-21Ms given to Syria, in 1973 JG 8 received twelve MiG-21MFs from JG 3, which made up for these transfers by reactivating fifteen MiG-21F-13s (!). Four years later, JG 8 returned the MiG-21MFs to JG 3 after it received the MiG-21bis. Others went to JG 7 and several even returned to JG 9. Between January 1978 and August 1982, during the introduction of the MiG-23, twenty-nine of JG 9's thirty-two remaining MiG-21MFs (and one MiG-21UM) were transferred to JG 3, and these aircraft were used to equip the 3rd Fighter Squadron and then the 2nd Fighter Squadron. As a result, JG 3 was completely equipped with this version of the MiG-21. In July–August 1982, the 1st Fighter Squadron and its MiG-21MFs moved to Rothenburg to assist JAG 15 in training Libyan officer students. After the MiG-29 entered service with the 1st Fighter Squadron of JG 3 in 1987–88, JG 1 received that squadron's MiG-21s. With the arrival of the new type in the 2nd Fighter Squadron in 1989, it also sent its

MiG-21MFs to JG 1's new base at Holzdorf, and only the 3rd Fighter Squadron continued using the MiG-21MF, with twelve aircraft. Eight aircraft were written off in accidents.

In October 1975, JG 9 received fourteen MiG-21bis LAZUR (designated Flugzeug 75A by the NVA and 75 I by the Flugzeugwerft Dresden). This was the beginning of the introduction of the fourth-generation MiG-21 by the LSK/LV. The Geschwader was thus operating four versions of the MiG-21 at that time: in addition to the MiG-21bis, it had twenty-three MiG-21MFs, six MiG-21Ms, and nine MiG-21UMs. In July 1976 followed seventeen of the SAU version of the MiG-21bis (after the type 75B or 75 II landing system was installed), which were also received by JG 9. Eleven more MiG-21bis SAUs were delivered in October 1977, these going to JG 8. Four more MiG-21bis SAUs arrived for this Geschwader in May 1978, ending the procurement of the MiG-21 for the NVA. With the exception of the aircraft built in 1978, all the MiG-21bis for the NVA were delivered in a smart pale-gray paint scheme, but by major overhaul at the latest they were repainted in the standard green-and-brown NVA

Flight operations on snow-covered surfaces—here by a MiG-21UM—are standard practice in Finland.

A MiG-21bis makes a low pass in afterburner. The small national emblems indicate that this photo was taken late in the type's service life. *Alexander Golz*

camouflage scheme, which on closer examination proves to be not so standardized. Not least because of a shortage of resources in the East German economy, which of course also affected the National People's Army, the aircraft were painted in whatever colors were available at the time they were refinished. This led to considerable differences in colors between individual machines. Furthermore, there were major differences between the aircraft that received perfect paint finishes at the Flugzeugwerft Dresden and those that were sprayed at the *Staffel* level, often by nonessential personnel.

By November–December 1977, all thirty-one of *JG* 8's MiG-21bis had been transferred to *JG* 8, since the *Geschwader* was preparing for the introduction of the MiG-23 at Peenemünde. All of the NVA's MiG-21bis were thus concentrated at Marxwalde, where they remained until the NVA was disbanded in 1990. By then, five MiG-21bis SAUs had been lost.

In 1983, *JG* 1 moved from Cottbus to the newly constructed airfield at Holzdorf. Construction had begun in 1973, after it became clear that flight operations by the MiG-21 near residential areas were unacceptable because of the noise and potential danger to the residents.

In 1989, the disarmament initiatives decided on by the National Defense Council of the GDR, previously mentioned, resulted in the disbandment of *JG* 7. Prior to this action, which was carried out under the eyes of the press, including foreign representatives, the oldest active MiG-21s from all the wings were concentrated at Drewitz. *JG* 1 and *JG* 2 turned in their MiG-21PFMs, and in return, *JG* 2, along with

TAFS 47 and 87, received *JG* 7's MiG-21Ms. As a result, each of the remaining five MiG-21 wings and two squadrons was equipped with roughly equal numbers of MiG-21s of the PFM, M, MF, and bis versions. *JG* 7's last day of flight operations was on August 31, 1989, and on October 23, the *Geschwader* was officially disbanded.

After the upheavals of autumn 1989, the NVA and the LSK/LV found themselves in the midst of a constant reformation process, which on the one hand was marked by hopes of maintaining independent forces on the territory of the GDR, and on the other resulted in constantly changing political directions and a massive reduction in personnel resulting from the shortening of service periods for draftees and regular soldiers. The wings continued flying with restrictions, and the remaining personnel faced heavy workloads. The last day of flying by all *Geschwader* came at the end of September (*JG* 1, the 26th; *JG* 2, *JG* 3, and *JG* 8, the 27th; and *FAG* 15, the 20th), in which for the first (and last) time they performed public formation overflights and demonstrations by individual aircraft.

When the German Democratic Republic joined the Federal Republic of Germany on October 3, 1990, 251 MiG-21s of various versions became part of the *Bundeswehr*. In detail, these consisted of forty-five MiG-21PFMs, fifty-six MiG-21Ms, forty-seven MiG-21MFs, forty-one MiG-21bis, thirteen MiG-21Us, thirteen MiG-21USs, and thirty-six MiG-21UMs. These aircraft were distributed as follows: *JG* 1 had seven MiG-21PFMs, thirty-five MiG-21MFs, and nine MiG-21UMs; *JG* 2 had thirty-one MiG-21Ms, twelve MiG-21PFMs, and

Ready for the farewell flight: Yrjö Rantamäki and his technicians Seppo Hattunen and Erkki Reponen.

eight MiG-21UMs; *JG* 3 had twelve MiG-21MFs and three MiG-21UMs; *TAFS* 47 had thirteen MiG-21Ms and two MiG-21UMs; *TAFS* 87 had twelve MiG-21Ms and two MiG-21UMs; *JG* 8 had fourteen MiG-21bis LAZUR, twenty-seven MiG-21bis SAU, and eight MiG-21UMs; and *FAG* 15 had twenty-six MiG-21PFMs, thirteen MiG-21Us (already grounded), thirteen MiG-21USs, and three MiG-21UMs.

The MiG-21 saw no regular service in the united Germany. Prior to reunification, the Federal Ministry of Defense and the *Bundeswehr* had made it clear that it had no interest in continuing to use the assets inherited from the NVA. Originally this also applied to weapons systems that were superior to their counterparts in the *Bundeswehr*. From the beginning, those responsible ruled out any continued use of the MiG-21. Despite this, former East German insignia and serial numbers were overpainted, but the Iron Cross was applied only to a few aircraft. These included one MiG-21MF (513, which became 23+17) and one MiG-21bis (846, which became 24+20), which were sent to WTD 61 (Technical and Airworthiness Center for Aircraft) at Manching for test purposes but did not fly there, as well as several aircraft

whose nationality markings were completed at the initiative of the personnel carrying out the work.

In the course of the disbandment of all NVA fighter wings (with the exception of *JG* 3, which was equipped with the MiG-29 and continued to exist as the MiG-29 testing wing), by December 31, 1990, all aircraft were gathered and stored at Drewitz (*JG* 1, *JG* 8, *TAFS* 87), Rothenburg (*FAG* 15, *JG* 3, *TAFS* 47) and Trollenhagen (*JG* 2). All flyable aircraft were flown in from Holzdorf, Marxwalde, and Preschen, while the training aircraft from Kamenz and Bad Düben technical schools were brought by road or slung beneath helicopters.

The last transport took place in June 1993. After absorbing the NVA aircraft, the Bundeswehr had a total of 1,040 combat aircraft, but under the terms of the Treaty on Conventional Armed Forces in Europe (CFE), it was permitted to have only 900 such aircraft; 140 aircraft thus had to be destroyed, but this affected only the MiG-21. Scrapping of the MiG-21s officially began at the Elbe Flugzeugwerke, successor to the VEB Flugzeugwerke, on September 22, 1992, the company falling back on its experience with the aircraft disassembled in 1989 and those originally destined for Iran. The program continued until October–November 1993. The scrapping of other aircraft, such as those MiG-21F-13s and PFs previously retired, some of them used as decoys, was decentralized, taking place at Trollenhagen and various other bases. A number of aircraft were donated to museums in Germany and elsewhere and were thus preserved for posterity.

Finland

Despite its special role during the Cold War as a neutral, capitalist country with close economic and political ties to the Soviet Union, Finland aligned itself with the West when it came to the procurement of new weapons systems in the late 1950s–early 1960s. Thus for the *Ilmavoimat* (Finnish air force) the jet age began with the de Havilland Vampire, the Folland Gnat, and the Fouga Magister. Concerned about the technical state of the Finnish air force and the associated weakness of its northern flank, but at the same time also trying to reduce its trade deficit, in the spring of 1960 the USSR made an offer to Finland to provide it with the MiG-19. After several test flights, the Finns rejected the type as obsolete and one year later began evaluating the Mirage III and the Saab J-35. The Soviet Union subsequently increased its political pressure on Finland and simultaneously offered the MiG-21. Due to the performance figures for this type—of which the Finns had knowledge only from documents—and because political conditions forbade the acquisition of Western types, on February 1, 1962, a Finnish delegation signed a contract for the delivery of twenty-one MiG-21F-13s, associated air-to-air missiles, and four MiG-15UTI trainers. On May 10 of the same year, an agreement was reached for the training of personnel in the USSR. This took place between August and September 1962 for sixty-two Finnish pilots and technicians at Lugovaya (Kazakhstan).

On November 10, the four MiG-15UTI two-seat trainers, produced in the ČSSR, were flown by Soviet pilots to Finland. The first ten MiG-21F-13s arrived from the Soviet Union on April 24, 1963. They were received by *Hävittäjälentolaivue* (HavLLv, or fighter squadron) 31 of the *Karjalan Lennosto* (Karelian Wing) at Kuopio-Rissala. In keeping with the Finnish designation system, which consisted of two letters for the aircraft type and a one- to three-digit aircraft number, the aircraft were given the codes MG (for MiG) 1 to 10. These were later changed to MG-31 to MG-35, and MG-46 to MG-

50. The aircraft from the first Moscow production batch still had an IFF antenna on the fuselage spine. This was later removed, however, since the system was not used in Finland.

Eleven more MiG-21F-13s (MG-61 to MG-65, MG-76 to MG-80, and MG-91) followed in November 1963. Because the number of available aircraft exceeded HavLLv 31's personnel capacities, six of these were placed in storage at Tikkakoski-Luonetjärvi. After MG-64 crashed due to engine failure on May 20, 1964, in October the Soviet Union delivered a replacement aircraft (MG-92), one of the last MiG-21F-13s built. The first air-to-ground firing by the new type, using rockets and cannon, took place in February–March 1964. Air-to-air firing against target missiles was first carried out in 1968.

While regular checks of the MiG-21F-13s were carried out at the unit level (after 25, 50, and 100 hours), the Valmet Company at Halli carried out 500-hour checks. Seven aircraft underwent major overhaul at Lvov in the USSR between 1973 and 1975. The aircraft were flown there by Soviet

Guido E. Bühlmann

In Yugoslavian service the MiG-21F-13 was given the local designator L-12.

pilots, who picked up the aircraft at their base or, later, also at Pulkovo airfield near Leningrad.

After training with HavLLv 31, in 1966 HavLLv 11 of the *Hämeen Lennosto* (Häme Wing; Häme is a Finnish region) began operating the six MiG-21F-13s that had been in storage at Luonetjärvi. The aircraft had numerous technical problems, caused mainly by having been idle for two years, and the unit's activities were limited mainly to training flights. This did not change until the unit began specializing in reconnaissance duties in the late 1960s–early 1970s. Basically, it was possible to modify some of the MiG-21F-13s for the reconnaissance role by installing an AFA-39 camera in place of the starboard landing light. This installation did not, however, meet Finnish requirements. In 1966, therefore, the Finns began developing their own reconnaissance equipment. In 1968, they tested a camera made by the French manufacturer Omera in an empty napalm tank. This solution also failed to live up to expectations, and consequently the Finns turned their attention to the reconnaissance pod made by the British company Vinten. After the manufacturer adapted the pod for use on the MiG-21, tests were completed

successfully in 1971. A program began in December 1971 in which nine MiG-21F-13s were converted. In 1973, these were issued to the *Tiedustlentolaivue* (reconnaissance squadron, TiedLLv) formed at Luonetjärvi. In the interim, all aircraft were stationed at Rissala after the *Hämeen Lennosto* received the Saab J-35 Draken in 1972. With the arrival of the MiG-21bis at HavLLv 31 in 1980, the remaining eight MiG-21F-13s were gradually transferred to the TiedLLv. From 1966 to 1985, one MiG-21F-13 also flew with the *Koelentue* (test center) at Halli. Two aircraft (MG-61 and MG-80, the latter replaced by MG-76) were also fitted with a special flight data–recording system. The last flight by a Finnish first-generation MiG-21 was carried out by TiedLLv at Luonetjärvi on January 17, 1986. Five aircraft (MG-62, MG-63, MG-64, MG-79, MG-80) were lost during the type's twenty-three years of service, with one pilot losing his life. Fourteen remaining aircraft were converted into decoy targets, with folding wings and tailplanes for easier handling, and were painted in the colors of the MiG-21bis. All but three examples of the MiG-21F-13 were scrapped between 1999 and 2001.

22832 is the last active MiG-21MF in the Serbian air force and also the oldest machine in the fleet. The cannon was removed to enable the LORAP reconnaissance pod.

The Finns began pilot training in their own country in 1964, no easy undertaking without a two-seat trainer. Beginning in 1970, the student pilots—as in the GDR at about the same time—went from a jet trainer straight to the MiG-21, with no intermediate type. Also at the beginning of the 1970s, the Finns began developing their own training program, which was clearly different from the rigid Soviet syllabus. Training focused on dogfighting and operations from roads and unpaved strips. As a result, the Finns were among the best MiG-21 pilots anywhere in the world.

Pilot training was considerably simplified by the arrival of two MiG-21U-400 two-seat trainers. They arrived at Rissala on April 1, 1965, and wore the codes MK-103 and MK-104 ("MK" standing for MiG *Kaksipaikkaiset* = MiG two-seater). Both were assigned to HavLLv 31 but were also used by TiedLLv and Koelentue. MK-104 was retired on September 6, 1979. It was subsequently used for training purposes, then became a decoy target, and was finally scrapped in 1999. MK-103 flew for the last time on May 29, 1981, after which

it was used for braking-parachute experiments, and today it is on display in the Air Force Museum at Tikkakoski.

To expand its training capacity, on June 18, 1974, the Finnish air force received two more two-seat trainers, both more up-to-date MiG-21UMs (MK-105 and MK-106). Both were equipped with the R-11F2S-300 engine when delivered, but these were later replaced with the R-13. Like their predecessors, the MiG-21UMs were assigned to Rissala and were lent to other units as required. The delivery was preceded by conversion training for two pilots and several technical personnel in the Soviet Union. In March 1981, two more MiG-21UMs were acquired in connection with the procurement of the MiG-21bis, and they were flown to Rissala on September 25, 1981. Prior to this, a Finnish pilot had had the opportunity to make several test flights in a MiG-21UM equipped with the R-13 engine. Upon delivery the aircraft were found to have so many problems that the Finns refused to accept them, and in June 1982, Soviet pilots had to return the aircraft. The replacement aircraft with the same codes arrived by rail in August 1982. Once again there were

In addition to Soviet-made S-5 unguided rockets, Yugoslavian MiG-21s can carry the domestically developed L-128-04 Munja 128 mm unguided rocket (front left). *Guido E. Bühlmann*

numerous problems that had to be addressed, and it was not until October 15 that the aircraft could be handed over to HavLLv 31.

The MiG-21UMs were maintained exclusively in Finland, both by the units and at Valmet. At the same time, Western avionics and navigation equipment were installed in the aircraft. Externally these aircraft can be identified by the presence of ILS antennas beneath the auxiliary input doors on the fuselage in place of the deflector panels. While the earlier versions flew exclusively in natural metal finish, the first two MiG-21UMs were delivered in a camouflage finish, and the last two were painted pale gray overall. Later they were finished in different variants of the gray and camouflage schemes.

When, in the mid-1970s, a decision had to be made as to a successor to the MiG-21F-13 because of the previous procurement of the Draken, it was obvious that the successful design would have to come from the Soviet Union. The Soviets offered the MiG-23MS, Su-20, and the MiG-21bis. The Su-20, a fighter-bomber, was never in the running, while the MiG-23's high procurement and operating costs were a negative factor, but the Finns had more than ten years of operating experience with the MiG-21. The decision in favor of the MiG-21 was again made with no opportunity to test the

aircraft. Not until autumn 1976 did two Finnish pilots have the opportunity to fly this version at Krasnodar. A conversion course with fifty-nine participants was held at the same place in February and March 1978, but it contained only theoretical instruction with no flight training.

The first two MiG-21bis, MB-111 and MB-114 (MB for MiG bis), were flown to Rissala by Soviet pilots on September 21, 1978. While MB-111 remained there for pilot training, MB-114 was used by the flight test center at Halli for type testing and creation of operating manuals.

After the identifying letters had been changed to MG, the first major delivery of six aircraft (MG-115 to 118, 120, 127) took place in June 1980. Six more were delivered both on July 17 ((MG-122, 124, 125, 129 to 131) and September 10 (MG-132, 133, 135, 138 to 140). The procurement was completed with two deliveries, each of three aircraft, which reached Finland in February 1985 (MG-119, 128, 136) and July 1986 (MG-121, 123, and 134). All six had incorrect serial numbers when delivered. The aircraft delivered in 1986 were among the last MiG-21s produced in the Soviet Union.

Finnish MiG-21s made friendship visits to the USSR a total of four times—1981, 1985, 1988, and 1991. Each time, their destination was the base at Kubinka near Moscow. Like the MiG-21UMs before them, the avionics of the MiG-

21bis were modified to suit Finnish requirements. This included the installation of Western radios, ILS, and transponders. Unused components, such as the LAZUR ground control intercept system, were removed. Once again Valmet carried out the work. The company also adapted a KTS-4 MiG-21PFM simulator, purchased in 1978, to simulate the MiG-21bis.

Six MiG-21bis were converted into MiG-21T reconnaissance aircraft, and these replaced the MiG-21F-13s at TiedLLv, which had been retired. Outwardly, these modifications could be identified by containers on the wingtips—similar to those of the MiG-21R. In addition to a Vicon 18 camera pod, these aircraft could also carry a Philips 9CM120X chaff/flare dispenser or a Selenia SL/ALQ-234 jamming pod—each on the fuselage pylon. One MiG-21bis was also permanently assigned to Koelentue. In 1988, MG-131 was fitted with a flight data recorder specifically for this purpose. In addition to testing operational procedures and new avionics, the test center was also responsible for acceptance flights of aircraft overhauled at Valmet.

Finland first achieved full political independence at the beginning of the 1990s, with the collapse of the Soviet Union. Preparations for the procurement of a new combat aircraft began in 1987, with the Mirage 2000, F-16, JAS-39 Gripen, MiG-29, and F/A-18 Hornet under consideration. In 1992, the decision was made to purchase the American F/A-18 to replace the MiG-21 and the J-35 Draken. From that time on, the usage of the MiG-21 fleet was kept to a minimum, and no more spares were purchased. Valmet stops major overhaul after 600 or 750 hours. Instead, the scope of the 300-hour checks was expanded. TiedLLv, the reconnaissance squadron, was disbanded at the end of 1996, and all its aircraft were reassigned to Rissala. With the arrival of the first F-18D in Finland in November 1985, the end of the MiG-21's service life in the Finnish air force was just a matter of time. On March 7, 1998, a big farewell celebration at Kupio-Rissala marked the retirement of the MiG-21. At 1234 that day, MG-138 made the last landing by a Finnish MiG-21, flown by the commander of HavLLv 31.

According to official statements, all the aircraft had reached the end of their service lives. An examination of the airframe documents, however, reveals that no more than half had flown their design lives of 3,600 hours. Six MiG-21bis (MG-115, 117, 120, 122, 128, 139) were lost in accidents, and two pilots lost their lives. Eight MiG-21bis continued in

Postflight checks: while one pilot is still going through the postflight checklist, the ground crew is already at work: one man is removing the cassette from the SARPP flight data recorder in the vertical tail.

use as instructional airframes. The best-preserved aircraft, MG-129, rolled down the runway in afterburner at the MiG pilot meet at Kuopio in 2003. The rest, with the exception of a few display aircraft, were scrapped.

Yugoslavia

After the Second World War, the Socialist Federal Republic of Yugoslavia, under partisan leader Josip Broz Tito, steered a socialist course. The right to its own path to socialism demanded by Tito resulted in a break with the Soviet Union in 1948. Relations between Yugoslavia and the Soviet Union resumed in 1955. The first Soviet combat aircraft subsequently delivered to the *Jugoslovensko Ratno Vozduhoplovstvo i Protivvazdušna Odbrana* (JRV i PVO; Yugoslavia air force and air defense) was the MiG-21F-13. In preparation for the first delivery, in January 1962 seven pilots were sent to Lugovaya airfield in the Soviet Union for conversion training.

The first five Gorki-produced MiG-21F-13s arrived by rail shipment at the 204th *lap* (*lovački avijacijski puk*; fighter regiment) at Batajnivca airfield (Yugoslavian cover designation Base 177), near Belgrade. Prior to delivery of the aircraft, the Yugoslavian side expressed an interest in building the type under license; however, the Soviet side refused.

The JRV i PVO used its own designation system for aircraft and components, which was also used on the MiG-21. The MiG-21F-13 was designated L-12, with the letter standing for *lovac* (fighter aircraft). The abbreviation for the two-seat

Serbian MiG-21bis on QRA standby are armed with four R-60 air-to-air missiles and a 130-gallon external fuel tank on the fuselage pylon.

trainer was NL (*nastavni lovac*; practice fighter aircraft). The system also included designations for engines (MM: *mlazni motor*; turbojet engine) and missiles (SR: *samonavodena raketa*; guided missile).

All subsequent delivery batches of MiG-21F-13s—seven aircraft in 1963 and twenty-eight in 1964—came from Moscow and also went to the 204th *lap*, which as a result was equipped completely with this type. Previously, the regiment had been the only flying unit in Europe to simultaneously operate Soviet and American types—in this case, the F-86E. The new MiG-21s were shown to the public for the first time on the occasion of the May Day parade in 1964. With the arrival of more-modern versions in 1967–68, the MiG-21F-13s were transferred to the 117th *lap*, which at that time moved from Pleso (Base 151) to Željava near Bihać (Base 200). Then, in 1970, the 117th *lap* passed the MiG-21F-13s on to the 83rd *lap* at Priština-Slatina, where they replaced F-86Ds. Other MiG-21F-13s were received by the 83rd *lap* directly from Batajnica. The 83rd and 117th *lap* had underground bunker installations in the mountains to shelter their equipment.

All subsequent versions of the MiG-21 also went first to the 204th *lap*. Deliveries of two-seat trainers began with three MiG-21U-400s (NL-12) in the summer of 1965. At the same time, five pilots were sent to the USSR on an instructor's course—this time at Krasnodar. The MiG-21U-400s were followed one year later by fifteen MiG-21U-600s (NL-12M). The last of these were retired in 1991. The next single-seat version to be received was the MiG-21PFM (L-14), thirty-six

of which were received by Yugoslavia between 1967 and 1969. The last machines to be delivered came with fittings for the GP-9 cannon pod. The eight aircraft delivered in 1969 were from the final production batch of this version. Once again, conversion training for the new pilots was carried out in the Soviet Union, where the pilots were given the opportunity to carry out live firing with air-to-air missiles at the Astrakhan range.

The JRV i PVO was placed on alert on August 21, 1968. The invasion of Czechoslovakia by forces of the Warsaw Pact caused the Yugoslavian leadership to fear that a similar action might take place against their own country. In an action code-named Avala, all aircraft then operational—including thirty-eight MiG-21F-13s, twenty-eight MiG-21PFMs, and sixteen MiG-21U two-seat trainers—were armed and then dispersed in the country, and their crews were ordered to maintain a state of readiness. Even though the fear of aggression proved unfounded, defending against attacks from east and west remained a key part of Yugoslavian defense planning.

In October 1968, the 126th *lae* (*lovačka avijacijska eskadrila*; fighter squadron) of the 204th *lap* began receiving the MiG-21R reconnaissance version. Twelve aircraft, with the Yugoslavian designation L-14i, were delivered. The 126th *lae* functioned as the training unit for the 352nd *iae* (*izvidjacka avijacijska eskadrila*; reconnaissance squadron), which—stationed in the underground facilities at Željava—took charge of the aircraft in April 1970. That same year, nine MiG-21US arrived to bolster the two-seat trainer fleet.

In September 1970, the first twenty-one MiG-21Ms (L-15) were commisioned with by the 126th and 127th *lae*. A second delivery in January 1972 comprised four aircraft. The MiG-21PFMs of both squadrons made available by the delivery of the MiG-21M were assigned to the 128th *lae*. The L-15M (MiG-21MF) was acquired in smaller numbers than the L-15. Just six examples were placed in service by the 204th *lap* in 1975. They were the last MiG-21s built in Moscow. In 1984, four aircraft were modified to serve as reconnaissance aircraft and were equipped with the Fairchild long-range aerial panoramic photographic system (LORAP), carried in pods beneath the fuselage. Designated L-15i, these aircraft—unlike the MiG-21R—were considered strategic reconnaissance assets, since with their KA-112 panoramic cameras, from an altitude of 49,200 feet they were capable of photographing targets deep inside neighboring countries.

MiG-21bis about to touchdown at Batajnica. All ex-Yugoslavian air forces practice very flat, soft landings.

The first of twenty-four Yugoslavian MiG-21UMs (NL-16) arrived in 1974, the last not until 1985. The main version in the Yugoslavian inventory was the MiG-21bis. Deliveries to the 204th *lap* began in 1977, following a conversion course at Krasnodar. Twelve MiG-21bis SAUs (L-17) were issued to the 126th *lae*, while thirty-three more aircraft arrived in 1978 for other units. These were followed by thirty-six MiG-21bis LAZUR (L-17K), in part for the 127th *lae*, and that same year they were used to train Iraqi pilots. In June 1982, there followed ten aircraft of this version, three L-17s, and more MiG-21UMs. MiG-21PFMs that became available as a result were issued to the 117th *lap* and the 128th *centar za preobuku* (pilot training center), formed from the 128th *lae*. From the latter, which also trained Palestinian pilots, the 129th *lae* and the 185th Training Regiment (*školsom puk*) were created at the base in Pula in 1985. MiG-21Ms from the units now operating the MiG-21bis went to the 123rd and 130th *lae* of the 83rd *lap*. Also in 1983, Soviet technicians modified the MiG-21bis to use the R-60 short-range air-to-air missile. In addition to these and other Soviet missiles (R-3, R-13, S-5, S-24) and bombs (FAB-50 to 500), Yugoslavian MiG-21s were armed with British BL-755 cluster bombs and 128 mm (0.4 in.) *Munja* rockets, developed in Yugoslavia and carried in four-round launchers.

A total of 261 MiG-21s flew with the Yugoslavian air force. With the exception of the MiG-21F-13s already retired and

the aircraft lost in accidents (seventy-two since 1972), in 1991 the complete MiG-21 fleet was transferred to the Federative Republic of Yugoslavia. With the exception of the 127th *lae*, which had converted to the MiG-29, all the named units continued flying the MiG-21. After most of the constituent republics declared their independence in the summer of 1991, the latent tensions between the ethnic groups of Yugoslavia turned into open hostilities. The Serbian JNA dominated, and with it the JRV i PVO became increasingly involved in the conflict. In August 1990, after the declaration of the autonomous Serbian Republic of Krajina, the threat of MiG-21s operating from Željava was sufficient to deter the Croatians from taking countermeasures, and the air forces of the federal republic were deeply involved in the subsequent hostilities. The MiG-21 received its baptism of fire in the unsuccessful attempt to prevent the breakaway of Slovenia. From June 28 to July 2, 1991, aircraft of the 117th *lap* flew missions in support of Serbian ground forces. Much more significant, however, was the MiG-21's part in the war in Croatia, which began at the same time. The MiG-21s flew several hundred missions from Batajnica and Željava. In doing so they repeatedly violated the airspace of Austria and Hungary; however, there were no encounters with fighter aircraft from the neighboring countries. In August 1991, Yugoslavian MiG-21s forced a Ugandan Boeing 707 carrying arms to Croatia to land. In January 1992, a MiG-21bis based

Until modernization of its MiG-21 fleet, aircraft with outwardly visible serial numbers were the exception in the Croatian air force. Most aircraft flew with just national insignia and unit crests.

at Željava shot down an Italian helicopter of the EU observer mission with an R-60 missile. In the subsequent fighting the MiG-21s, which operated from forward bases such as Petrovec in Macedonia, covered the withdrawal of ground forces, especially against the Croatians. During a mission against a crossing over the Save River near Slavonski Brod on May 2, 1992, the JRV i PVO recorded the seventh and last loss of a MiG-21 during the war, when MiG-21bis 17152 was shot down. The Yugoslavian air force lost a total of five MiG-21bis and two MiG-21Rs to Croatian air defenses, while two more were lost to reasons other than enemy action. One pilot was killed, and another is listed as missing. Three MiG-21bis and one MiG-21R were also lost when Croatian pilots deserted with their aircraft.

When hostilities in Croatia began, the federal army moved all aviation units based there to Serbian-controlled parts of the country. The MiG-21 units affected by this were the 129th *iae* of the 185th *lap* at Pula, on the Croatian coast of the Adriatic, which in 1991 had been based at Tuzla (Base 399), in the eastern part of Bosnia, and there continued pilot training. After the ultimate disintegration of the country in 1992, when the Yugoslavian federal army withdrew from the now-independent Republic of Macedonia and from Bosnia-Herzegovina, it took all the weapons and equipment there with it. The 129th *iae* moved again—on May 12, 1992, to the 83rd *lap*'s base at Priština in Kosovo—and soon afterward was disbanded. After all the MiG-21s of the 352nd *iae* and the 117th *lap* had left Željava airfield between April 22 and

May 4, 1992, on May 16 the underground airfield installations there were blown up. The 352nd *iae* moved to Batajnica, and the 124th *iae* went to Ponikve, where it was attached to the 83rd *lap*. The 125th *iae* was disbanded and its equipment was passed on to other units.

With its withdrawal from Croatia the JRV i PVO also lost an importance maintenance facility—the Zmaj depot at the Zagreb-Pleso airport. Prior to the breakup of the country, not only had Yugoslavian MiG-21s been overhauled there, but MiG-21s and MiG-23s from Libya and Iraq had as well. Eight of these remained in Yugoslavia after the outbreak of the Gulf War in 1991 and—like all the equipment at the depot—were moved to Batajnica by the federal army during its withdrawal. Three MiG-21s wearing Iraqi camouflage colors and Yugoslavian markings saw action during the civil war.

Also removed from the direct control of the Yugoslavian government were the Orao aeronautical plant in Bijeljina and the Kosmos plant in Banja Luka, which maintained engines and avionics. Located in the Serbian part of Bosnia-Herzegovina, these facilities were still available to the JRV i PVO, however. All significant maintenance capacities were concentrated in the Moma Stanojlovič aeronautical plant in Batajnica.

The new political reality caused by the separation of the republics was de facto acknowledged by the Serbian side by the reconstitution of the Federal Republic of Yugoslavia, now consisting of just Serbia and Montenegro, on April 27, 1992. Despite this, there was no peace for the MiG-21 units following the federal army's withdrawal to within the borders of the new state. After the imposition of UN sanctions and a naval blockade by NATO in July 1992, the fighter forces were kept at a permanent state of increased readiness. This essentially continued until the end of the NATO Operation Deliberate Force to guard the protected zones in Bosnia-Herzegovina, even though the JRV i PVO did not intervene in this conflict.

The retirement of the older machines concentrated in Yugoslavia began in 1992, with the MiG-21PFM and MiG-21US. The 204th *lap* at Batajnica subsequently still had two MiG-21 squadrons equipped with the MiG-21bis/UM (126th *iae*) and MiG-21MF/R (352nd *iae*). The 83rd *lap* at Priština and Ponikve flew two squadrons of MiG-21bis/UM (123rd and 124th *iae*) and one squadron of MiG-21M/UM (130th *iae*). After the signing of the Dayton Peace Treaty in June 1996, the JRV i PVO was obliged to reduce the number of

At Pleso a MiG-21UM waits for its crew.

MiG-21bisD 108 on approach to land at Zagreb. This aircraft and sister machine 120 were destroyed in a midair collision in 2010.

Chapter 9: In Action on the Front Lines of the Cold War

combat aircraft to 155 within sixteen months. This resulted in the scrapping of sixteen MiG-21PFMs, four MiG-21MFs, five MiG-21Rs, four MiG-21Us, and five MiG-21USs. The 230th *lae*, which had been created from the 130th *lae* and was based at Ponikve, was disbanded. Four of its sixteen MiG-21Ms were issued to the 1st AO (*avijacijsko odeljenje*; aviation division) of the 353rd *iae*, formerly the 352nd *iae*, as replacements for its MiG-21MF fighters. This brought its total complement of MiG-21s to sixty-seven aircraft. Nine MiG-21UMs were converted into unarmed training aircraft. Nineteen aircraft had been lost to enemy action and accidents between 1992 and 1999. A total of fifty MiG-21 pilots lost their lives in service since the start of the 1970s.

The next cuts were not long in coming: after massive actions by Serbian security forces against Kosovar separatists, on March 24, 1999, NATO attacked numerous targets in Yugoslavia as part of Operation Allied Force. Because of NATO's total air superiority, the MiG-21s were not used to intercept the air attacks. The bombing, which destroyed almost all of the Yugoslavian air force's bases, claimed

twenty-five MiG-21bis, two MiG-21Ms, and six MiG-21UMs, several of which had been moved to Niš, Ponikve, Sjenica, and Podgorica. The Moma Stanjolovič maintenance facilities at Batajnica were also largely destroyed. Despite this, through the use of camouflage and decoy targets, but mainly by hiding aircraft in the underground bunker facilities at Priština, the RV i PVO succeeded in preventing part of its fleet of MiG-21s from being destroyed. There were only enough aircraft left to equip one regiment, however, and in September 1999 the 83rd *lap* at Priština was disbanded and the remaining twelve (eleven MiG-21bis and one MiG-21UM) of its original force of thirty-seven MiG-21s were flown to the 204th *lap*. Batajnica was thus left as the sole remaining MiG-21 base. With the end of Operation Allied Force, the fleet of thirty-two MiG-21s began intensive training in anticipation of further hostilities—a phase that lasted until the end of the Milošević era in October 2000. At the same time, the MiG-21 took over the air defense role from the MiG-29, since the latter was no longer able to carry out this role due to heavy losses in the war.

A MiG-21UMD taxis out for takeoff at Pleso. The condition of the aircraft's exterior shows that the modernization in Romania is already several years in the past.

The annual flying hours by the RV i PVO of Serbia and Montenegro, as the state was designated as of February 2003, dropped rapidly due to shortages of fuel and spare parts. The last flying MiG-21R was retired in December 2003. In April 2004, the remaining MiG-29s were grounded, leaving the country's air defense in the hands of the MiG-21s of the 126th *lae*. The sole remaining serviceable MiG-21MF, the oldest combat aircraft in the inventory, was converted into a reconnaissance machine, carrying the reconnaissance pod previously used by other aircraft of this version. Two MiG-21bis were also fitted with reconnaissance pods. These were created by installing British-made Vinten 880 and 753A cameras in 130-gallon drop tanks.

When the Federation of Serbia and Montenegro split apart in early 2006, the MiG-21 fleet, all of which was in Serbia, was not affected. At that time, twenty-four MiG-21bis (probably twenty-three, plus one MiG-21MF) and four MiG-21UMs were reported to the OSCE (Organization for Security and Co-operation in Europe), and operated by the 101st *lae* and the 1st *izvidačko avijacijsko odeljenje* (reconnaissance flight; *iao*) of the 204th *Avijacijska Baza Batajnica*. An overhaul proposed by Russia after inspection of the MiG-21 fleet fell victim to the bad economic situation, so the last two MiG-21bis were decommissioned in 2014 and 2015 respectively. This leaves only three MiG-21UM in service which, due to the lack of fighter aircraft, were armed with R-60 AAM. In this configuration they perform QRA duty together with MiG-29. These three MiG-21s will probably be retired when overhaul of the MiG-29s delivered by Russia in 2017 is finished.

Croatia's declaration of independence in June 1991 was the beginning of a struggle lasting several years against the Yugoslavian army, which used all the means at its disposal to prevent a further breakup of the federation.

After its founding on December 12, 1991, the *Hrvatske zračne snage* (Croatian air force or HZS) had a considerable number of personnel, since many Croatians had left the federal army (where they made up a large percentage of aircrew and technical personnel) and gone home. What the air force lacked was combat aircraft, since the Yugoslavian army had either taken them with it when it withdrew or had

At overhaul in Ukraine, Croatian MiG-21s received a striking grey colour scheme.

MiG-21PFM on approach to land at Poznań. The 3rd Fighter Regiment, which was based there, operated this version until March 1998. *Stefan Büttner*

destroyed them. This did not change until, between October 1991 and June 1992, four Croatian pilots deserted with their aircraft from Yugoslavian airfields. While Rudolf Perešin, later commander of the 21st *lovačka eskadrila* (fighter squadron), landed his MiG-21R at Klagenfurt, Austria, on October 25, 1991, the others were able to reach Croatian airfields. One MiG-21bis escaped from Željava to Pula on January 4, 1992, while two flew from Ponikve to Zagreb and Split on May 15. These formed the basis for the subsequent development of the air force.

Within a short time, the Croatians succeeded in forming their personnel and equipment into a significant combat force and put its newly acquired aircraft to use. The first loss occurred on June 24, 1992. While attacking surface-to-surface missile sites of the federal army, a MiG-21bis crashed near Slavonski Brod for reasons that remain unexplained; the pilot was killed. Another aircraft was shot down by Yugoslavian surface-to-air missiles in the Vrginmost region. Once again the pilot was killed—his ejection seat failed to function.

Despite UN sanctions against all former Yugoslavian states imposed in 1992, Croatia succeeded in procuring twenty-three MiG-21bis fighters and four MiG-21UM two-seat trainers from Kirgizstan. The aircraft were given the serial numbers 104 to 126 and 160 to 163 and were sent to ZTZ (Zrakoplovno-Tehnicki Zavod—an aviation company, formerly Zmaj) at Velika Gorica for major overhaul. The poor mechanical condition of the aircraft (which had been in open-air storage for a long time) required considerable work by the maintenance personnel to restore them to operational

condition. One MiG-21bis could not be made flyable again and was used as a source of spare parts. Other aircraft spent only a short time in service with the *Hrvatsko ratno zrakoplovstvo i protuzračna obrana* (HRZ i PZO—the service's designation since 1993.

Even before the MiGs received their baptism of fire, an aircraft was lost during a practice flight on April 16, 1995. Operation Lightning, to liberate western Slavonia, began in May 1995. On May 2, 1995, a MiG-21bis was shot down by a Strela shoulder-fired SAM, and its pilot was killed. Operation Storm followed on August 4, 1995. For four days the Croatians attacked Bosnian-Serbian troops on a front of 420 miles, capturing from them the region known as Krajina and thus gaining control of the internationally recognized border. According to Croatian sources, the MiG-21s taking part in the operation flew at least six sorties per day—purely in the air-to-ground role. Both sides agree that there was no aerial combat. There were also no aircraft losses, and just one aircraft was damaged and had to be repaired.

After the end of fighting, there began a period of consolidation, with the focus on the training of new pilots. After several hundred hours on the PC-9 trainer, these proceeded directly to the MiG-21. The first graduates bolstered the two flying units—the 21st *eskadrila lovackih zrakoplova* (*elz*, fighter squadron) and the 91st *zrakoplovna baza* (air base) at Zagreb-Pleso and the 22nd *elz* at the 92nd *zrakoplovna baza* at Pula in 1996.

Two aircraft were lost in peacetime. One MiG-21bis crashed while on approach to land at Zagreb-Pleso in August

This MiG-21R on approach to the base at Sochaczew was photographed shortly before the 32nd Tactical Reconnaissance Regiment was disbanded on December 31, 1998. *Alexander Golz*

1996. Another was written off after a fire on the ground and was subsequently scrapped.

In the late 1990s, planning began for a modernization of the MiG-21 fleet in order to extend the lives of the by-then-aging fighters. Negotiations were carried out with SOKOL in Russia and with IAI and Elbit in Israel. In February 1999, a contract worth ten million US dollars was signed with the latter company for the modernization of twenty-four aircraft, but it was canceled in February 2001 due to a lack of funds. In November of the same year, it was reported that a contract had been signed with Russia, and in January 2002 the Croatian defense minister finally announced that AEROSTAR in Romania was going to modernize eight MiG-21bis and four MiG-21UMs. While the MiG-21bis came from Croatian stocks, the MiG-21UMs were supposed to come from Poland but were then procured from the CIS. The first two updated two-seat trainers arrived in Croatia in May 2003. The remaining aircraft were delivered by the end of the year. The updated aircraft, which were designated MiG-21bisD and MiG-21UMD (see "Modernization: MiG-21 for the Twenty-First Century"), were fit for another ten years of service. Since plans for a follow-up type have gotten no further than the preliminary study stage at best, in 2013, the Croatian government decided to overhaul the MiG-21s again and to purchase a few replacement aircraft. The order went to Ukrspezeksport in Ukraine. Of six operational MiG-21bisD— two MiG-21bisD aircraft were lost in a midair collision in September 2010—and four UMD, seven aircraft (three bisD and four UMD) were sent to be overhauled; five originally intended for Yemen were delivered by Ukraine. The overhaul took place at OdesAviaRemServis; the first overhauled MiG-21 arrived at Pleso Airbase in April 2014. Until July 2015, the fleet was complete again. However, after that, massive technical problems occured in flight operations. At the same time, one non-upgraded MiG-21bisD crashed due to a technical fault. Subsequent investigations revealed numerous irregularities in overhaul and corruption in procurement. In early 2018, the Croatian Ministry of Defense requested Ukraine to take back four MiG-21bis and replace them with defect-free aircraft. Almost at the same time, the delivery of used F-16s is agreed with Israel. The aircraft are to be delivered between 2020 and 2022, and will replace the MiG-21s.

Poland

In 1947, the communists who had followed the Red Army back into Poland took sole power in the country; however, they frequently came into conflict with the Soviet controlling power. Nevertheless, Poland's *Wojska Obrony Powietrznej Kraju* (WOPK; Troops of the Air Defense of the Land) was equipped with the future standard fighter aircraft of the Warsaw Pact. On September 29, 1961, the first Polish MiG-21F-13 arrived at the *Centrum Szkolenia Lotniczego* (CSL, or flight training center) at Modlin, where the training of pilots of the 1st *Pułk Lotnictwa Mysliwskiego* (PLM, or fighter

MiG-21M on approach to land at Malbork. The P-62 launch rail on the port outer stores pylon with R-60 training round is an indication that at least some Polish MiG-21Ms were modified to use this missile. *Alexander Golz*

regiment) from Mińsk Mazowiecki, the 11th PLM from Debrzno, and the 62nd PLM from Poznań-Krzesiny took place. It was more than a year after this before the unit received another eight aircraft. The first operational unit was the 1st Squadron of the 62nd Fighter Regiment, which received four MiG-21F-13s. Like their predecessors, these machines had been manufactured in Gorki, and they replaced the Lim-5s (MiG-17) that the unit had previously flown. Further aircraft were delivered until the autumn of 1963. Six were assigned to the 1st PLM and six went to the 11th PLM. That same year, the 62nd Fighter Regiment took part in a Warsaw Pact maneuver with nine aircraft. In 1964, the total of twenty-five MiG-21F-13s were assigned to eight units. In addition to those named above, they were the 3rd PLM at Wrocław, the 13th PLM at Łęczya, the 26th PLM at Zegrze Pomorskie, the 40th PLM at Świndin, and the 41st PLM at Malbork, while Modlin turned in its aircraft. In 1965, all MiG-21F-13s were concentrated in the 4th (from 1967 onward, the 2nd) Fighter Regiment at Goleniów, where they remained until phased out in 1973. That same year the last twelve serviceable aircraft were sent to Syria. Two were used for training purposes at aviation engineering schools in Olesnica and Zamosc and were scrapped in 1977. Three survive in collections and museums, while the remaining eight were destroyed in accidents.

Deliveries of the MiG-21PF began in April and May 1964, with twelve Gorki-built aircraft (four each for the 62nd and 1st PLM and four more divided between the flight training

center and the 11th PLM). Deliveries continued until August 1965, and at eighty-four aircraft the PF clearly outnumbered the F-13. Built in Moscow beginning with the thirteenth aircraft, the MiG-21PFs were assigned to regiments at Minsk Mazowiecki (1st), Wrocław (3rd), Debrzno (11th), Zegrze Pomoskie (26th), Świdwin (40th), Malbork (41st), and Poznań-Krzesiny (62nd). Later transfers from these units made it possible for the 10th Fighter Regiment at Łask (from March 1968 onward) and the 39th Fighter Regiment at Katowice-Mierzęcice to convert to the MiG-21. Further large transfers took place in 1966, from the 40th to the 4th PLM, and in 1968, from the 26th to the 1st PLM. In 1980, the 39th PLM gave its MiG-21PFs to the 1st and 10th PLM, which then became the last regiments flying this type. The service life of the MiG-21PF with the Polish air force was clearly longer than that of its predecessor—the last aircraft were phased out at Minsk Mazowiecki and Łask in December 1989, after sufficient MiG-21PFMs became available from disbanded regiments and the 1st Fighter Regiment began flying the MiG-29. Many MiG-21PFs were stored—like the surplus aircraft of later versions—at Katowice-Mierzęcice and were scrapped only later. By the time the MiG-21PF was retired, eight had been lost in accidents.

In parallel with the MiG-21PF, the first two-seat trainers were delivered between January and June 1965. Six Moscow-built MiG-21U-400s were delivered to the CSL at Modlin. Later, two were sent to Świdwin (40th PLM) and two went to Minsk Mazowiecki (1st PLM), plus one to Malbork

This MiG-21MF of the 10th Fighter Regiment at Łask wears the unit emblem on its nose and a white stripe on the aft fuselage for identification during air-to-air exercises. *Stefan Büttner*

After the ground crew has given the all-clear for takeoff, a MiG-21UM taxis past empty parking spaces left by aircraft already in the air.

Chapter 9: In Action on the Front Lines of the Cold War

MiG-21bis of the 41st Fighter Regiment at Malbork taxis in preparation for takeoff.

A MiG-21UM undergoes maintenance at Gdynia-Babie Doły. The bird-of-prey eyes on the nose were supposed to prevent bird strikes.

(41st PLM). One initially remained at Modlin and later flew at Katowice (39th PLM). The MiG-21U-400 was followed by the MiG-21U-600, five of which were delivered in July and August 1966. Of these, the 40th PLM received three and the 41st PLM got two. Later, these aircraft were also passed on to other units. As of November 1969, the 10th PLM had one MiG-21U-400 on strength, and from 1980 onward, one MiG-21U-600. All MiG-21Us were subsequently concentrated in the 1st Fighter Regiment, where they remained in service until February 1990, by which time three MiG-21U-400s had been lost.

The most numerous version of the MiG-21 to serve with the Polish air force was the MiG-21PFM, deliveries of which began in February 1966, with the 40th Fighter Regiment receiving ten aircraft from the Gorki plant. The 41st Fighter Regiment received twenty-one aircraft beginning in August of the same year. Next was the 34th Fighter Regiment at Gdynia-Babie Doły, which for the first time received MiG-21s. Seventeen aircraft were received, and these replaced the Lim-5Ps operated by the 1st Squadron. One month later, thirteen MiG-21PFMs were issued to the 26th Fighter Regiment. In 1968, forty-three aircraft were delivered, and these were issued to two squadrons of the 26th and two of the 34th Fighter Regiments. A total of 132 examples arrived from Moscow by 1968 and were subsequently flown by all the named units. The last twelve aircraft, delivered in September 1968, were the nuclear-capable MiG-21PFMN version and were divided among the 2nd, 9th, and 41st Fighter Regiments. With the repurposing of the 40th Fighter

Regiment as a fighter-bomber regiment (40th PLM-B), twenty-one of its MiG-21PFMs went to the 2nd Fighter Regiment. Through transfers from other units, the MiG-21PFM also joined the inventories of the 9th, 10th, and 11th Fighter Regiments in 1968, and the 39th Fighter Regiment in 1970. In 1981, MiG-21PFMs replaced the last Lim-5s in service with the 62nd Fighter Regiment. The 10th PLM retained its MiG-21PFMs until 1989, when they were transferred to the 1st PLM. Simultaneously the 32nd PLRTiA (*Pułk Lotnictwa Rozpoznania Taktycnego i Artyleryskiego*; tactical and artillery reconnaissance regiment) at Sochaczew received eight aircraft of this type, which were used for training purposes. In 1987, the 39th Fighter Regiment at Katowice-Mierzęcice was disbanded, and the regiment's MiG-21PFMs were passed on to the 1st and 62nd Fighter Regiments and from there to the 10th Fighter Regiment. Twenty more aircraft came from the 2nd Fighter Regiment, which ceased operations in 1989 as part of the Warsaw Pact disarmament initiative. This also meant the phasing out of the aircraft of the PFMN version, which were concentrated there. Three remained in service with the 10th PLM, however.

On September 28, 1968—just a few days after the last MiG-21PFM—the first MiG-21s of the third generation, two MiG-21Rs, were received by the 41st Fighter Regiment at Malbork. At the end of 1968, therefore, the WOPK had a total of 237 MiG-21s in five versions in its inventory. Entirely or partly equipped with this type were the 1st (MiG-21PF), 2nd (MiG-21F-13 and MiG-21PF), 9th, 11th, 13th, 34th, and 40th Fighter Regiments (all with the MiG-21PFM), plus the

During a DOL (*Drogowy Odcinek Lotniskowy* = road landing section) exercise, aircraft carried out flight operations from a specially prepared and sealed-off section of ordinary road. Here a MiG-21bis of the 41st Fighter Regiment lands on one such auxiliary landing strip. *Alexander Golz*

41st (MiG-21PF, PFM, R), and 62nd (MiG-21PF) Fighter Regiments.

The two MiG-21Rs delivered in 1968 were handed over to their unit, the 21st PLRTiA at Powidz, in July 1969. The next ten aircraft went directly to the regiment between July 1969 and April 1970. On January 13, 1972, Soviet pilots flew fourteen MiG-21Rs to the base at Bielice. Ten more followed on January 26, all destined for the 32nd PLRTiA at Sochaczew. The introduction of this type was assisted by Soviet factory representatives, who remained on site for one year. The new aircraft were used for extended reconnaissance flights over the Baltic, where there were frequent, more or less peaceful encounters with West German, Danish, and Swedish combat aircraft, consisting of F-104 Starfighters and J-35 Drakens. With the restructuring of the 21st PLRTiA into a fighter-bomber regiment (21st PLM-B), in December 1982, the unit's MiG-21Rs were transferred to Sochaczew, where they replaced the last SBLim-2A trainers (MiG-15UTI). From then on, the entire fleet of thirty-three aircraft was concentrated at that location. Simultaneously, the last remaining reconnaissance unit of the WL i OPL was renamed

the 32nd PLRT (*Pułk Lotnictwa Rozpoznania Taktycnego*; tactical reconnaissance regiment).

As in other countries, the reconnaissance aircraft did not just carry the standard Soviet type D and R reconnaissance pods, but also a Polish-developed Saturn-2 pod. This consisted of UB-16 rocket pods, each with two cameras. The exposed film could be developed in flight and jettisoned in shockproof cassettes.

The first MiG-21M reached its base of operations with the 41st PLM at Malbork on December 30, 1969. The unit received a total of twenty-four aircraft of this type by the beginning of February 1970. Twelve more were delivered to the 9th Fighter Regiment at Debrzno in March 1970. In 1985, two of these went to the 10th PLM at Łask, and the rest went to the 2nd PLM at Goleniów when the 9th Fighter Regiment was disbanded at the end of 1988. Twelve MiG-21US two-seat trainers arrived between August 1969 and July 1970. Nine of the aircraft assigned to the CSL were subsequently divided among the 1st, 11th, 39th, and 62nd PLM, and the 21st PLRTiA. Two and one, respectively, went directly to their future users, the 34th and 26th Fighter Regiments. During

For the Miedzynarodowe Pokazy Lotnicze Radom 2002 air show, two Polish MiG-21UMs, including aircraft 9292, were finished in this special paint scheme. They retained the finish until all Polish MiG-21s were retired in December 2003.

the formation of fighter-bomber regiments, the 2nd PLM (from the 40th PLM-B) and the 32nd PLRT (from the 21st PLM-B) also received MiG-21US two-seat trainers. In 1989, the 62nd PLM had the largest complement of this version. Six of them were passed on to the 1st PLM as replacements for its MiG-21U trainers and remained there until phased out. One MiG-21US crashed in 1977.

From the beginning of the 1970s, *Wojskowe Zakłady Lotnicze* (WZL, or military aircraft establishment) No. 3 at Deblin was responsible for industry-level maintenance of the Polish MiG-21s. The first aircraft overhauled there were the MiG-21PFs of the 1st, 10th, and 39th Fighter Regiments. Such an overhaul required six to eight months. Work on the MiG-21PFM did not begin at Deblin until 1983, followed soon afterward by the MiG-21M/MF.

The MiG-21UM two-seat trainer version had the longest delivery period of any Polish MiG-21. The first batch of twenty aircraft arrived between July 1971 and October 1975 (the aircraft with the number 5006 did not arrive until about two years after its completion). The first of these—all powered by the R11 engine—were received by the 41st PLM. Other units followed—the 32nd PLRTiA and the 34th, 9th, 26th,

and 28th PLM. After various transfers, MiG-21UMs were flown by every Polish regiment.

The delivery of 120 MiG-21MFs to Poland began in December 1972 and ended in December 1975. The 1st Squadron of the 34th Fighter Regiment at Gdynia-Babie Doły was first, receiving nine aircraft. Twenty-four aircraft for the 41st PLM at Malbork followed in August and September 1973, replacing that unit's MiG-21PFMs. The 28th Fighter Regiment at Słupsk, where the MiG-21MF replaced the last MiG-19s in Polish service, received aircraft from the 34th PLM. Beginning in February 1974, the 26th PLM at Zegrze Pomorskie received twenty examples of the MiG-21MF, where they replace MiG-21PFMs. In December 1975, twenty Gorki-built MF-75s, the last ones delivered, were assigned to the 34th Fighter Regiment, which was then completely equipped with the MiG-21. The number of MiG-21s in service with the WOKP had grown to more than 400. In 1978, the 2nd Fighter Regiment received the MiG-21MF aircraft transferred from other units. Following the delivery of the MiG-23MF to the 28th Fighter Regiment and the MiG-21bis to the 26th and 34th Fighter Regiments, their MiG-21MFs went to the 9th, 10th (from May 1978 onward), 11th, and

After modernization by Israel Aircraft Industries (IAI) in Tel Aviv, a number of Polish MiG-21s were sold to Uganda.

Like many other MiG-21s from Polish, Czech, Hungarian, and East German stocks, MiG-21UM 7505 is now owned by a private citizen in the United States. It was retired in 1992, after just nineteen years of service, and sold a short time later.
Alexander Golz

Chapter 9: In Action on the Front Lines of the Cold War   **209**

The first MiG-21F-13s produced at Gorki arrived in Romania in October 1962. Several of these aircraft have remained virtually unchanged to this day.

41st Fighter Regiments. These regiments' pilots had first been trained on the new type by the original units. With the disbandment of the 9th Fighter Regiment in 1988, its MiG-21MFs returned to Zegrze Pomorskie, where the 26th Fighter Regiment was renamed the 9th Fighter Regiment.

The economic crisis in Poland, which in 1980 led to the formation of the Solidarność Labor Union and to the takeover by General Wojciech Jaruzelski, and became worse in the years that followed, had its effects on the air force. Aircraft numbers and flying hours fell.

For this reason, the WL i WOPK was very late in receiving the fourth generation of the MiG-21. At first Poland did not plan to acquire the MiG-21bis at all, intending instead to adopt the MiG-23, but for cost reasons the MiG-23MF/UB was procured only for the 28th PLM. Instead of additional MiG-23s, in March 1980 thirty-six MiG-21bis LAZUR were delivered to the 34th Fighter Regiment at Gdynia-Babie Doły.

In parallel with the MiG-21bis, thirty-four additional MiG-21UM two-seat trainers with the R13 engine arrived between January 1980 and May 1981 and were divided between the 9th, 11th, 26th, 34th, and 41st Fighter Regiments. Another thirty-six MiG-21bis were delivered between July and September 1981, going to the 26th Fighter Regiment at

Zegrze Pomorskie, and this ended procurement of the MiG-21 by Poland. The fleet thus reached its highest level of 486 aircraft. By that time, eighty-one aircraft had been destroyed in accidents.

At the beginning of 1989, the political change in Poland was initiated from above. In the Republic of Poland—the state's new name—as well, development of the air force, which had been renamed *Wojska Lotnicze I Obrony Powietrznej* (WLiOP, or air force / air defense), continued to be overshadowed by shrinking budgets and, with these, a reduction in the MiG-21 fleet. At the same time, the political leadership oriented itself toward the West and entry into NATO.

In January 1991, the 34th Fighter Regiment, with thirty-two MiG-21bis and six MiG-21UMs, was attached to the *Lotnictwo Marynarki Wojennej* (naval air force). By the end of 1992, there were about 280 MiG-21s in service with nine regiments. The 1st Fighter Regiment had two squadrons with MiG-21PFMs and MiG-21USs. Completely equipped with the MiG-21 were the 2nd Fighter Regiment with MiG-21Ms, the 9th with the MiG-21bis, the 10th with the MiG-21MF, the 11th with the MiG-21M/MF, the 34th with the MiG-21bis, the 41st with the MiG-21M/MF, and the 62nd Fighter Regiment

All two-seat trainers in Romania were combined under the designation MiG-21DC (*dublă comandă* = dual controls). Aircraft 1120 was the first MiG-21 trainer taken on strength. *Stefan Büttner*

with the MiG-21PFM, plus the 32nd PLRT with the MiG-21R. All these units also had MiG-21UM two-seat trainers on strength.

In keeping with the terms of the Treaty on Conventional Armed Forces in Europe, in 1993 the scrapping of the PF and PFM versions took place at Mierzęcice. With the disbandment of the 2nd Fighter Regiment at Goleniów in September of the same year, its MiG-21Ms were reassigned to the 1st PLM at Minsk Mazowowiecki, the 10th PLM at Łask, and the 41st PLM at Malbork. At that time, the pilots were flying an average of seventy to eighty hours a year. In 1993, the 62nd Fighter Regiment was renamed the 3rd Fighter Regiment. That same year, the commander of the WLiOP ordered the end of major overhauls of MiG-21s and the concentration of means on more-modern types, which made the end of operational use of the MiG-21 in Poland merely a matter of time. Two years later, WZL-3 Deblin delivered the last overhauled aircraft to the air force.

In January 1995, *Eskadry* (squadrons) A and B of the 1st *Dywizion Lotnictwa Marynarki Wojennej* (DLMW; naval air division) were formed from the 34th PLM. In March 1996, the 1st PLM received Czech MiG-29s, ending its use of the MiG-21. The unit's MiG-21s were passed on to the 10th and 41st PLM.

The closing of the base at Sochaczew on December 31, 1997, marked the end of the MiG-21R's use in the reconnaissance role. In August, nine MiG-21Rs and three MiG-21UMs of the 32nd PLRT had been given to the 3rd

Fighter Regiment at Poznań-Krzesiny, where together with the last MiG-21PFMs they were used in the training role. All reconnaissance-related equipment was removed. Three more MiG-21Rs went to the newly created *Grupa Doświadczalna* (testing group) of the 45th *Eskadra Lotnicza* (EL, or air squadron) at Modlin. This unit later became the *Eskadra Lotnicza Specjalna* (ELS, or special air squadron) and was based at Deblin. The 23rd ELS's tasks included acceptance flights of overhauled aircraft and testing of modifications within various development programs. The last active MiG-21R was lost in an accident on July 11, 2000. The MiG-21M took over the reconnaissance role for a short time, but from 2000 onward this was completely transferred to other types.

The MiG-21US two-seat trainers were retired from service individually between 1990 and 1995. The MiG-21PFM was able to remain in service for a relatively long time. The last fourteen examples with the 1st Fighter Regiment at Minsk Mazowiecki were retired in 1993 with the arrival of the MiG-21M. Not until March 27, 1998, did the MiG-21PFMs of the 3rd Fighter Regiment at Poznań-Krzesiny make their last flight, after which they were stored at Mierzęcice. Eleven aircraft are known to have been lost in crashes. On July 1, 1998, the WLiOP still had 124 MiG-21s of the R, M, MF, bis, and UM versions in service. One year later the number had fallen to just fifty.

At the end of 1999, the 11th PLM at Wrocław-Strachowice, which also included a section stationed at Katowice after the

A MiG-21RFMM, the Romanian designation for the MiG-21PFM, at Bačau. Like most of the Romanian MiG-21s, it is in the open, since Feteşti is the only base with shelters for its aircraft. *Stefan Büttner*

39th PLM based there was disbanded, ceased operations. Its MiG-21Ms, MiG-21MFs, and MiG-21UMs were divided among the 3rd, 10th, and 41st Fighter Regiments. The last examples of the MiG-21M were retired by these units in 2000.

Long before Poland entered NATO, which finally took place on March 12, 1999, consideration was given to modernization of the MiG-21 fleet to make it compatible with the countries' new allies. Plans to equip the aircraft with a Western radar were soon dropped. Eighteen MiG-21bis were fitted with a new IFF system by Thomson-CSF, built under license by Warszawa Radar. These aircraft were the only ones that occasionally took part in exercises in other NATO countries.

While in the late 1990s, Polish MiG-21 pilots normally logged 100 to 120 flying hours annually, as of 2001 this figure fell below ninety hours, because an attempt was being made to extend the service lives of existing aircraft for as long as possible. In January 2001, the former fighter regiments were reorganized into tactical fighter squadrons (ELT, *Eskadra Lotnicztwa Taktycznego*). The MiG-21 units affected by this were the 3rd, 9th, 10th, and 41st Fighter Regiments, which had a combined strength of twenty-four MiG-21MFs, twenty-nine MiG-21bis, and seventeen MiG-21UMs. Another twenty-one MiG-21bis and five MiG-21UMs were in service with the 1st DMLW of the naval air service. Eight of these were transferred to the *Agienca Mienia Wojskowiego* (AMY, or military utilization agency), and nine and eight more followed in 2002 and 2003, respectively. After four aircraft were flown for the last time on January 23, 2003, on January 30 the LMW phased out the MiG-21 for good. The remaining aircraft went to the 3rd and 41st ELT. A demonstration team with four MiG-21MFs was formed at Łask in 2002. These aircraft were finished in a finish made up of several shades of gray, which was noteworthy in that almost all Polish MiG-21s had flown in natural metal finish, while a very few were painted gray. The demonstration team gave ten shows before the MiG-21s were officially retired at Łask on January 24, 2004. The 23rd LES at Deblin and the 9th ELT at Zegrze Pomorskie had previously been disbanded. Their last thirteen MiG-21bis (and five MiG-21UMs) were received by the 3rd ELT as replacements for its twelve MiG-21MFs, which had been

A LanceR A undergoes maintenance at Câmpia Turzii. The hangar, a remnant from socialist days, has since been replaced by a new building.

While refueling of LanceR B 176 is still going on, the tow bar is attached in order to tow the machine to the flight line.

This LanceR C wears a special marking that was applied to mark the twenty-fifth anniversary of Baza 71 Aeriana and its predecessor units.

Preflight preparations for a LanceR C at Šiauliai in Lithuania during Baltic Air Policing 2007.

phased out. The 10th ELT's last eleven MiG-21MFs were "replaced" by TS-11 Iskra jet trainers, and it kept just four MiG-21UMs in service. In the end, the 41st ELT had sixteen MiG-21bis and three MiG-21UMs on strength.

On December 27, 2002, it was announced that Poland would procure forty-eight F-16s and also obtain additional MiG-29s from Germany, officially sealing the fate of the MiG-21. On December 16, 2003, a ceremony and farewell flyby by MiG-21bis 9507 brought an end to the MiG-21 era with the 3rd Tactical Fighter Squadron at Poznań-Krzesiny. Three days later, on December 19, the 41st Tactical Fighter Squadron at Malbork phased out its MiG-21s, ending the aircraft's use by the Polish air force. The very last flight was undertaken by a MiG-21UM, with the serial number 9323. MiG-21s remained at QRA at Malbork until January 4, 2004, but they were no longer used operationally.

The remaining MiG-21s were stored at Poznań and Malbork, after planned sales—including to RSK MiG-21, which planned to modernize the aircraft and sell them to southern African countries—failed to materialize. Three MiG-21UMs had been sold to private interests in the United States and Australia at the beginning of the 1990s. Six MiG-21bis and one MiG-21UM were modernized by Israeli Aircraft Industries and sold to Uganda. The rest of the fleet will probably be scrapped.

Romania

Despite its independent and noninterventionist foreign policy, Romania received every new weapons system at the same time as the other Warsaw Pact nations—including the MiG-21 from April and September 1962. Two groups of pilots and technicians of the 93rd *Regimentul Aviatie Vânãoare* (Regt. Av. Vt.; fighter regiment), based at Timişoara-Giarmata, were sent to the Soviet training center at Krasnodar for conversion training, to prepare for the introduction of the new type into service with the *Forţele Aeriene ale Republicii Române* (air force of the People's Republic of Romania). The first aircraft, twelve MiG-21F-13s built in Gorki, were delivered by Soviet pilots to the regiment, which at that time was stationed at Caracal-Deveselu, in October of the same year. Romanian pilots made their first flights in the new type in November.

A second MiG-21 squadron with twelve aircraft, built in Moscow, was formed at the base at Constanţa-Mihail Kogălniceanu as part of the 57th Fighter Regiment in August 1963. Pilots and technicians of this unit were instructed in the use of the new fighter in courses at the military academy in Medias given by their colleagues of the 93rd Fighter Regiment. In 1968, the MiG-21F-13s were assigned to the regiments at Deveselu (91st) and Feteşti-Borcea (86th), where they remained in use until 1975–76. The official phasing out of the MiG-21F-13 did not take place until 1993. In the intervening period they were used for training at the military technical school in Medias. Just three MiG-21F-13s are claimed to have been lost in their first ten years of operation. Four now belong to the National Aviation Museum

Traditionally, preflight preparations in Romania differ from flight line operations by central European MiG-21 users. Here, returned aircraft are lined up one behind the other for refueling from the trucks parked beside them.

A MiG-21 LanceR C armed with two Matra Magic 2 AAMs leaves its weatherproof shelter for a night flight.

The last takeoff from German soil by a MiG-21 to date was made by a Romanian LanceR on July 15, 2008. The aircraft stopped at Erfurt on its way home from Bastille Day, the French national holiday, in Paris.

Though the succesor is already in service with the RoAF, the spectacular performances by the Romanian MiGs may still be seen for several more years.

in Bucharest. There is also one at each of the bases at Bacău and Feteşti.

Deliveries of the MiG-21PF (designated RFM, or *radar fortaj modernizat*, radar afterburner modernized) began in 1965—that year the air force was renamed the *Forţele Aeriene ale republicii Socialiste Române* (air force of the Socialist Republic of Romania). Roughly the first dozen aircraft produced in Moscow were received by the regiment at Feteşti-Borcea in January of that year. Twenty-four more were delivered to Caracal-Deveselu in July. Aircraft of this version were later flown by the 57th Fighter Regiment and the 93rd Fighter Regiment. From the early 1970s onward, the *Centrul de Instructie a Aviatiei* (pilot training center) operated about twenty aircraft. The MiG-21PF remained in service until the beginning of the 1990s. In 1999, all remaining aircraft were assembled at Craiova and Caracal, where they remain in storage; four have been lost in the interim. The first two-seat trainers, two MiG-21U-400s, were delivered to the Romanian air force in May 1965, followed by two more in December. They came from the Moscow production line and, like all subsequent two-seat trainers, in Romania were given the designation MiG-21DC (*dublă comandă*; dual controls). Three aircraft delivered in October 1966 and February 1968 were of the MiG-21U-600 version.

The MiG-21U remained in service with the Regt. 86 Av. Vt. at Borcea and the 91st Regt. Av. Vt. at Caracal-Deveselu until the early 1990s. One MiG-21U-400 was lost in a flying accident.

The next operational version was the MiG-21PFM (Romanian-designated RFMM), of which Romania received fourteen examples in 1966, another fourteen in February 1968, and twenty-two more in February 1968. The MiG-21PFM was eventually flown by all four existing regiments and by the pilot training center.

The MiG-21R reconnaissance version (Romanian-designated MiG-21C for *Cercetare*, or reconnaissance) was procured immediately after the MiG-21PFM. The aircraft, which were delivered from Gorki in December 1968 (two), September 1970 (three), and 1972 (five), formed the equipment of the 31st *Escadrila Aviatie Cercetare* (31st Reconnaissance Squadron) at Timişoara-Giarmata.

The first MiG-21Ms were delivered in two batches in 1969, with the first batch of thirteen in August followed by five more in September. Forty more aircraft were delivered in 1970. As a result, all four fighter regiments were equipped with MiG-21s. Of the total of fifty-eight aircraft, in 1975 forty-two were assigned to the regiment at Mihail Kogălniceanu, which after the arrival of the MiG-23 passed these aircraft to

The Hungarian air force retired its MiG-21F-13s quite early, in 1977. Several monuments, such as this one in Kecskemét, are the only reminders of their service.

Until 1990, the air forces of Hungary, Romania, and Bulgaria wore very similar national insignia, which differed only in the colors of the concentric circles in the centers of the stars. Seen here is the Hungarian variant on a MiG-21MF. *Guido E. Bühlmann*

other regiments. Despite this, in 1983, in addition to twenty-three MiG-23s, the 57th Regiment still had twenty-eight MiG-21Ms and four MiG-21 two-seat trainers.

More two-seat trainers were received, with ten Tblisi-built machines arriving in 1969 and two more in 1970, with the pilot training center receiving the majority. In 1969 eight MiG-21PFMs and two MiG-21US were in service there, but by 1971 the training center's inventory consisted of twenty each of the MiG-21PFs and MiG-21PFMs plus ten MiG-21US two-seat trainers. Additional MiG-21US trainers were used by the operational regiments, such as Regt. 91 Av. Vt. at Caracal.

To the current day, the MiG-21MF forms the backbone of the Romanian MiG-21 fleet. Twelve examples of this version were received in September 1972; six, in November 1973; twenty, in September 1974; and thirty-five, in November 1975. The latter were Gorki-built MiG-21MF-75s, while all previous aircraft had come from Moscow. The regiments at Deveselu and Borcea were equipped with the MiG-21MF. Beginning in 1982, the newly formed 48th *Escadrila Aviatie Vânătoare* (fighter squadron) at the base in Luna near Câmpia Turzii received aircraft of this version plus MiG-21Ms, both transferred from other units. From the squadron and its equipment was created the 71st Regt. Av. Vt. at the same base in 1986. The MiG-21MF-75s were primarily concentrated in the 91st Regt. Av. Vt. at Timişoara-Giarmata, and this unit was equipped exclusively with the MiG-21MF and MF-75.

The first deliveries of the MiG-21UM coincided with that of the first MiG-21MFs. Five aircraft in September 1972 were followed by two more in September 1973 and four in January 1974. Ten examples were delivered in 1976, and a final four arrived in 1980. The arrival of the MiG-21UM, which ultimately flew with every MiG-21 unit, ended procurement of the MiG-21 by the *Forţele Aeriene ale Republicii Socialiste Române*. Romania did not receive the MiG-21bis. The reason for this could have been because Soviet-Romanian relations had reached a low point at that time, since in 1978, Romania had allowed Chinese specialists to analyze every detail of a MiG-21MF (see the "Chinese MiG-21s"). Pending availability of the MiG-23, which entered service in 1979, may also have been why Romania did not receive the MiG-21bis.

In 1968, the *Uzina de Reparatii Avioane* (aircraft repair facility), which had been established at Bacău in 1953, assumed responsibility for overhauling Romanian MiG-21s. The facility at Bacău was capable of overhauling all of the aircraft's components, including engines.

After the bloody fall of dictator Nicolae Ceauçescu in 1989, the tense economic situation forced severe cuts in military spending, which resulted not just in a reduction in equipment but also in a considerable tightening of funds for day-to-day operations. As a result, the previously low accident rate of the *Forţele Aeriene Române* (Romanian air force, as designated since 1990) rose sharply. Eight aircraft (including four MiG-21s) were lost in accidents in 1994 alone.

Nevertheless, in 1995, 186 single-seat MiG-21s and thirty-five two-seat trainers still remained; in 1999, a total of 218 MiG-21s of all versions.

In the 1990s, Romania procured five used MiG-21UM two-seat trainers. Claims that these came from East German stocks can be ruled out definitively, and the aircraft probably came from the CIS. With the goal of entering NATO and in view of a shrinking budget, Romania became the sole MiG-21 user in Europe to opt for an extensive modernization of its fleet. In 1997, the first MiG-21 LanceR (see "Modernization: MiG-21 for the Twenty-First Century") was delivered to the air force. Almost at the same time as the first flight of the LanceR, there was a massive restructuring of the Romanian air force. The former fighter regiments were reorganized as airfield bases (*Baza Aeriană de Aviatie Vânătoare*) and the groups (*Grupul Aviatie Vânătoare*), consisting of two squadrons (*Escadrile*), that were stationed there. The affected MiG-21 units were *Grupul* 71 at Câmpia Turzil, *Grupul* 86 at Fetești-Borcea, *Grupul* 91 at Caracak-Deveselu, *Grupul* 93 at Timișoara-Giarmata, and *Grupul* 95, the former pilot training center, at Bacău. The title of the MiG-21R squadron at Timișoara was shortened to 31st *Escadrila Cercetare*.

Between 1997 and 2003, the *Forțele Aeriene Române* received a total of seventy-one LanceR As, fourteen LanceR Bs (MiG-21UM), and twenty-five LanceR Cs. Of the previously named units, the ones at Bacău (from 1997), Fetești-Borcea (from 1998), Timișoara-Giarmata (from 2000), and Câmpia Turzil (from 2001) were reequipped.

With the introduction of the LanceR, the older MiG-21s that had not been modernized were phased out. At Bacău the LanceR had completely replaced the MiG-21PFM by 1997. *Grupul* 86 at Borcea stopped flying this version in 1999, while *Grupul* 91 at Deveselu flew some examples of this version and the MiG-21US until it was disbanded in 2001–2002. The closing of Deveselu also meant the end for the MiG-21 M/MF and UM, which because of higher flying hours could not be modernized. Of the forty-eight MiG-21PFM delivered to Romania, only eight did not survive until retirement. Five of twelve MiG-21USs were lost, at least fifteen of fifty-eight MiG-21Ms, just four of 73 MiG-21MFs, and nine of thirty MiG-21UMs were lost.

Reconnaissance drones assumed the role of the MiG-21Rs of the 31st *Escadrila Cercetare*; the unit was disbanded in 1998, by which time one machine had crashed.

Since the phase-out of all MiG-23s and MiG-29s, the MiG-21 LanceR has been the *Forțele Aeriene Române*'s sole combat aircraft for more than a decade. The fleet has undergone numerous changes in this time. The base at Timișoara was closed on August 31, 2004, and the aircraft based there were transferred to other bases. Dozens of aircraft have been in storage for years and will probably never fly again. Eleven LanceR aircraft (three of the A version, two of the B version, and six of the C version) have been lost since introduced into service.

Despite a shrinking fleet, the fully NATO-compatible Romanian MiG-21s have also been active internationally. From August 1 to October 31, 2007, the Lithuanian Zoknai Air Base near Šiauliai was the showplace for the first operational mission by the Romanian air force since the Second World War. Four MiG-21 LanceR C aircraft of Baza 71

MiG-21bis on land approach. From this angle it is possible to see that in Hungary even the missile launch rails were camouflaged. *Stefan Büttner*

Aircraft 6115 was finished in a special paint scheme for the farewell flight marking the retirement from service of the Hungarian MiG-21s. Here it is stopped in front of the technical checkpoint (TKP) before taking off on its last solo display flight. *Stefan Büttner*

The last few meters on its own power: a MiG-21UM turns into the flightline at Papá.

Aeriană based at Câmpia Turzii spent four months guarding the airspace over the Baltic. Annually, at Romanian air force bases, which since 2010 are designated Flotila Aeriană participate in joint maneuvers with other NATO air forces, in particular the USAF, where the MiG-21 LanceR is a popular sparring partner. Occasionally, the aircraft also spend time abroad—in Germany, the last time was at Elite 2007 at Lechfeld.

Discussions about procuring a follow-on type have taken place since 2006, but it was not until October 2013 that a contract with Portugal, for the supply of twelve used and modernized F-16As and Bs, was signed. These arrived in Fetesti between September 2016 and September 2017, where they equipped the newly-established *Escadrila 53 Aviaţie Vânătoare*, while *Escadrilele 861 Aviaţie Vânătoare* continued to operate the MiG-21. During the modernization of the base for the deployment of the F-16, the unit's MiG-21s were based at Mihail Kogălniceanu. The only other MiG-21 unit today is *Escadrila 711 Aviaţie Vânătoare* in Câmpia Turzii. Procurement of further F-16 is to be expected in the near future, as the lifespan of the MiG-21 ends in 2019–20. After all LanceR As have been decommissioned in the meantime, B and C versions will remain in service; a total of about thirty aircraft.

Hungary

After the defeat of Hungary, which had been allied to Germany in the Second World War, and the communist takeover in 1948, the rebuilding of the *Magyar Legiérő* (Hungarian air force) began in 1948 with Czech and Soviet technology. The service's first jet aircraft, the MiG-15, entered service in 1951, and prior to the Hungarian uprising in 1956, the Hungarian LSK was one of the most powerful air forces in the region. After 1956, the Hungarian air force was rebuilt on a smaller scale, and since Hungary was again considered a trusted ally, it received the latest aircraft.

Between February and June 1961, the technical personnel of the 47th *Vadászrepülő* (VE, or fighter regiment) went to Krasnodar in the Soviet Union for training on the MiG-21. The course for the pilots was given at the same place between March and August. At the same time, the unit switched bases with a Soviet one and moved from Sármellek to Pápa. The delivery of MiG-21F-13s began in October 1961, comprising forty aircraft from GAZ 21 in Gorki. These then equipped the 1st, 2nd, and 3rd *Vadászrepülő Szazad* (VS, or fighter squadron), while the 4th VS continued operating its MiG-15s. Thirteen additional aircraft from Gorki, this time for the 31st *Honi Vadászrepülő* (HVE, or home defense regiment) at Taszár, followed at the end of 1962. Deliveries of the MiG-21F-13 ended with twenty-seven Moscow-built aircraft, which were allocated to the 1st and 2nd VS of the 59th VE at

Kecskemét. Hungary thus had eighty MiG-21F-13s, a huge number given that it had just three operational regiments. Following the delivery of MiG-21PFs in 1964, the 47th Fighter Regiment's surplus MiG-21F-13s were sent to Kecskemét, and as a result the 59th Fighter Regiment was completely equipped with this version. In October 1973, each of the three regiments handed over four aircraft to serve as replacements for aircraft lost by Syria in the October 1973 war. After deliveries of the MiG-21MF ended, in 1974, all remaining MiG-21F-13s were sent to Kecskemét, where they continued in service until phased out in 1977. By that time, thirty aircraft had been lost in crashes or had been taken out of service.

In 1965, the Pestvidéki Gepgyár state maintenance facility at Tököl airfield near Budapest began carrying out overhauls of Hungarian MiG-21F-13s, the last of which left the facility in 1975. They were followed by every version in service: the MiG-21PF from 1969 to 1982, and the MiG-21U from 1970 to 1986, plus the MiG-21UM, MiG-21MF, and MiG-21bis from 1974, 1976, and 1980, respectively, until the end of the MiG-21's service life. The facility's records show that 411 aircraft were overhauled, and it can be assumed that all Hungarian machines passed through the facility, which was privatized as *Dunai Repülőgépgyr RT* at least one or two times.

At the end of 1964, fourteen MiG-21PFs reached the 47th Fighter Regiment at Pápa, where they were used to reequip the 1st Fighter Squadron. Ten more MiG-21PFs were issued to the 31st Home Defense Regiment at Taszár in mid-1965. With the MiG-21s already there plus its MiG-15s and MiG-19s, the total strength of the regiment, which consisted of three air defense and one close air support squadrons, rose to sixty aircraft! In 1971, the 4th Fighter Regiment released nine more MiG-21PFs, which had first been overhauled, to Taszár. There the MiG-21PF, which was succeeded by the MiG-21MF, replaced the last MiG-19s in 1974. The last flight by a MiG-21PF of the Hungarian air force took place on March 6, 1989. The aircraft flew from Taszár to Kecskemét, where they were placed in outdoor storage. Seven aircraft of this version had been lost in crashes, with three pilots losing their lives.

The introduction of the two-seat trainer began with nine MiG-21Us for the 47th Fighter Regiment in April–May 1965. Nine more arrived before the end of 1965 and in mid-1967 and were issued to the 31st Home Defense Regiment and

the 59th Fighter Regiment. The MiG-21U remained in service until 1997. Two aircraft were lost in crashes, and nine were sold to India after overhaul by AEROSTAR Bacău in Romania.

Since Hungary did not procure the MiG-21PFM, MiG-21R, or MiG-21US, it was several years before the next new MiG-21s arrived. In autumn 1971, the 2nd Squadron of the 47th Fighter Regiment received the first fourteen MiG-21MFs. Twelve machines for the 3rd Fighter Squadron of the 31st Home Defense Regiment followed in October 1973. Between June and August, twenty-seven more MiG-21MFs arrived, completing deliveries of this version—all produced in Moscow. Twenty-four aircraft from the final deliveries formed the equipment of the 1st and 3rd Squadrons of the regiment at Pápa, which then had thirty-eight MiG-21MFs and eight MiG-21UMs. The 59th Fighter Regiment received its first MiG-21MFs from the stocks of the 31st Home Defense Regiment in 1976, and more from the 47th Fighter Regiment followed the next year. As a result the regiment was again operating a single type.

Coincident with the MiG-21MFs, the first MiG-21UM two-seat trainers also arrived at the 47th Fighter Regiment in the autumn of 1971. Further deliveries followed in 1972 (three), 1973 (three), 1974 (five), 1976 (three), 1979 (five), 1980 (two), and finally 1983 (four). The total of twenty-eight MiG-21UMs was divided among the three MiG-21 regiments and remained in service until the entire fleet was phased out in 2000.

Deliveries of the MiG-21bis to the Hungarian air force began in 1975. In contrast to previous practice, the first aircraft went to Taszár and not to Pápa. The first fourteen MiG-21bis LAZUR arrived there in July. This made it possible to retire the regiment's MiG-21F-13s. At that time, the regiment had MiG-21PFs with the 1st Fighter Squadron, MiG-21bis with the 2nd, and MiG-21MFs with the 3rd. In May 1976, eleven MiG-21bis SAUs replaced the MF version with the 2nd Squadron. In 1977, twelve MiG-21bis SAUs went to Pápa, where they relieved a squadron of MiG-21MFs. In both cases the regiment at Kecskemét received the aircraft that had been made available by the arrival of the new MiG-21s. Then, in 1978, thirteen MiG-21bis SAUs were delivered to Taszár, while seven aircraft were delivered to Pápa in 1979, and five in 1980. Both deliveries resulted in the transfer of aircraft to Kecskemét.

When, in August 1979, the 1st Fighter Squadron of the 47th Fighter Regiment began operating the MiG-23MF, its

MiG-21MFs were transferred to Kecskemét. At that time the regiment had thirty MiG-21bis and nine MiG-21UMs in its 2nd and 3rd Squadrons.

In the mid-1980s, as the result of growing foreign debt, Hungary began reducing its military responsibilities. The result, beginning in 1987, was a reduction in the number of flying hours. In 1989, as part of the Warsaw Pact initiative, the 3rd Squadron of the 47th Fighter Regiment, which that year was given the name Aurél Stromfeld, was disbanded. The same thing happened to the 59th Fighter Regiment on January 1, 1990.

After the political changes, the Hungarian air force was renamed *Magyar Honvéd Repülő Csapat* (air force of the Hungarian defense force). In April 1990, the flying units were renamed *Vadászrepülő Osztály* (home defense division) then in August 1991 became the *Harcászati Repülőezred* (HR, or tactical air regiment). The name of the 47th Tactical Air Regiment was changed to Pápa, the 31st Tactical Air Regiment was given the name *Kapos*, and the 59th was named Dezső Szentgyörgyj after a Hungarian fighter ace of the Second World War.

Because of the growing tensions in Yugoslavia and the increasing number of border infringements by aircraft of the Yugoslavian People's Army, at the beginning of the 1990s as many as five MiG-21bis of the 47th Tactical Air Regiment were moved to Taszár. In order to be able to react to different threat scenarios, the 47th Regiment formed a mixed QRA consisting of three MiG-21MFs, two Mi-24s, and two Mi-8 helicopters and two surface-to-air missile complexes.

At that time Hungary still had an impressive fleet of MiG-21s: the 1st and 2nd Squadrons of the 31st *Harcászati Repülőezred* at Taszár were equipped with twenty-four MiG-21bis, four MiG-21Us, and six MiG-21UMs. The 2nd Squadron of the 47th Tactical Air Regiment at Pápa had 23 MiG-21bis and six MiG-21UMs. Finally, at Kecskemét (59th HR) there were two squadrons with a total of thirty-five MiG-21MFs and six MiG-21U and MiG-21UM two-seat trainers each. Cuts were not long in coming, however: after the introduction of the MiG-29 and the retirement of the MiG-21 by the 59th Tactical Air Regiment on August 31, 1994, that unit's MiG-21MFs and UMs were flown to Pápa. They were followed by the MiG-21bis/UM of the 31st Tactical Air Regiment, whose base at Taszár was handed over to the US Air Force for implementation force (IFOR) operations over Yugoslavia in December 1995. The last QRA takeoff from Taszár took place on December 14. Fourteen MiG-21bis and four MiG-21UMs stationed there flew to Pápa. The 31st HVE's aircraft were, however, serviced at Taszár, where the aircraft due for overhaul also remained. Personnel commuted between the two bases until the 31st Tactical Air Regiment was disbanded at the end of 1996. By then, the nineteen MiG-21bis and ten MiG-21UMs at Taszár had also been flown to Pápa, and finally, all MiG-21s were concentrated there. Twelve examples of the still-flyable MiG-21bis and MiG-21UMs were used in rotation.

There was no real modernization of the MiG-21 fleet. The only measure taken by the Hungarians was to equip the MiG-21bis and MiG-21UMs with American-made transponders and IFF systems in 1994.

The MiG-21MF ceased flying operations on December 4, 1996, and one year later it was officially phased out. Of the total of fifty-three Hungarian MiG-21MFs, nine had been lost in crashes during the type's service life. The last twelve MiG-21MFs were placed in open-air storage at Pápa. The 47th Tactical Air Regiment subsequently had ten MiG-21UMs in the 1st Squadron and eighteen MiG-21bis in the 2nd Squadron. After Hungary entered NATO in 1999, the latter stood quick reaction alert (QRA) as part of NATO's integrated air defense system (NATINADS).

After the MiG-23 and Su-22 stopped flying operations in 1997, in the spring of 2000 Hungary announced that it was going to ground the rest of its MiG-21 fleet and close several bases in 2001. Because of growing financial problems, the end-of-service date was moved up, and on September 1, 2000, the 47th Tactical Air Regiment was disbanded. Previously, on September 1, 2000, the regiment had marked the end of almost forty years of MiG-21 operations in Hungary with a large-scale farewell ceremony. The very last flight by a Hungarian MiG-21 was made by the commander of the 47th Tactical Air Regiment on August 31 in a MiG-21bis. Of the total of sixty-two MiG-21bis delivered to Hungary, twenty had been lost in accidents and three pilots were killed. The defense of Hungarian airspace was subsequently left to the MiG-29, which has since been replaced by the JAS-39 Gripen.

The retired MiG-21bis and MiG-21UMs all are supposed to be scrapped. Because of the considerable airframe life remaining, this decision was revisited; however, no sales were made nor were other uses found. The last machines retired are still at Pápa and may make their way to the crusher in the foreseeable future.

Appendix

ASCC Reporting Names

Created in 1948, the Air Standardization Coordinating Committee (ASCC, now Air and Space Interoperability Council) is a multinational body made up of the United States, Great Britain, Canada, Australia, and New Zealand. Among the duties of the ASCC is assigning code names to all new Soviet/CIS (and Chinese) military aircraft, which are then binding within NATO. In the past, because of secrecy and deception, the assignment of main and subvariants often reflected technical reality less than the perceptions of the West, which in the case of the MiG-21 resulted in some blurring. In some cases, versions that differed outwardly were assigned the same code names, since classification was based on their radar signatures, which because of similar components were identical or at least very similar.

Fighter aircraft code names began with the letter *F*, and the MiG-21 was assigned the name "Fishbed." When they first appeared, the MiG-21 two-seat trainers were placed under "Miscellaneous," resulting in the code name "Mongol."

MiG-21 Designations

Reporting Name	Version(s)
Faceplate	Ye-2A (prototype)
Fishbed-A	Ye-6 (prototype)
Fishbed-B	Ye-5 (prototype)
Fishbed-C	F, F-13
Fishbed-D	PF, PFS, FL
Fishbed-E	
Fishbed-F	PFM
Fishbed-G	PD (prototype)
Fishbed-H	R, S
Fishbed-J	M, MF, SM
Fishbed-K	SMT, MT
Fishbed-L	bis LAZUR
Fishbed-M	
Fishbed-N	bis SAU
Mongol-A	U
Mongol-B	US, UM

Bibliography

A 107/1/327 Flugzeug 96 mit Triebwerk 95—Elektro-Spezialausrüstung—Nutzung, 1974.

A 187/1/104 Katapultsitze KM-1, KM-1U, KM-1I—Beschreibung, 1971.

A 187/1/105 Flugzeug 96 und dessen Modifikationen—Zelle, Triebwerk und Bordsysteme, 1972.

A 187/1/105 Neufassung der für das Flugzeug 96 mit Triebwerk 95 geänderten Abschnitte/Unterabschnitte der Beschreibung A 187/1/105 und ergänzende Abschnitte/Unterabschnitte.

Banach, Dietrich. J-7/F-7. Unpublished manuscript.

Banach, Dietrich, Thomas Bußmann, Thomas Girke, Klaus Meißner, Jürgen Willisch, and Lutz Freundt. MiG, Mi, Su & Co. Diepholz, Germany: Aerolit, 2002.

Bulgarian Air Force, MoD of the Republic of Bulgaria.

Büttner, Stefan. Rote Plätze: Russische Militärflugplätze, Deutschland 1945–1994. Edited by Lutz Freundt. Berlin: AeroLit-Verlag, 2007.

Страницы Истории 32-го Гвардейского Истребительного Авиационного Полка: Исаев. Часть I + II. Арбор, 2006–2009.

Freundt, Lutz. Sowjetische Fliegerkräfte in Deutschland 1945–1994. 4 vols. Diepholz, Germany: Freundt, 1998–2000.

Gordon, Yefim. Soviet/Russian Aircraft Weapons since World War Two. Hinkley, UK: Midland, 2004.

Gordon, Yefim, Keith Dexter, and Dmitriy Komissarov. Mikoyan MiG-21. Famous Russian Aircraft. Hinkley, UK: Midland, 2008.

Hottmar, Ales, and Stanislav Mackovík. Soviet Air Force over Czechoslovakia, 1968–1991. Part I. Hradec Králové, Czech Republic: JaPo, 2008.

Irra, Miroslav. MiG-21 "Jednadvacítka": Letoun MiG-21 v čs. a českém vojenském letectvu v letech 1962–2005. 2 vols. Bučovice, Czech Republic: Jakab, 2007–2009.

K 167/3/004 Ausstattungs- und Zeitnormen der Flugzeugmunition. 1988.

Kopenhagen, Wilfried. Die andere deutsche Luftwaffe. Berlin: Transpress, 1992.

Krachunova, Zoia, ed. История на Авиобаза Граф Игнатиево/The History of Graf Ignatievo Air Force Base. Sofia, Bulgaria: Voenno Izdatelstvo, 2003.

Kreißig, Die Funk-Funkmeßausrüstung des Flugzeugs L-39. Kamenz, Germany: OHS der LSK/LV.

Kreißig, Lehrheft für das Fach Funk-Funkmeßausrüstung. Kamenz, Germany: OHS der LSK/LV, 1985.

Lahtela, Heikki, and Jukka Nykänen. MiG-21 Suomen Sinessä. Vuorela, Finland: Karjalan Lennosto, 1998.

Laukkanen, Jyrki. MiG-21 in Finnish Air Force. Tampere, Finland: Apali Oy, 2004.

Lorenc, Miroslav, and Stanislav Rogl. Zrušená křídla. Olomouc, Czech Republic: Votobia, 2000.

MiG-21. Modřany, Czech Republic: 4+Publication, 1991.

Mikolajczuk, Marian. Uzbrojenie ZSSR i Rosji 1945–2000. Vol. 1, Lotnicze Systemy Rakietowe. Warsaw, Poland: Iglica, 2000.

Mikolajczuk, Marian. Sowjetische Fliegerkräfte in Deutschland 1945–1994. Pułk Lotnictwa Rozpoznania 32. Warsaw, Poland: Rossagraph, 2004.

Müller, Robert. Typeneinweisung in die Erzeugnisse 37, 95 und 25. Kamenz, Germany: OHS der LSK/LV.

ОКБ им. А.И. Микояна. 60 лет: Центр Авиации и Космонавтики, 2000.

Oluić, Saša, Goran Antić, and Bojan B. Dimitrijević. 204. Lovački avijacijski puk. Belgrade, Serbia: Vojska, 2005.

Sandachi, Paul. Aviaţia de luptă reactivă în România 1951–2001. A 187/1/158 Triebwerk 37F2S—Technische Beschreibung 1970. Editura Regina din Arcadia, 2001.

Vándor, Károly. Soviet Air Force in Hungary and Austria. Budapest: VPP, 2004.

Инженерно Авиационната Служба на Военната България / The Engineering and Aviation Service of the Bulgarian Air Force. Sofia, Bulgaria: Еър Груп / Air Group, 2000.

Articles from the magazines Fliegerrevue, Fliegerrevue Extra, Air Forces Monthly, and letectví+kosmonautika.